DIGITAL REASON:
A GUIDE TO MEANING, MEDIUM AND COMMUNITY IN A MODERN WORLD

Digital Reason

A Guide to Meaning,
Medium and Community
in a Modern World

Jan Baetens, Ortwin de Graef and Silvana Mandolessi

Leuven University Press

© 2020 by Leuven University Press / Presses Universitaires de Louvain / Universitaire Pers Leuven.
Minderbroedersstraat 4, B-3000 Leuven (Belgium).

ISBN 978 94 6270 206 6
D / 2020/ 1869 / 2
NUR: 610

Cover design: Anton Lecock
Cover illustration: Impression from a woodcut of a small portion of Mr. Babbage's Difference
Engine, No.1, Babbage, Henry Prevost https://digital.library.cornell.edu/catalog/ss:8329889.
Typesetting: Crius Group

Foreword

Tomorrow's humanities scholars grow up in a unique and restless era. They will have to explore and mold a boundless cultural space, while demographic, ecological, economic, political, religious and technological forces are constantly calling traditional agendas, laws and even the legitimacy of that space into question. The Leuven Faculty of Arts wants to prepare its students for this dynamic. It does not only want to train critical domain experts, it also wants to form creative and multifaceted thinkers who, starting from a broad conceptual and theoretical basis, can transcend their discipline's template and in so doing can weigh on topical social and scientific debates. Five common courses in the arts constitute the cornerstone of this ambition, which is a unique project. What began as free reflection by professors, staff and students of all study programmes, culminated in courses and textbooks that examine the power of fundamental thinking and the possibilities and challenges of digital (r)evolution and inter-cultural society.

The substantive plan that underlies the book *Digital Reason. A Guide to Meaning, Medium and Community in a Modern World* was developed by Stijn Carpentier, Raf De Bont, Mark Delaere, Elias De Mulder, Mark Depauw, Hendrik De Smet, Silvana Mandolessi, Paul Sambre, and Jeroen Van Craenenbroeck, under the guidance of Anke Gilleir. We are very grateful to them for their commitment and for the generosity with which they shared their knowledge.

Jo Tollebeek, Liesbet Heyvaert and Koenraad Brosens
Coordination and general editing

Table of Contents

Part Two   Medium

Part Three   Community

Index

Introduction:
We Have Always Been Digital

We have always been digital, but we have been getting better. Or at least better at it. For have we really been getting better? In this book we want to explore the ways in which the digital turn has affected our relationship with the material *medium* to which we as human beings have committed our insights, anxieties, doubts and desires (or whatever we want to call what goes on in our brains) ever since we started to leave traces of them for others to read. We also want to look at the ways the dynamics of *community* formation and deformation have been dramatically changed by the advent of digital social media and other digitally enabled forms of (dis)information sharing. But before we address those issues of medium and community, we want to engage with the more nebulous notion of "*meaning*"—as in "what is it all about?" or even "what's the point?," in short: the question of *purpose*, of what it means to be human. It is not a question we will even begin to answer—its point is in the asking and we ask because we do.

Our main reason for turning to the question of meaning or purpose before we explore the digital turn is that we think a proper appreciation of this turn for students of the humanities can benefit from some long-term historical perspective on human beings as symbol-using hyper-social animals. This long-term perspective should be complemented with a shorter-term perspective taking on board in very general terms some responses to material and social realities of historical modernity (roughly from the late 18th century onwards), as well as the fading, displacement or reconfiguration of religion as an undisputed answer ("undisputed" being the operative word) to the question of purpose. We do not think that the digital turn in and of itself can give us better purchase on this question of purpose, but we do believe that keeping this question online in the background is helpful for a critical understanding of what digital developments may or may not mean for the study and especially the sharing of human culture.

But first: we have always been digital, and we have only been getting better at it. Another way of putting this is that we have always used tools, and for better or worse have become the most accomplished technological animal in the history of the planet. Other animals use tools, too, but none do so as intensively and with such sophistication as humans. Yet what arguably singles out humans most among other animals is the extent to which our technologies—the broad spectrum of tool-complexes we routinely use—have amplified our activities far beyond what we can meaningfully think of as "natural." On the one hand, yes, technologies do allow us better to perform tasks that fit the four Fs of natural animal life (feeding, fighting, fleeing and fornicating). As media scholar Siva Vaidhyanathan puts it, echoing Marshall McLuhan, "technologies are extensions of ourselves," allowing us to "supplement" and "extend" activities we were already doing. (Cohen 2018) But on the other hand human technologies have given rise to practices of such complexity that reducing them to the four-F regime, while in principle always possible, is intellectually unsatisfying, if not dishonest. Again following McLuhan, Vaidhyanathan insists that in order properly to understand technologies, we must "denaturalise" them: "Don't assume the chalkboard in my classroom is a given and the computer in my classroom is technology—that one is natural and one is unnatural. The chalkboard and the computer that displays PowerPoint slides do similar work in different ways." Vaidhyanathan's example is felicitous in that it invites us to go one step further: not only are the piece of chalk and the computer keyboard both "unnatural" technologies, they also both do "digital" work in different ways.

The word "digital" is of course related to *digitus*, Latin for "finger." In present-day usage, it mostly refers to the electronic storage and transmission of data in binary form, but it makes sense to reconnect it to our fingers—not in order to naturalise digital processing but rather to denaturalise what we have been doing with our fingers all along. *Homo sapiens* has been around for a few hundred thousand years, but we know very little about what our oldest conspecifics might have been up to.[1] To date, the oldest probable evidence of traces deliberately left by humans was found on a flake of stone recently discovered in Blombos Cave in South Africa. Analysis confirmed "that red ochre pigment was intentionally applied to the flake with an ochre crayon" some 73,000 years ago, thereby establishing, backed up with other evidence, "the ability of early *Homo sapiens* in southern Africa to produce graphic designs on various media using different techniques" (Henshilwood *et al.* 2018, 115). According to archaeologist Paul Pettit (not a member of the team working in Blombos Cave), "If there is any point at which one can say that symbolic activity had emerged in human society, this is it" (Barras 2018). While we have no idea *what* the Blombos design may have meant, what matters is *that* it very likely must have meant, and that whatever meaning its early human maker sought to share with her or his community was entrusted to the medium of ochre on stone by means of a crayon held by a human hand. The Blombos design is therefore not only probably the oldest instance of human symbolic activity discovered to date, it may also quite literally be the oldest piece of digital art.

Image of the Blombos Cave silcrete flake L13 displaying the drawn lines that form a cross-hatched pattern. C. Foster (Henshilwood *et al.* 2018, 116)

Human hands are extraordinary. We are not the only primates with digits and opposable thumbs, and indeed there are other animals besides primates with opposable thumbs or functionally similar body parts, but the dexterity and precision with which humans manipulate objects and tools and touch each other and themselves is unmatched. As is the case for all other anatomical features of the human body, hands are the result of natural evolution, but precisely when and why something like the *anatomically modern* human hand first got selected for further evolution we will probably never know. What is clear is its importance for *behaviourally modern* humankind, characterised by such features as a fully developed language, ritual and artistic practices, extensive tool-use, self-decoration and the controlled use of fire.

A particularly intriguing question in this connection involves the relationship between the production of material symbolic traces such as the Blombos design, the development of language and the emergence of writing. Counterintuitive as it may seem, there are good reasons to take seriously the Algerian-French philosopher Jacques Derrida's contention that writing precedes speech—or, more precisely, that spoken language is constitutively marked by the same features that are typically considered characteristic of written language only, and are typically taken as evidence of the inferiority or secondariness of writing to speech (Bennington & Derrida 1991, 43–63). We can dispense with the larger context of Derrida's deconstruction of the metaphysics of presence here; what matters is the observation that language as a system of symbolic communication can only do its work when it functions as if it were always already writing. This does not mean that *Homo sapiens* could not speak before she could write, or that human babies cannot be touched into thought by their mother tongue before they can type. What it does mean is that the system of symbolic communication we call human language can only work if it works in the radical absence of both the sender and the receiver of any given series of signifiers—and let "any given" here maximally signify that that is what "data" etymologically are: material givens the presence of whose original givers and getters is not material to their functioning as data. What Derrida's notion of writing—or, as he sometimes calls it, "archi-writing"—invites us to think about is the potential of language in general as a technology used by humans to transmit their intentions (their concern for others, for the world and for themselves) through time and space by producing symbolic traces (like the Blombos design) that are in principle eternally able to elicit other such traces (for instance, our speculations about the meaning of the Blombos design). Writing so conceived names humans as specifically *historical* animals, using their hands to share what occupies them so that in principle all other humans alive and yet to be born or built may be their witness. The fact that these historical traces can often no longer be read is not just an accident: it is only because it is always possible that it cannot be read that writing can be read at all.

In contrast to the early humans of Blombos Cave, consider the white-spotted puffer fish. The male of the species, measuring a good 10 cm in length, takes some seven days to build a two-metre-wide 3D-circle in the sand on the seabed. These "mystery circles"—as they were called before we found out who made them—are stunning geometric structures it is hard not to mistake for creative art. Seven days says it all. And even though we know the fish builds this discworld to attract a mate (or a series of them), the sheer complexity and perfection of the design seem so disproportionate to the purpose of mere procreation (F#4) that it must at least also appear as an instance of real symbolic creation asking to be read.

To think this is not just to give in to anthropomorphism but to commit theriomorphism by stealth: it takes the difference out of human symbolic practice and returns it to the order of what natural life makes living things make. It demystifies the symbolic process by mistake. When science suggests that the intricate design of the circle with its radial ridges and valleys is entirely functional as a means to collect fine particles of sand at the centre of the structure where they form a soft bed perfectly suited for spawning, that is not demystification: it just gives us a good four-F reason why *Torquigener albomaculosus* builds his mystery whorl this way (Kawase *et al.* 2013). What is demystifying and missing the point no sound science or scholarship should is to call it an act of creation, an instance of artistic or symbolic activity. Not only is the white-spotted pufferfish's circle-building obviously not digital, it is also not art, even though it undeniably looks more impressive than the Blombos design. Symbolic activity is other: it makes a difference that is only really made when it is read for the differences it demands. The digital turn offers us powerful new tools to meet that demand, but it also makes it easier to ignore it in favour of more measurable differences.

This is the sense in which humans have always been digital animals: only humans write. This is not to suggest that what is called the digital turn never happened. On the contrary: we take the digital turn so seriously that we do not want to take it too seriously. Essentially, it has not changed anything much: it is just a further extension of the human capacity for symbolic technology use—we are only getting better at it. Yet "essentially" is not how we live, and as historical animals we still want to know whether we are getting better.

A note on pronouns

We have written this book together, but each of us has taken principal care of one part: Ortwin de Graef for Part One, Jan Baetens for Part Two, Silvana Mandolessi for Part Three. So sometimes we will use the first person plural, when we are writing in the name of the book or in the name of everyone thinking along; at other times we will use the first person singular, when we do not want to burden the others (or you) with responsibility for what one of us came up with.

PART ONE
Mass Meaning

1 Starry Sky and Moral Law

The emergence of the public sphere as a site where individuals can freely think for themselves about the organisation of society, and share their thoughts with others, is a crucial feature of (Western) modernity, made possible in part by the development of an extensive infrastructure for public communication (especially newspapers and journals). Given the gradual erosion of dogma and autocratic rule on the one hand, and the growing prestige of natural science on the other, a crucial cause of concern was the truth-value of this new public political discourse, especially as regards the moral purpose of human life and the possibility conditions for a just community of self-interested yet social subjects. Immanuel Kant's writings for the general public are an exemplary instance of the modern project to educate human beings in the right use of reason, rejecting authoritarian dogma while recognising and respecting the difference between natural science and the science of humankind. Although they acknowledge the absence of objective evidence for the progress of humankind, these writings still seek to install a state of mind that furthers such progress, calling on the State to take responsibility for the education of its citizens in the service of cosmopolitan civil society.

Keywords: Enlightenment, public sphere, community, social contract, sympathy, education, progress, State action

The Purpose of Historically Modern Humans

We may always have been digital, but our digital condition in the early 21st century is obviously dramatically different from that of our early human ancestors. The specific technological infrastructures of modern digital communication account for much of that difference, but much of it is also due to momentous changes characteristic of historical modernity in general: massive demographic expansion, the emergence of modern democracy, a series of industrial and service revolutions, the institutionalisation of formal education, full-scale globalisation, the spectacular rise of science as a truth regime rivalling religion and culture, and the achievements of engineering in the modification of living conditions—to name just a few of those changes in no particular order. Before we address the differences made by the digital turn in present-day culture and society, it is useful to reflect on some of the conditions of modernity from which or against which it emerged. Our focus in this part will be on the question of what it means to be human in modern times by looking at some answers given to this question by a very few of the very many who have given it thought over the past two-and-a-half centuries or so.

What follows is, as will be evident soon, not in any way a comprehensive survey of modern thought: I could have chosen other authors who came up with very different answers; the authors I did choose are typically just those I happen to be more or less familiar with, and most of them wrote a lot more than what I engage with here. Yet I do think that the ways in which these authors address the question of the purpose of humanity provide a useful sample of an important strand in modern thought on this matter. There are other strands, more explicitly engaged with political and economic issues, and less parochially Western. None of them are discounted here, but to get the conversation going we have to start somewhere and the thought-narrative that follows is intended to welcome objections, corrections and developments in alternative detail.

The principal characters in this thought-narrative find themselves challenged in various ways by three fundamental and interrelated developments characteristic of (Western) modernity: (i) the spectacular rise of science as a truth regime complementing or displacing the traditional truth regimes of religion and philosophy; (ii) the gradual emergence of the notion of the self-determining human being, no longer unquestioningly subject to autocratic rule but worthy of recognition and respect as an essentially independent member of a democratic community; and

(iii) the increasingly urgent need to involve an unprecedentedly rapidly expanding population in public discourse.

This third point is particularly important in the context of this book. As already mentioned, it is not our ambition to answer the question of human purpose. But we are also not primarily interested in listing historical answers to that question which we think are particularly compelling or instructive or just right in their own right. Rather, what we will mainly focus on are articulate (as opposed to dogmatic or knee-jerk) engagements with the question of human purpose that are explicitly concerned with the task of *sharing* that engagement with the whole of humanity—the task, in the broadest sense of the word, of *education*. Whether human beings *can* be educated or even *want to be* educated to become what whoever educates them thinks they essentially are, and therefore should be, is less important from our perspective than the deployment of technologies broadly conceived to ensure that they *are* educated—or at the very least informed, or efficiently fed bits of fact and feeling.

The overall relevance of this techno-educational history to the digital turn should be clear, given the massive increase in the sharing of bits or bytes of fact and feeling it has made, and continues to make, possible. But we also want to draw specific attention to the *rhetoric* of this modern pre-digital public discourse: the textual techniques used to relay the question of purpose in public space. To this end, rather than just providing sustained summaries of arguments, I have regularly liberally quoted from the original texts (sometimes in translation). Most of the texts I focus on are relatively short—as befits contributions to wide public deliberation—and I hope students will want to turn to the full texts themselves. But if not, this way at least everyone will end this part having read some of the featured authors first-hand.

For the sake of clarity, and to avoid confusion and frustration, I emphasise that the d-word will not appear all that often in the course of this first part, mainly dealing as it does with thought pre-dating the digital turn. Now and then there will be brief flashforwards to the digital condition in the narrow sense, but on the whole I will stick to spinning a story of what preceded it. Whether this pre-history also documents a precondition for the digital condition, in the sense that it identifies past developments without which the digital turn would never have taken place, is doubtful but well worth asking. A thought experiment to complement this question would be to imagine what the world would have looked like if computers had already become mainstream in the course of the 19th century. A recommended read in this regard is the alternative history novel *The Difference Engine* (1990) by

William Gibson and Bruce Sterling, which does exactly that. The novel takes its cue from the work of Charles Babbage (1791–1871), whose Difference Engine and Analytical Engine designs are widely credited as the first precursors of modern computers, though neither engine was ever properly operational during Babbage's lifetime. Gibson and Sterling imagine Babbage's engines up and running by the middle of the 19th century already and have thought-provoking steampunk fun with the idea, but since what-if narratives only really work against the backdrop of what did take place, we stick to the record here and begin with Immanuel Kant.

Enlightenment and the Public Sphere

Immanuel Kant (1724–1804) is arguably one of the chief architects of the set of ideas with which Western modernity has been trying to make sense of itself. At the core of that set of ideas is the injunction with which Kant, in a 1784 article in the *Berlinische Monatsschrift,* answered the question "What is Enlightenment?": "*Sapere aude!* Have courage to use your *own* understanding!" (Kant 1784b, 54). Only when they have the courage to think for themselves can humans find release from their "self-incurred immaturity" and become enlightened. But for that courage not to be self-defeating, Kant adds, there must be freedom: "freedom to make public use of one's reason in all matters" (55).

Kant uses two different terms for human mental faculties here: "understanding" (*Verstand*) and "reason" (*Vernunft*). In his major works of critical philosophy, these are strictly distinguished though complementary: *understanding* involves applying rules to empirical evidence in order to attain objective knowledge; *reason* involves applying principles in order to attain insight in matters of morality. But in the non-specialist discourse of the monthly magazine, Kant dispenses with such philosophical niceties: what matters is the idea that the enlightened subject thinks for her- or himself, instead of lazily or cowardly submitting to authority. Yet of course it also matters *what* the enlightened subject is thinking about: for instance, the place of the planet in the solar system (a matter of understanding), or the question whether we are getting any better or are merely more and more of the same (a question of reason).

Before we turn to those issues, let us also underscore that Kant's definition of enlightened thinking for oneself is not just a public practice but specifically a *pub-*

lishing practice: "by the public use of one's own reason I mean that use which any-one may make of it *as a man of learning* addressing the entire *reading public*" (55). Enlightenment, in other words, requires freedom of the press, and Kant explicitly condemns any monarch or ruler who would subject his subjects' public exercise of their own reason in writing to "governmental supervision" or censorship: the ruler would thereby "expose himself to the reproach: *Caesar non est supra Grammaticos*" (58). The allusion is to an anecdote about the Council of Konstanz in 1414, where King Sigismund of Luxembourg made a grammatical mistake and, when corrected, retorted that as King of the Romans *he* would decide what was grammatically correct or not, upon which one of the members of the Council protested that the Emperor does not overrule the grammarian.[1] The suggestion is that the structure of language has an autonomy that should not be subject to political arbitrariness: we all know that political power always involves the manipulation of language—Orwell's New-speak and the current climate of fake fake news come to mind as brutal examples—yet our outrage at such manipulation bespeaks a deeply rooted if not quite coherent conviction that language is a core component of our human heritage no-one has the right to change at will. Evidently, language is constantly changing, but what offends is the idea that political rule can wilfully impose changes in grammatical rules.

The more precise point of the allusion, though, is the difference between the early-15th-century Council and the late 18th-century *Berlinische Monatsschrift*: the former is a closed negotiation between secular and religious authorities to sort out a crisis in the Catholic Church; the second is an open medium for public discussion by private persons, one of the very many such publications made technologically possible by the print revolution and politically possible by the gradual erosion of autocratic rule. In other words: what distinguishes 15th-century Konstanz from 18th-century Königsberg (where Kant lived, now called Kaliningrad) is what Jür-gen Habermas has described as the *Strukturwandel der Öffentlichkeit*: "the struc-tural transformation of the public sphere," arguably one of the crucial characteristics of modernity broadly conceived.

Habermas's analysis focuses on the emergence of the public sphere as a site of "political confrontation" where "private people come together as a public" to nego-tiate with "public authorities" (the State) about the general rules regulating society (Habermas 1989, 27). In the late 18th century, these "private people" engaging in public debate are mostly male members of the bourgeoisie in possession of suffi-cient property to ensure their relative autonomy—as Habermas points out, for Kant being male and financially independent is even an explicit prerequisite for participation in the public sphere. Yet stripped of its sexist (and, as is elsewhere evident, racist) prejudice, the underlying principle of Kant's vision of an ideal society is that all humans must have the right not to be prevented by others from trying to attain the status of a citizen exercising his or her reason in public debate about politics (109–11). To the extent that we approximate this "pleasant dream", as he calls it elsewhere (Kant 1798, 188), Kant believes we may really be getting better—or may at least be beginning to behave better. He warned against "expect[ing] too much of human beings in their progressive improvements" and did not believe that "the basic moral capacity of mankind" would ever change much; yet he did think that, given the right conditions, this basic moral capacity could lead to a superior political constitution in accordance with reason. It was the central article of faith for the "universal history" of humanity he liked to imagine was running its course (Kant 1784a).

Before we take a closer look at some of Kant's various attempts to picture this "universal history," let us underscore once more the importance of an infrastructure for public communication as a possibility condition for true public enlightenment. As Habermas emphasises, the central principle of the bourgeois public sphere is "supervision," allowing citizens to "transmit the needs of bourgeois society to the state, in order, ideally, to transform political into 'rational' authority" (2006, 76). Newspapers play an exceedingly important role in this regard: they are (or were) the chief technology of public opinion—initially restricted to the bourgeoisie, but as democracy and literacy develop increasingly extending to the entire public body. As a result of this further extension, the public sphere necessarily becomes more conflictual, as public opinion splits up in response to the often incompatible interests of different groups. Yet at the same time, as Benedict Anderson has noted, the mass consumption of newspaper print is also one of the central practices by means of which an "imagined community" is represented (Anderson 2006, 25). Newspapers not only transmit (various strands of) public opinion; the very act of reading them gives shape to the fiction of a nation or even of a global human community:

> The significance of this mass ceremony—Hegel observed that newspapers serve modern man as a substitute for morning prayers—is paradoxical. It is performed in silent privacy, in the lair of the skull. Yet each communicant is well aware that the ceremony he performs is being replicated simultaneously by thousands (or millions)

Starry Sky and Moral Law

of others of whose existence he is confident, yet of whose identity he has not the slightest notion. Furthermore, this ceremony is incessantly repeated at daily or half-daily intervals throughout the calendar. [...] At the same time, the newspaper reader, observing exact replicas of his own paper being consumed by his subway, barber-shop, or residential neighbours, is continually reassured that the imagined world is visibly rooted in everyday life (Anderson 2006, 35–36).

The medium of the newspaper creates a sense of connection between a multitude of readers who may never meet but nonetheless feel part of the same community. That that community is indeed *imagined* does not make it less real—to the contrary: its reality is a function of its being imagined in the first place. Like other communities more directly dependent on face-to-face intercourse, it can of course be challenged or even disrupted by alternative reality effects, such as economic or political change, but if and when that happens newly imagined communities typically take shape instead.

It is not much of a leap of the imagination to see the newspaper in this sense as a precursor of today's social media, which may also be said to forge imagined communities. But the differences are more arresting than the similarities. For one thing, unlike Anderson's newspaper readers, users of social media like Facebook can in principle form a fairly precise notion of the individual identity of other users—the fact that that identity is often substantially embellished or downright fake seems less important than its availability in the form of an image, specifically a face, or an image functioning as a face, accompanied by a list of likes and dislikes identifying the user as a particular person. But arguably the more important difference is the fact that the newspaper as social medium in the public sphere not only creates the sense of community in the ritual of its consumption but also in its more or less successful efforts at *editing* public opinion in such a way that it assumes a kind of equally imaginary but nonetheless effective coherence.

In its ambition to supervise the political in the name of its readers, the newspaper also supervises these readers themselves by observing certain standards of deliberation for the representation of what these readers are imagined to think, including the demand that information be verifiable and argument consistent. Obviously, newspapers will bend these standards in the service of whichever segment of the potential readership they seek to give shape to, but on the whole their function is

25

to act as a respectable mouthpiece for (a section of) public opinion ready to engage with other players in public space in the name of the imagined community of readers whose opinion they supervise. Social media as a rule do not supervise in this sense: instead, they typically surveil their users for commercial purposes, at best suppressing only content considered offensive. Properly editing the sharing'n'shaming bonanza that its billions of users indulge in into something like democratic deliberation is no longer an option, if ever it was.[2] Newspapers, needless to say, also have commercial purposes when supervising their readers, but that (at least in principle) involves securing a readership in whose name they propose to supervise the political sphere, not so much securing data about individual preferences they can sell to the highest bidder eager to use these data to shift more products, or to shaft the political process.

For Kant, the standards of deliberation in public debate are of paramount importance: opinions circulating in public must be based on objective information and must be argumentatively coherent if they are to earn the right to challenge political authority. Yet Kant was keenly aware that in matters involving the question of what it means to be human, what counts as "objective information" is itself open to debate. Indeed, as suggested above, it was a debate central to his critical philosophy's ambition to monitor the possibility conditions for a proper balance between certain knowledge about facts of nature and rational certainty about the moral purpose of human freedom. To articulate that balance, he repeatedly resorts to an analogy between the study of the movements of stars and planets and the study of human history. That the analogy never quite works is less interesting than Kant's attraction to it, particularly in his writings for the wider public, which testifies to his recognition of the well-earned and increasingly publicly applauded confidence of modern natural science even as he sought to claim respect for an alternative *Wissenschaft* up to the task of investigating human purpose.

The Science of Nature and the Science of Humankind

In the conclusion to his *Critique of Practical Reason* (1788), Kant comes clean on what moves him most: "Two things fill the mind with ever new and increasing admiration and reverence, the more often and more steadily one reflects on them:

the starry heavens above me and the moral law within me" (269). It seems a pretty straightforward statement, but when pressed a little it goes straight to the core of Kant's critical project and indeed to the core of the modern predicament. For the important difference between stars and the moral law is that stars are open in principle to empirical natural-scientific observation in ways that the moral law is not, which also suggests that the methods and discourse of natural science may not be adequate to deal with what matters to humans: not just "what, where, whence, whither, when"—all answerable within the objective space-time coordinates of natural science—but "*why*." As a scientist himself—his first book was *General History of Nature and Theory of the Heavens* (1755)—Kant was particularly keen to study human conduct with the discipline and rigour expected of science, but precisely because he was a good scientist, he was also acutely sensitive to the need to recognise that feature of human existence that appears to exceed the life of humans as "animal creatures" that are destined to return the matter of which they consist to the planet they inhabit (itself "a mere speck in the universe" [269]): the thought (for it may not quite be a fact, which is why natural science may not in itself be able to grasp it) that humans are persons whose purpose it is to live in accordance with moral law.

In previous phases of human history, Kant continues his conclusion, the observation of the stars landed us with astrology, while thinking about the moral law led to superstition and fanaticism (*Schwärmerei*). But just like the proper development of scientific method backed up by mathematics eventually led to the replacement of astrology by astronomy, so the principled study of human "moral capacities" can lead to a true knowledge of what it means to be human. Such, at least, is what Kant hopes for: that there can be a true science (*Wissenschaft*) of human morality just as there already is one of the material universe, and that this science will replace fanaticism and superstition with a confident account of wisdom.

> In a word, science *[Wissenschaft]* (critically sought and methodically directed) is the narrow gate that leads to the *doctrine of wisdom*, if by this is understood not merely what one ought *to do*, but what ought to serve *teachers* as a guide to prepare well and clearly the path to wisdom which everyone should travel, and to secure others against taking the wrong way; philosophy must always remain the guardian of this science, and though the public need take no interest in its subtle investigations it has to take an interest in the *doctrines* which, after being worked up in this way, can first be quite clear to it (270–71).

Although Kant is too modest to say so, the big book of which these are the closing sentences is itself intended as a substantial contribution to this "doctrine of wisdom". The *Critique of Practical Reason* is certainly full of "subtle investigations" that have kept philosophers occupied over the past centuries. Fortunately perhaps, these need not detain us here: we are interested not so much in the precise detail of Kant's (or anyone else's) philosophy, but rather in the way these philosophical ideas circulate in the public sphere, in their potential function in public deliberation about the right way forward for humankind.

Kant's emphasis on the role of "teachers" in the quotation above indicates that he too was actively interested in this public circulation of the results of his investigations. It confirms the role he himself played in the *Berlinische Monatsschrift*, by publishing articles for the general reading public such as the piece on "What is Enlightenment?" we have already looked at. In another piece published in that same journal one month earlier, he addresses the question of the way forward for humankind head-on, under the title "Idea for a Universal History with a Cosmopolitan Purpose" ("Idee zu einer allgemeinen Geschichte in weltbürgerlicher Absicht"). Here too, Kant resorts to the analogy between astronomy and the science of humanity, but a revealing absence in the analogy demonstrates its limitations.

The article's intent is to find a "guiding principle" for a universal history of humanity that makes rational sense, and to this end Kant draws up nine "propositions" which, taken together, form the blueprint for such a universal history (1784a, 42). According to the eighth proposition, the realisation of the highest purpose of nature is the constitution of a conglomerate of peaceful cosmopolitan states, a perspective which is projected as the outcome of "a hidden plan of nature" into a distant future (50). Kant acknowledges that for this "hidden plan" to sound plausible, some indication of "a purposeful natural process of this kind" is required, though he admits that not much evidence can be expected since human history has not been up and running for long enough for us to be able accurately to determine its course. Still, he adds, this is no more difficult than it is to determine "the path which our sun […] is following within the vast system of the fixed stars," and although we do not yet have sufficient astronomical observations to determine the exact path the sun will follow, "from the general premise that the universe is constituted as a system and from the little which has been learned by observation, we can conclude with sufficient certainty that a movement of this kind does exist in reality" (50).

Note that "a movement of this kind" refers to the path of the sun, not the course of human history, and that what is crucially missing in the analogy is the *point* or *purpose* of the movement of the sun. In the framework of natural science available to Kant and his contemporary readers, the exact course of the sun may be *difficult to determine*, but "the premise that the universe is constituted as a system" guarantees that that course is *in principle determinable*, as it must be the result of physical forces whose impact can be plotted mathematically. No such premise or principle is available for human history, other than the assumption that human reason itself guarantees this determinability—an assumption for which there is as yet no evidence that can stand the test of natural-scientific objectivity, which renders the analogy between astronomy and history, and specifically future-oriented history, quite literally pointless, or at least a case of wishful thinking.

Kant knows this, of course, and almost admits as much when he notes that "it appears that we might by our own rational projects accelerate the coming of this period" in which the "hidden plan of nature" for the history of humankind will be realised. No astronomical observation is likely to affect the course of the sun, and if human rational projects can plausibly affect the course of universal human history, that is where the analogy stops before it has even started. But Kant also knows that his readers are as impressed with the advances of natural science as he is, and that aligning his political thought with the prestige of scientific progress may well amplify the impact of his "rational project" even though this may be seen to compromise its rational coherence.

To be clear: this is not a matter of finding fault with Kant. On the contrary: what is impressive about his writings for the general public is the effort he makes to *imagine* what an ideal organisation of human society might look like (the *purpose* or *Absicht* in the title of the article flags his commitment to a peaceful cosmopolitan world order governed by enlightened human reason), while using the emerging truth regime of natural science (which has little to say about notions like the ultimate meaning of human history) as a frame within which this imagination becomes compelling. Importantly, this frame is quite specifically a frame, like that of a picture: it demarcates an area within which something is to be seen—and in this particular case something that cannot strictly speaking be seen. The "*bestirnte Himmel*" is visible in ways the "*moralische Gesetz*" that Kant hopes to discern in human history is not—the latter residing, as he notes in the conclusion to the *Critique of Practical Reason*, in the "invisible self" (Kant 1788, 269).

Put in slightly more technical terms, the stars belong to the *phenomenal* order, the order of appearance, open to empirical inspection, while the moral law pertains to the realm of the *noumenal,* the domain of *ideas* which in principle is not available for objective observation. Yet as Kant will come to say explicitly in his third and final major philosophical work, the *Critique of Judgement* (1790), we human beings do want at least some indication of the "objective reality" of ideas (even though this is strictly speaking "impossible"), and such an indication can be supplied in the form of intuitions (*Anschauungen*), *images* or *symbols* that provisionally embody what is in principle beyond vision (225). For an answer to the question about what it means to be human to have some kind of impact, it needs body, and time and again Kant borrows that body from celestial bodies or other large-scale natural phenomena.

Self-interest and Sympathy

In the opening paragraph of the article on "Universal History," Kant declares his interest in discovering "a regular progression" of the human race: by studying the apparently disjointed individual actions of individual subjects on a large scale, history hopes to uncover a "steadily advancing but slow development of man's original capacities" (41). And here, too, he resorts to natural science (this time meteorology) for support through analogy—though not without first having activated another kind of science: the science of the State we now call *statistics,* often without thinking about its etymological origin. In themselves, "the actions of individuals" may appear "confused and fortuitous", but "we may hope" that when looked at "in the history of the entire species," "a regular progression" can be discerned:

> Thus, marriages, births, and deaths do not seem subject to any rule by which their numbers could be calculated in advance, since the free human will has such a great influence upon them; and yet the annual statistics *[die jährlichen Tafeln]* for them in large countries prove that they are just as subject to constant natural laws as are the changes in the weather, which in themselves are so inconsistent that their individual occurrence cannot be determined in advance, but which nevertheless do not fail as a whole to sustain the growth of plants, the flow of rivers, and other natural functions in a uniform and uninterrupted course (41).

Human animals, driven by whatever drives them, engage with other humans, have sex, and die; but when you bracket whatever *they think* drives them, and just look at the numbers in the "annual tables" of statistics, what we now call demographic patterns (essentially *images*) begin to emerge—patterns that appear as stable as the cycles of the seasons emerging from otherwise apparently random meteorological occurrences. Statistics are a crucial part of the imaging technology enabling the state to "see like a state," as James C. Scott has argued in his book of that title, but that vision is also necessarily narrow and simplifying (Scott 1998, 11). Kant is refreshingly candid about this simplification, admitting in so many words that since we "cannot assume that mankind follows any rational *purpose of its own* in its collective actions," the writer of his projected "law-governed history of mankind" must factor out human intentions. Paradoxically, the possibility of a purposive history of humanity depends on the dismissal of not just individual but also collective human purpose.

> Individual men and even entire nations little imagine that, while they are pursuing their own ends, each in his own way and often in opposition to others, they are unwittingly guided in their advance along a course intended by nature. They are unconsciously promoting an end which, even if they knew what it was, would scarcely arouse their interest (41).

This closely echoes the remarkable passage in the Scottish philosopher Adam Smith's *Theory of Moral Sentiments* (1759) on the workings of the invisible hand. Smith seeks to establish the principle that even though "the rich" may only be driven by "their own vain and insatiable desires", in effect they share "the produce of all their improvements" with "the poor":

> They are led by an invisible hand to make nearly the same distribution of the necessaries of life, which would have been made, had the earth been divided into equal portions among all its inhabitants, and thus without intending it, without knowing it, advance the interest of the society, and afford means to the multiplication of the species (Smith 1976a, IV.I.10).

What Smith and Kant have in common here is the intent to describe aggregated human activity, irrespective of individual intentions, as driven towards a purpose that makes sense—which Kant calls "a civil society which can administer justice universally" ("*einer allgemeine das Recht verwaltenden bürgerlichen Gesellschaft*") (Kant 1874a, 45), and Smith more neutrally calls "the interest of the society" and "the multiplication of the species." It is important to underscore that this shared intent is resolutely anthropological: it amounts to the rational attempt to uncover the first principles of human sociality on the basis of scientific description—i.e. without taking *a priori* recourse to a religious narrative or myth. A religious account would argue that humans act the way they do because they were created to act in accordance with a higher purpose designed by God or Gods. An anthropological account merely states: humans act the way they do because they are human—and then proceeds to extract first principles from this tautology.

An important precursor for this enterprise in Western modernity is Thomas Hobbes, whose *Leviathan or The Matter, Forme and Power of a Common Wealth Ecclesiasticall and Civil* (1651) is one of the first fully developed social contract theories. Crucially for our purposes here, Hobbes's account is based on a principled refusal to describe the so-called *summum bonum* or greatest good, the ideal to which humankind should aspire—instead, he just starts out from what he describes as human nature, establishing that humans in the state of nature are involved in a war of all against all, each individual driven only by rapacious self-interest.

> In such condition [the state of nature], there is no place for Industry; because the fruit thereof is uncertain: and consequently no Culture of the Earth; no Navigation, nor use of the commodities that may be imported by Sea; no commodious Building; no Instruments of moving, and removing such things as require much force; no Knowledge of the face of the Earth; no account of Time; no Arts; no Letters; no Society; and which is worst of all, continuall feare and danger of violent death; And the life of man, solitary, poore, nasty, brutish, and short (Hobbes 1651, 89).

This is the *summum malum*, the greatest evil, and the only way out is to arrive at a social contract that limits individual self-interest under sovereign command.

Frontispiece of Thomas Hobbes, *Leviathan*, by Abraham Bosse (1651).

Possibly the central difference between Hobbes and Smith one century later is that Smith, as the opening sentences of *The Theory of Moral Sentiments* make clear, insists that humans are naturally driven not only by self-interest but also by something else:

> How selfish soever man may be supposed, there are evidently some principles in his nature, which interest him in the fortune of others, and render their happiness necessary to him, though he derives nothing from it except the pleasure of seeing it. Of this kind is pity or compassion, the emotion which we feel for the misery of others, when we either see it, or are made to conceive it in a very lively manner (Smith 1976a, I.i.i.1).

The human animal is a selfish creature that only seeks to further its own interest, yet one of these interests turns out to be the well-being of other humans. What Smith describes here is in line with what more recent anthropological, primatological and more generally behavioural-biological or zoological research establishes: no matter how selfish they undeniably are, human beings have highly developed "natural inclinations of sympathy and fairness towards others" (Tomasello 2016, 162).

The question is: how far do these inclinations stretch? Some scientists have argued that the evolutionary basis for modern human intersubjective relations is the practice of "cooperative breeding" or "alloparenting" (Hrdy 2009), whereby infant-rearing tasks are not just left to the mother but are shared with other members of the group. While it is relatively easy to imagine how such a practice may have evolved in a context of physical proximity in small groups, it is not immediately clear how this natural sympathy can be expanded to cover larger societal structures such as the nation or, at the limit, for now, planetary humanity. Smith's answer to this question is that such expansion takes care of itself as long as humans do not start to meddle with it too much. If it ain't broke don't fix it, and for Smith it is far from broke, spinning away under its own steam, though "led by an invisible hand." Again, what Smith programmatically cancels out here is knowledge and intention: there is a natural process of distribution of material which needs no intentional human interference to arrive at something like justice. The fanciful notion of an "invisible hand" leading all this is just that: a fanciful notion, an aftertrace of the theological tradition which the argument in its basic confidence in the rightness of things as they are does not really need.[3]

Significantly, Smith seeks to ground confidence in the invisible hand by appealing to a "natural" trick of the "imagination," whereby humans confuse the material comfort they might derive from wealth with "the regular and harmonious movement of the system, the machine or oeconomy by means of which it is produced" (Smith 1976a, IV.i.9). When confronted with the spectacular wealth of the rich, the poor are not naturally driven to envy but instead enjoy the spectacle of wealth-production for its own sake: "[i]t is this deception which rouses and keeps in continual motion the industry of mankind" (IV.i.10). Motivated though we are by interest in "the happiness of our fellow-creatures," we are inclined to confuse "end" and "means" and admire what appears as a "beautiful and orderly system" in its own right (IV.i.11).

It is no coincidence that Smith should also have been the author of the much better known *An Inquiry into the Nature and Causes of the Wealth of Nations* (1776), which was to become retrospectively canonised, rightly or wrongly, as the foundational document of capitalism. In that later work, Smith once more invokes the invisible hand as a trope advertising the soundness of a system of commodity circulation unhindered by misplaced human intention:

> He [the individal entrepreneur] generally, indeed, neither intends to promote the publick interest, nor knows how much he is promoting it. [...] he intends only his own gain, and he is in this, as in many other cases, led by an invisible hand to promote an end which was no part of his intention. Nor is it always the worse for the society that it was no part of it. By pursuing his own interest he frequently promotes that of the society more effectually than when he really intends to promote it. I have never known much good done by those who affected to trade for the publick good. It is an affectation, indeed, not very common among merchants, and very few words need be employed in dissuading them from it. (Smith 1976b, IV.ii.9)

The passage has become famous as evidence of Smith's confident reliance on the self-regulating powers of the economy, which has an in-built teleology ("an end") favourable to the "publick interest" but unaffected by whatever "intention" individual humans may have. What is less often noted is that this also implies that the faculty of sympathy Smith acknowledged as a distinctive feature of the human being apparently ceases to function in the wider context of society: all that matters there is personal gain; the relief of suffering is taken care of by the system itself. The material system of capital and commodity circulation naturally produces the public good and all is well with the world.[4]

Both Smith and Kant seek to describe human conduct in such a way that it makes sense in terms of a higher purpose, though without assuming that human individuals are intent on that higher purpose as they go about their business. Both, in other words, are sceptical about human beings' ability properly to conceive of the higher purpose and to strive for it in an appropriate way, yet they do not therefore wish to abandon this higher purpose. But while Smith seems confident in the capacity of the system of free capital and commodity circulation to deliver that higher purpose without human interference, Kant favours a more interventionist model based on *education* delivering *moral culture* rather than mere *civilisation*:

> We are *cultivated [cultivirt]* to a high degree by art and science. We are *civilised [civilisirt]* to the point of excess in all kinds of social courtesies and proprieties. But we are still a long way from the point where we could consider ourselves *morally* mature. For while the idea of morality is indeed present in culture, an application of this idea which only extends to the semblances of morality, as in love of honour and outward propriety, amounts merely to civilisation. But as long as states apply all their resources to their vain and violent schemes of expansion, thus incessantly obstructing the slow and laborious efforts of their citizens to cultivate their minds *[die langsame Bemühung der inneren Bildung der Denkungsart ihrer Bürger]*, and even deprive them of all support in these efforts, no progress in this direction can be expected. For a long internal process of careful work on the part of each commonwealth is necessary for the education *[Bildung]* of its citizens (Kant 1784a, 49).

The English translation misses the repetition in the original of the important term *Bildung*, which can be rendered as "education" or "cultivation" but also carries more embodied or plastic undertones suggesting "creation," "formation," "shaping," all related to the root sense of *Bild* as image, visual representation, what appears to the eye. Kant's last work published during his lifetime contains further evidence of the importance of this visual or spectacular register for thinking about the purpose of humanity, but this time with a remarkably vivid *historical* twist.

The Spectacle of Progress and the Machinery of Education

In *The Contest of Faculties* (1798) Kant once more turns to the question "Is the Human Race Continually Improving?" To answer that question, one would have to be able to predict the future, for even if we were to agree that the present state of humanity is a vast improvement on the past, "no-one could guarantee that its era of decline was not beginning" (180). We can predict future events in nature (for instance "eclipses of the sun and moon" [177]), but the "free actions" of humans in the future we cannot foresee (181), and what we *can* see of past and present human actions does not seem to make much sense in terms of an ultimate purpose. Perhaps, Kant suggests, we may have to choose another point of view: just as celestial mechanics only really began to add up when Copernicus left the point of view of the earth and looked at the movement of the planets as if he were standing on the sun, so the logic of human history may perhaps be revealed when we look at events from a perspective that is uncompromised by the illusions of our particular position. Intriguingly, here, too, Kant does not quite complete the analogy: instead of demarcating a point of view analogous to that of the sun in Copernican observation, he comes up with a historical "experience" which demonstrates that such an alternative perspective is possible and which therefore can function as a "*historical sign*" proving a "*tendency*" towards progress "within the human race as a *whole.*"

That significant event turns out to be itself an experience of looking on at unfolding events: not the French Revolution itself, but the way in which its events were enthusiastically witnessed by spectators "more than a hundred miles removed from the scene *[Schauplatz]*" (183). What Kant focuses on is "the attitude of the onlookers as it reveals itself *in public* while the drama of great political changes is taking place: for they openly express universal yet disinterested sympathy for one set of protagonists against their adversaries, even at the risk that their partiality could be of great disadvantage to themselves" (182). The onlookers, importantly, are not themselves involved in the *Spiel* of the revolution (for that would cloud their vision with self-interest): they are only *Zuschauer* aroused to "a *sympathy* which borders almost on enthusiasm" by the spectacle of a people fighting for a just constitution committed to the rights of the individual and the avoidance of wars of aggression, and this unselfish sympathy itself is sufficient proof of "a moral disposition within the human race."[5]

Let us note once more Kant's emphasis on the *public* nature of this expression of sympathy: not only are the facts of the revolution reported through media of the public sphere, but the enthusiastic response of the sympathisers themselves is also registered only because it takes place in public space and can therefore figure as an image of the public for the public. Kant calls the "*historical sign*" he brings to our attention a "*signum demonstrativum*" (180),[6] which invites us to recognise its logic as similar to what we would now call a public demonstration, a march or rally in protest against or support of something. As in the case of public sphere print discussed above, here, too, we can think of the global reach and diversification of such phenomena today: while Kant was pointing mainly to relatively local Prussian expressions of support for the revolution, the most massive more recent phenomenon of this kind is arguably the February 2003 anti-war protest, which mobilised millions across the world. Research on the role of mass media in this mobilisation has yielded interesting results: in countries where both government and opposition were supportive of war against Iraq, mobilisation was largely the result of initiatives taken by activist organisations and the group of demonstrators was less diverse ("the usual suspects") than in contexts where government and opposition, and thus also public opinion, were more divided and mass media did play a more important role in rallying support from protesters more representative of the population as a whole (Walgrave & Verhulst 2009, 1377). The *signum demonstrativum* may have become easier to send than two centuries ago, but it may also have become harder to read as unmistakable evidence in the face of the powers that be that humanity is improving.[7]

We may or may not be convinced by Kant's reasoning, but he is cautious enough not to conclude from it that the ideal society will be fully achieved anytime soon. In the meantime, what is to be done? Kant has made us see the ultimate purpose of humanity, but he has also told us he cannot predict when it will finally come about—and indeed he adds that it might never come about if an "epoch of natural convulsions" like that which "engulfed the animal and vegetable kingdoms before the era of man" were to destroy the human race, "For man in turn is a mere trifle in relation to the omnipotence of nature, or rather to its inaccessible highest cause" (185). We will return to this shift from the register of astronomy to the equally natural but more disturbing register of cataclysmic changes in life on earth (anticipating the findings of geology and evolutionary theory in the 19th century). For now, let us note Kant's insistence that the scientific recognition of the futility of humanity in the face of the forces of nature is precisely what humans should *not* act on:

> But if the rulers of man's own species regard him as such and treat him accordingly, either by burdening him like a beast and using him as a mere instrument of their ends, or by setting him up to fight in their disputes and slaughter his fellows, it is not just a trifle but a reversal of the *ultimate purpose* of creation (185).

So even if the actual unfolding of progress cannot be predicted, and even though it may never actually occur, mankind must act in the essentially *aesthetic* mode of "as if," in accordance with belief in such purposive progress powered by sympathy, and for such acting the role of the State is essential—just education in and of itself is not enough.

> To expect that the education of young people in intellectual and moral culture, reinforced by the doctrines of religion, firstly through domestic instruction and then through a series of schools from the lowest to the highest grade, will eventually not only make them good citizens, but will also bring them up to practise a kind of goodness which can continually progress and maintain itself, is a plan which is scarcely likely to achieve the desired success. For on the one hand, the people believe that the expense of educating their children should be met not by them but by the state; and on the other, the state itself [...] has no money left over to pay qualified teachers who will carry out their duties with enthusiasm, since it needs it all for war (188–89).

Yet without the intervention of the State, "the whole mechanism of education [*das ganze Maschinenwesen dieser Bildung*]" will be disjointed: it must be "designed on the considered plan and intention of the highest authority in the state, then set in motion and constantly maintained in uniform operation thereafter" (189). Again, Kant's choice of tropes is significant: *Bildung* should operate like a well-designed and well-maintained machine, and the term *Maschinenwesen* carries a positive charge, appealing as it does to a bourgeoisie which, while suspicious of State intervention, is beginning to take on its role as an agent of industrialisation in "revolutionising the instruments of production," as Friedrich Engels and Karl Marx were to note with more than mixed feelings half a century later (Engels & Marx 1848).

Ironically, Kant was only able to publish the text in which he puts responsibility for the design of public education in the hands of "the highest authority in the state" because that highest authority had recently died. In 1794, Friedrich Wilhelm II of Prussia, clearly convinced that he was *supra Grammaticos*, had expressed displeasure at Kant's unorthodox opinions and had effectively cancelled the philosopher's freedom of expression, but when the king died in 1797 and was succeeded by Friedrich Wilhelm III, Kant reclaimed his right to publish again (Lehman 2009, 71–72). In a further twist of irony, a decade or so after his accession Friedrich Wilhelm III entrusted the organisation of public education in Prussia to the author of an article published in the *Berlinische Monatsschrift* for December 1792 which had boldly stated that public education was none of the State's business. The author of that article, Wilhelm von Humboldt (1767–1835), would go on to become a driving force in the organisation of Prussian public education supervised and supported by the State so as "to provide the conditions in which each student could develop to the maximum, and as harmoniously as possible, his various capacities, moral, intellectual, and aesthetic," thereby "promoting the ideal of *Bildung* among students of all ages and of all social origins" (Sweet 1980, 36).

As Humboldt had originally conceived it, that ideal of individual *Bildung* was something to be preserved from state interference. The *Berlinische Monatsschrift* article of 1792 (which had ended on the statement that "national education *[öffentliche Erziehung]* seems to me to lie wholly beyond the limits within which the State's activity should properly be confined") was part of a larger work eventually published only after Humboldt's death under the title *Ideen zu einem Versuch die Grenzen der Wirksamkeit des Staats zu Bestimmen*, a book whose basic scepsis about state intervention is more assertively advertised in its 1969 English translation as *The Limits of State Action* (Humboldt 1993, 52). Yet as the cultural critic Matthew Arnold (1822–1888), an admirer of Humboldt and a fervent advocate for state-controlled education later in the century, argued, Humboldt may have been committed to an ideal of individual self-reliance, but when confronted with the demands of the modern condition, he also realised that in order to "enabl[e] the individual to stand perfect on his own foundations and to do without the State, the action of the State would for long, long years be necessary" (Arnold 1869, 124).

To many the name Humboldt is now familiar from the Humboldt-Universität zu Berlin. Established in 1809 by Friedrich Wilhelm III on the advice of Wilhelm von Humboldt and others, it was first known as Friedrich-Wilhelms-Universität; its current name was given to it at its reopening (after closure in 1945) under Communist rule in 1949. Significantly, the new name honoured not only one of its original founders, Wilhelm, but also his younger brother, Alexander von Humboldt (1769–1859), arguably one of the greatest natural scientists of the 19th century, as well as a global celebrity who has more places named after him than anyone else (Wulf 2015, 7). Taken together, the Humboldt brothers may be said to embody science and culture, *Bildung* and *Wissenschaft*—closely related, but destined to differ. In the second half of the 19th century, that close difference is instructively enacted in an encounter between Matthew Arnold, one of Wilhelm's self-declared heirs, and Thomas Henry Huxley (1825–1895), one of Alexander's chief successors in the professionalisation of science—who also, by the way, puts in an appearance in Gibson and Sterling's *Difference Engine*. Half a century younger than the Humboldts, Arnold and Huxley faced a much wider audience: mass society had arrived.

2 Evolution and Culture

What we now recognise as modern democracy is essentially a 19th-century transformation of the political. A central challenge was (and remains) the administration of this transformation: to what extent is the State responsible for its massively expanding body of citizens? More particularly: how (if at all) should it educate them to become modern citizens? Public discussions on this issue typically involve the relative importance and specificity of natural science and cultural history, as well as the right balance between self-interest and solidarity. Meanwhile, the advent of evolutionary theory has given the question of human development or "destiny" in general a radically different inflection, calling for a new understanding of the history and dignity of human beings and of the future of all life on the planet. With the disasters of the twentieth century and the inexorable expansion of an increasingly globalised communications industry and digital infrastructure, the question of a democratic education adequate to the demands of our precarious present has only become more urgent.

Keywords: democracy, class, nature and culture, science and criticism, liberal education, practical knowledge, progress, evolution, communications industry, propaganda, genes, memes, altruism, empathy, machine learning

The "Middle Classes" and "the Masses Below Them"

Matthew Arnold's essay "Democracy" (1861) first appeared as the introduction to his official report as school inspector on "the Systems of Popular Education in France, Holland, and the French Cantons of Switzerland"—which explains its emphasis on the implementation of the principles of the French Revolution in the organisation of state schools in France. Arnold is all in favour of this, but he knows that the vast majority of British participants in public discourse is extremely suspicious of any substantial intervention of the State in the organisation of education, and indeed in most public matters, preferring instead a very minimal State whose primary responsibilities are foreign affairs and the protection of property and political rights, not the creation of greater equality.

For Arnold, the establishment of a comprehensive State administration is a necessary response to the central facts of the modern condition: the massive population explosion since the late 18th century, the substantial rise of the middle classes as agents of industrial and commercial expansion, and the growing demand of the even more substantially expanding lower classes to enjoy more of the accumulating wealth of the nation—three decisive factors in the emergence of modern democracy. An important fundamental observation is that Arnold sees the rise of democracy as a natural and inevitable phenomenon which "like other operations of nature, merits properly neither blame nor praise" (Arnold 1861, 5). It is just democracy doing its thing, as aristocracy had successfully been doing for centuries: "*trying to affirm its own essence*; to live, to enjoy, to possess the world"—in short, "the ceaseless vital effort of human nature itself" (6). This is not dissimilar to the ultimate purpose of human nature revealed to Kant in displays of enthusiastic sympathy for the French Revolution (though Kant himself was suspicious of democracy), and like Kant Arnold is convinced that this "operation of nature" needs to be given direction. The Smithian idea that the invisible hand will take charge will not do, as Arnold implicitly argues when he states that the "spectacle" of the affluence of the upper class, which according to Smith inspires admiration of "the system" in the lower reaches of society, can only lead to depression and disenchantment in the lower classes of modern times (6).

Arnold concedes that in previous centuries the wealth and power of the aristocracy may have inspired the people by adding what he calls "*the grand style*" to the nation, but that effect has now weakened, and the resulting spectacle is that of an uglier Body Politic. "[T]o the eye of the imagination," Arnold adds, a "popular order" obediently respectful of the wealth and power of the ruling classes "is certainly a more beautiful body" (7) than that of a disgruntled populace demanding more equality—but that uglier body is the body that is now in place. The "more beautiful" and perhaps even "happier body" of subjects "not questioning the natural right of a superior order to lead it" now exists "for the imagination" only (8): it is a community that can *only* be nostalgically imagined, no longer plausibly imagined as real.

Democracy may not be a pretty sight, but hiding it under a veil of upper-class opulence is a bad idea—and bad ideas are what the upper classes are good at. For the fundamental reason why the aristocracy in Arnold's diagnosis is no longer able to control the subordinate classes is the "incapacity of aristocracies for ideas" (8): they have splendour and grandeur, but no real culture. What is wanted, then, is an alternative to the spectacle of the grand style, adequate to the demands of democracy and able to give "a high tone to the nation" again (14)—and for that Arnold turns to the idea of the State itself, as the institutional embodiment of "an ideal of high reason and right feeling" (15) that can take over the aristocracy's role as political authority.

Yet the greatest enemy of the State is not the aristocracy, whose relevance is fading anyway, but the middle class, so Arnold's first priority is the education of the bourgeoisie, who elsewhere he calls the Philistines, those who are lacking in real culture—not because, like the aristocracy ("the Barbarians"), they cannot be bothered and prefer to be stuck in arrogant superiority and indifference, but because they are committed to narrow-minded individualism.

> It is of itself a serious calamity for a nation that its tone of feeling and grandeur of spirit should be lowered or dulled. But the calamity appears far more serious still when we consider that the middle classes, remaining as they are now, with their narrow, harsh, unintelligent, and unattractive spirit and culture, will almost certainly fail to mould or assimilate the masses below them, whose sympathies are at the present moment actually wider and more liberal than theirs. They arrive, these masses, eager to enter into possession of the world, to gain a more vivid sense of their own life and activity. In this their irrepressible development, their natural educators and initiators are those immediately above them, the middle classes. If these classes cannot win their sympathy or give them their direction, society is in danger of falling into anarchy (22).

So to Arnold the rise of democracy is a fact of nature that requires a concerted response by organising an education for the nation by the State. More specifically, schools for the middle classes where they acquire culture, and with culture the means to manage the masses—especially also to manage the powerful reservoirs of sympathy the masses possess and which undirected may lead to anarchy.

"Anarchy" as Arnold uses it is a pretty loose term, mainly meaning, as he puts in in *Culture and Anarchy*, "doing as one likes" (Arnold 1869, 81)—closer to the Sex Pistols' mindlessly amusing "don't know what I want but I know how to get it" than to anything advocated by, say, a committed anarchist political theorist like Pierre-Joseph Proudhon (1809–1865). What Arnold calls anarchy is not all that different from today's social media's like-icon culture, which Arnold would probably not credit as culture at all but would diagnose instead as the potential for public sympathy gone wrong.

In contrast, the central ethos of the schools Arnold envisages is the spirit of criticism, which elsewhere he defines as "*a disinterested endeavour to learn and propagate the best that is known and thought in the world*" (Arnold 1864, 50). Following this spirit is explicitly not favouring whatever one may happen to like, but instead committing oneself to "the endeavour, in all branches of knowledge, theology, philosophy, history, art, science, to see the object as in itself it really is" (26). The upshot of this endeavour is *culture*, Arnold's translation of Humboldt's *Bildung*. While Humboldt's *Bildung*, like Arnold's *culture*, does acknowledge the crucial importance of science or *Wissenschaft*, its principal emphasis is on what we would now call the humanities (as distinct from the natural sciences and the social and behavioural sciences), with a particular extra emphasis on the classics. In the organisation of education, that emphasis was increasingly questioned as science rose to further eminence in the course of the 19th century.

Science and Culture

In a speech later published as "Science and Culture," Thomas Henry Huxley outlined his idea about what modern education should deliver, and he did so in explicit disagreement with Arnold. The occasion for the speech was significant in its own right: the opening in 1880 of a new Scientific College in Birmingham with funding from a self-made industrialist, Josiah Mason (1795–1881), who ran the largest pen-making business in Britain. For Huxley, the establishment of the college was nothing less than "an indication that we are reaching the crisis of the battle, or rather of the long series of battles, which have been fought over education"—a crisis directly related to the relatively recent appearance of a new "army," "ranged round the banner of Physical Science" (T.H. Huxley 1880, 136).

> From the time that the first suggestion to introduce physical science into ordinary education was timidly whispered, until now, the advocates of scientific education have met with opposition of two kinds. On the one hand, they have been pooh-poohed by the men of business who pride themselves on being the representatives of practicality; while, on the other hand, they have been excommunicated by the classical scholars, in their capacity of Levites in charge of the ark of culture and monopolists of liberal education (136–37).

The opposition of the practical men, Huxley suggests, has meanwhile been overruled by the obvious practical value of science—as is indeed demonstrated by the decision of one such practical man, Mason himself, to set up a Trust to establish a university college dedicated to education in "sound, extensive, and practical scientific knowledge" (138). The defenders of culture and liberal education, on the other hand, are still very much in business, and to them one of the specific conditions stipulated for the College curriculum by Mason is an insult: "mere literary instruction and education" is prohibited, thus ruling out "the ordinary classical course of our schools and universities" for students of the new College (140–41). The "Levites in charge of the ark of culture" are up in arms, but Huxley wholeheartedly supports Mason's decision:

> For I hold very strongly by two convictions—The first is, that neither the discipline nor the subject-matter of classical education is of such direct value to the student of physical science as to justify the expenditure of valuable time upon either; and the second is, that for the purpose of attaining real culture, an exclusively scientific education is at least as effectual as an exclusively literary education.

Further to develop these convictions, Huxley then chooses Matthew Arnold, "our chief apostle of culture", as his sparring partner (142). Arnold, importantly, is not just a straw target for Huxley: the two of them are public intellectuals who respect each other and have much in common (White 2005). Both had fathers who were involved in education and carry on that concern, both are also modern professionals playing prominent public roles—Arnold as an inspector of schools and professor of poetry at Oxford; Huxley as a leading figure in the professionalisation and institutionalisation of science, a professor at the Royal School of Mines, and a vigorous spokesman for evolutionary theory (his nickname was "Darwin's bulldog").[8]

Huxley quotes a passage from Arnold's "The Function of Criticism at the Present Time" (1864) which sketches an ideal vision of Europe as it appears to the critical spirit that is the essence of culture, driven by the desire "to know the best that has been thought and said in the world." The function of this critical spirit is to regard

> Europe as being, for intellectual and spiritual purposes, one great confederation, bound to a joint action and working to a common result; and whose members have, for their common outfit, a knowledge of Greek, Roman, and Eastern antiquity, and of one another. Special, local, and temporary advantages being put out of account, that modern nation will in the intellectual and spiritual sphere make most progress, which most thoroughly carries out this programme. And what is that but saying that we too, all of us, as individuals, the more thoroughly we carry it out, shall make the more progress? (Arnold qtd. in T.H. Huxley 1880, 142–43).

For Huxley, the emphasis on "the intellectual and spiritual sphere" in this vision makes the achievement of real progress unlikely. What is needed for the modern outfit is input "from the stores of physical science" (144). Yet instead of arguing for a combination of Arnold's "criticism" on the one hand and "science" on the other, Huxley strategically takes over Arnold's signature term while expanding it into "scientific 'criticism of life'" (150). The rhetorical effect of this move is to scramble the customary distinction between "fact" and "value" typically resorted to by defenders of liberal education against the encroachment of science. If physical science, too, can claim to be not only committed to the ethos of objective evidence but also driven by the critical spirit, it has just as much claim to the province of culture as the proponents of classical humanist scholarship.

In general terms, there is no reason why science should not be thought of as a major contributor to culture, and in "Literature and Science," his response to Huxley two years later, Arnold readily admits as much. Yet an important difference between the ethos of natural science and the spirit of criticism as Arnold understands it remains, as is apparent in Huxley's fuller description of the "scientific 'criticism of life'":

> It is [...] certain that nature is the expression of a definite order with which nothing interferes, and that the chief business of mankind is to learn that order and govern themselves accordingly. Moreover this scientific "criticism of life" presents itself to us with different credentials from any other. It appeals not to authority, nor to what anybody may have thought or said, but to nature. It admits that all our interpretations of natural fact are more or less imperfect and symbolic, and bids the learner seek for truth not among words but among things. It warns us that the assertion which outstrips evidence is not only a blunder but a crime (T.H. Huxley 1880, 150).

The key to the difference between science and criticism is in the final sentence: for the assertions of criticism as Arnold conceives it cannot *not* outstrip evidence. Science, as Huxley insists, answers only to nature: it does not appeal to "what anybody may have thought or said"—the edited echo of Arnold's catchphrase definition of criticism's intent on "the best that is known and thought in the world" is unmistakable, as is the allusion to "nullius in verba," the motto of the Royal Society of London for Improving Natural Knowledge (of which Huxley was a fellow and whose President he would become in 1883). Criticism in Arnold's sense, in contrast, is committed to the bit edited out in Huxley's echo: "the best," a quasi-quality that strictly speaking only decisively applies when it cannot be reduced to evidence-based measurable qualities like size, weight or speed. In science, applying such quasi-qualities may indeed qualify as "crime"; in criticism it is core business, and it is core business because it addresses the human question of purpose which involves what takes shape "among words" more than what can be found "among things."

This is obviously not to say that what can be found among things does not matter. On the contrary: what criticism is interested in is how to make what can be established between things matter to humans. Arnold is clear about this when he takes on board the then (and in some quarters to this day) still contentious issue of the descent of humans. Slightly misquoting Darwin's *The Descent of Man* (1871), Arnold acknowledges that "our ancestor was a hairy quadruped furnished with a tail and pointed ears, probably arboreal in his habits" (Arnold 1882, 64). It is important to emphasise that, unlike many of his fellow-apostles of culture at the time, Arnold does not challenge this finding: it is an "interesting" and "important" piece of "natural knowledge" "we should all of us be acquainted with." But acquaintance with bits of natural knowledge—impressive and irrefutable though they may be, especially when integrated in what Huxley calls "the general conceptions of the universe, which have been forced upon us by physical science" (T.H. Huxley 1880, 149)—is not enough for humans. Human nature, Arnold asserts in a casual recycling of the old triad of the true, the good and the beautiful, is marked by "an invincible desire" to connect such knowledge to a "sense for conduct" and a "sense for beauty." And establishing this connection, Arnold adds, "the men of science will not do for us, and will hardly even profess to do" (Arnold 1882, 64–65).

Criticism, in contrast, is precisely intent on propagating culture as "the best" expression of the whole of human being. As I understand it (for Arnold does not quite put it this way), this means criticism must engage with what cannot reduce to the evidence base of natural knowledge, for the simple reason that nature has no history, just time and space. Human culture is the catch-all term for all the symbolic practices through which humans have expressed their concern for what is not available for empirical observation, especially the difference that will be made by their expression of this concern itself. In slightly more technical terms, borrowed from speech act theory (Austin 1976), culture is *performative*: it is obviously based on what can be established in terms of both natural knowledge and the material remnants of culture itself, but instead of expressing itself, as nature does in Huxley's view, according to "a definite order with which nothing interferes" and which science can in principle establish as fact in *constative* assertions, culture is essentially the expression of a search for purpose in an absence of order. Science establishes the definite order of which nature is the expression; criticism investigates the projections of purpose performed in culture.

The debate between Arnold and Huxley is instructive as an iteration—one of very many—of the attempt to think together *a* course for culture along lines of progress and *the* course of nature as an order with which nothing can interfere. Both, importantly, like Kant and the Humboldts, were fundamentally confident that this attempt was itself on the right track and that public educational infrastructure provided by a State following instructions from experts in culture and science would bring a brave new world of prosperity and peace. Meanwhile, Arnold's niece, Julia Ward, and Huxley's son, Leonard, got married, and two of their children were to add curious twists to this story of science and culture.

Bildung and Propaganda

Thomas Henry Huxley ended his speech at Mason College on a word of advice: next to instruction in physical science, and conceding some character-building exposure to modern (not classical) literary and artistic culture, the College should consider adding sociology to the curriculum.[9] For "the steady march of self-restraining freedom" to continue, "a clear understanding of the conditions of social life" and of "the machinery of society" is necessary, and any modern educational institution must supply this to its students in ways that conform to "the methods of investigation adopted in physical researches":

> They [the students] must learn that social phænomena are as much the expression of natural laws as any others; that no social arrangements can be permanent unless they harmonise with the requirements of social statics and dynamics; and that, in the nature of things, there is an arbiter whose decisions execute themselves (T.H. Huxley 1880, 158–59).

Half a century later, Huxley's grandson, Aldous Huxley (1894–1963), published his nightmare vision of a society engineered on the basis of "the nature of things." *Brave New World* (1932) is a dystopian novel depicting a future in which humans are governed and indeed bred by the application of scientific methods under supervision of the World State. The basic set-up of the novel is straightforward. The World Controllers have engineered a near-perfect society of stability and contentment for the World State population, itself divided into distinct classes whose members are designed from the start to be happy with their place. Drugs, entertainment and casual sex take care of whatever frustration may still be lingering, while some recalcitrant misfits in the higher classes critical of the State's hypermanagement of post-historical humanity are sent into exile. The novel's plot kicks off with the arrival of John, a naturally born and raised human considered a savage by World State standards. Unable to adapt to micro-engineered society, John ultimately flees into the countryside where he is tracked down by the media for the entertainment of the masses and eventually kills himself.

If *Brave New World* is not particularly good as a novel, that is partly because its satire of a State run on scientific principles is compromised by its nostalgic inability to imagine an alternative other than suicidal reality-denial or exile.[10] That has not prevented it from becoming an extremely popular work of speculative fiction. To the contrary: by serving its readers an entertaining vision of the terrible logic of wall-to-wall entertainment from the perspective of one of the few remaining unbrainwashed humans, it can comfortably sacrifice that one unmodified human as a victim of an inhuman future that drives him to kill himself, without having to engage with the messy question of what the future *should* look like to be better, apart from being different from what the World State has engineered, and closer to nice and natural. This is not so much an intellectual failure as it is a failure of imaginative nerve, though it is only fair to admit that dystopian fiction which does imagine convincing resistance to humanity gone bad is rare.

As it stands, though, *Brave New World*'s imagination of the production of humans along scientific principles is entertaining enough, but it acquires extra interest in light of its author's grandfather's grand vision of society. The novel opens on a guided tour through the World State's Central London Hatchery and Conditioning Centre introducing us to the artificial mass manufacture of human beings predestined and conditioned to remain complacent and content in whatever class they happen to be assigned to (Aldous Huxley 2005, 23–24). The lower classes are conditioned by electric shocks, while moral education for the higher classes, significantly, is replaced by "hypnopaedia": sleeping infants are disciplined into docile class consciousness by being played the same messages hundreds of times (33–34). As the Director of Hatcheries and Conditioning puts it: "wordless conditioning is crude and [...] cannot bring home the finer distinctions, cannot inculcate the more complex courses of behaviour. For that there must be words, but words without reason" (35–36). Such would seem to be the perverse outcome of the scientific truth regime advanced by Thomas Henry Huxley half a century before *Brave New World* was written: to properly manage the "machinery of society" in conformity with "the nature of things," words must be turned into things, and *Bildung* literally reconfigured as building or breeding.

Entertaining as it is, *Brave New World* disappoints in its failure to acknowledge its own complicity with the logic of entertainment it seeks to criticise. Ultimately, its nightmare vision is oddly comforting. It replaces the mess of modernity with a future in which science has miraculously succeeded in managing that mess, and the paradoxical effect is that, at least at first reading, the all too real mess of modernity in which its readers find themselves does recede, not through the miracles of science but through the mechanisms of amusement. Yet the mess, of course, remains, as the challenge of modernity itself. If the fantasy of a society micro-engineered by science can be seen as a facile fiction based on an uncritical *reproductio ad absurdum* of Thomas Henry Huxley's vision, its function as slick entertainment making fun of the hypermanaged SuperState risks forgetting the critical imperative issued by Matthew Arnold: to accept responsibility for "those vast, miserable, unmanageable masses of sunken people" created by "the mere unfettered pursuit of the production of wealth" (Arnold 1869, 175). In ridiculing and demonising both science and the state, *Brave New World* warns against what the designs of its author's late-Victorian ancestors might lead to, but it does so at the cost of forgetting what those designs were for—and indeed at the cost of forgetting history itself.

In the space of a fiction inventing a society six hundred years or so in the future that has itself cancelled history (as World Controller Mustapha Mond says, quoting Henry Ford, "History is bunk" [Aldous Huxley 2005, 40]), this history-denial may be part of the set-up, yet in the wider public sphere of discourse other considerations apply. Some twenty-five years after the novel's first publication, Huxley addressed those considerations in *Brave New World Revisited* (1958), a sequence of short essays investigating how much of his fable had actually come closer than he had imagined. Unsurprisingly, one of his principal targets in this is "the development of a vast communications industry, concerned in the main neither with the true nor the false, but with the unreal, the more or less totally irrelevant" (267). Appealing to human beings' "almost infinite appetite for distractions," this industry not only threatens to destroy all resistance to malevolent manipulation but also risks disabling "the rational propaganda essential to the maintenance of individual liberty and the survival of democratic institutions" (268).

Huxley's acknowledgement of the necessity of *rational* propaganda is striking in its own right, given the generally negative connotation of the term resonating also in the "Bureaux of Propaganda and the College of Emotional Engineering" in *Brave New World* (70). Yet it is specifically remarkable in its echo of Arnold's definition of the critical spirit of culture as "*a disinterested endeavour to learn and propagate the best that is known and thought in the world*" (Arnold 1864, 50). In classical Latin, *propagare* typically means the procreation of plants by means of cuttings or slips; its etymological root, which it shares with the word *page* (as in what you are reading now), is the stem of *pangere*, to fix, fasten, set, plant. More generally, *propagare* means to extend, enlarge, continue, spread, or increase. The post-classical Latin term *progaganda* itself came into use with the creation in the early 17th century of the *Congregatio de propaganda fide*, the congregation for propagating the (Catholic) faith—the Vatican body that eventually supervised the global spread of Catholic Christianity. So at the root of the term—pun inevitable—is the image of reproducing symbols along lines as predictable and manageable as those followed in the cultivation of plants; the word "culture" itself, of course, shares that imaginary legacy.

Huxley's concern for "rational propaganda", then, can be read as a positive echo of his great-uncle's plea for the propagation of culture—an echo amplified later on in *Brave New World Revisited* in the essay "Education for Freedom." "[A]ll the intellectual materials for a sound education in the proper use of language [and] in the art of distinguishing between the proper and the improper use of symbols" are available, Huxley writes, "yet children are nowhere taught, in any systematic way, to distinguish true from false, or meaningful from meaningless, statements" (Aldous Huxley 2005, 329). The reason for this is simple: "[b]ecause their elders, even in the democratic countries, do not want them to be given this education." To illustrate the point, Huxley invokes "the brief, sad history of the Institute for Propaganda Analysis"—as it turns out, a sobering because (at first at least) abortive instance of the kind of philanthropic educational initiative celebrated by Thomas Henry Huxley at the opening of Mason College, though this time directed by a desire to provide not so much "sound, extensive, and practical scientific knowledge" (T.H. Huxley 1880, 138) but rather something closer to the critical spirit envisaged by Matthew Arnold.

The Institute for Propaganda Analysis (IPA) was created in 1937 with funding from Edward A. Filene (1860–1937), who had made his fortune running a department store founded by his father, and had also played a major role in the introduction of credit unions in the United States. Filene's ambition was to advance the cause of "education for democracy" by "helping people learn how to think for themselves rather than telling them what to think" (Lee & Lee 1979, 118). With the money he made available for this, the IPA was created, though Filene died before it was up and running. The IPA board consisted mainly of academics who shared Filene's fear that the overload in biased information circulating in public space was increasingly threatening independent thinking—the "use of one's own reason" championed by Kant. The IPA sought to address this by designing various instruments to help the public to apply rational reasoning to the propaganda they were fed. It published monthly *Propaganda Analysis* bulletins, a couple of books and a series of "Decide for Yourself" packets containing conflicting propaganda treatments of the same topic, and it also reached out to schools and discussion groups with advice. The initial response was positive, but when US involvement in World War II increased, the mood changed, and the IPA was accused of instilling scepticism and left-wing sentiments in school pupils, leading it to suspend its activities in early 1942 (Lee & Lee 1979, 121).[11]

For Huxley, the moral of this "sad history" is that "the social order" cannot deal with too much critical spirit in "the common folk." They need to remain "suggestible enough to make their society work, but not so suggestible as to fall helplessly under the spell of professional mind-manipulators": "they should be taught enough about progaganda analysis to preserve them from an uncritical belief in sheer nonsense, but not so much as to make them reject outright the not always rational outpourings of the well-meaning guardians of tradition" (Aldous Huxley 2005, 330). Acknowledging that this does not sound very inspiring, Huxley adds a more positive flourish, "a set of generally acceptable values based upon a solid foundation of facts":

> The value, first of all, of individual freedom, based upon the facts of human diversity and genetic uniqueness; the value of charity and compassion, based upon the old familiar fact, lately rediscovered by modern psychiatry—the fact that, whatever their mental and physical diversity, love is as necessary to human beings as food and shelter; and finally the value of intelligence, without which love is impotent and freedom unattainable. This set of values will provide us with a criterion by which propaganda may be judged. The propaganda that is found to be both nonsensical and immoral may be rejected out of hand. That which is merely irrational, but compatible with love and freedom, and not on principle opposed to the exercise of intelligence, may be provisionally accepted for what it is worth (330–31).

Two points deserve to be underscored in this conclusion. First, its marked contrast in tone with the "philosophy of life" Huxley a decade or so earlier, when he wrote his preface to the 1946 re-edition of *Brave New World*, had felt was lacking in the novel. There, he had expressed a sense of regret that the book did not possess "philosophical completeness" and suggested that if he were to rewrite it, he would have added an alternative "philosophy of life":

> [a] kind of Higher Utilitarianism, in which the Greatest Happiness principle would be secondary to the Final End principle—the first question to be asked and answered

in every contingency of life being: "How will this thought or action contribute to, or interfere with, the achievement, by me and the greatest possible number of other individuals, of man's Final End?" (Aldous Huxley 2005, 7).

Compared to this "Higher Utilitarianism", a Bentham-based remix of Kant's second formulation of the categorical imperative,[12] the resignation twelve years later in *Brave New World Revisited* to relative irrationality compatible with love, freedom and intelligence is notably less ambitious, if therefore also more realistic.

But the second point about the conclusion to "Educating for Freedom" is arguably more significant: it involves the grounding of human freedom in "the facts of human diversity and genetic uniqueness", and this signals a different reading of what is real or realistic.

"A Race Between Education and Catastrophe"

In Kant the notion of the final end or purpose of humanity is what singles out humans as not just animals but always also creatures endowed with reason. The development of this reason in freedom is nothing less than "the *ultimate purpose* of creation *[Endzweck der Schöpfung]*" (Kant 1798, 185). With the advent and rise of fully-fledged evolutionary theory from the mid-19th century onwards, there is a shift in emphasis: no longer strictly speaking "creatures" created according to some kind of intelligent design, humans are simply the only extant species of animal on the planet in which reason has evolved. This "uniqueness of man," as they could still get away with calling it at that time, is the great theme of Aldous Huxley's older brother, the biologist, natural history entertainment pioneer and public intellectual Julian Huxley (1887–1975).[13]

Responsible for one of the world's first natural history documentaries (the Academy Award-winning *The Private Lives of the Gannets* [1934]) and instrumental in the creation of the World Wildlife Fund (now World Wide Fund for Nature, the changed name reflecting the increased urgency of its mission), Julian Huxley can be conveniently thought of as the original precursor of David Attenborough (Kellaway 2010). But he was also remarkably active more generally as an enthusiastic global ideology-engineer. If Aldous Huxley tends to take a fairly dim view of humankind, Julian Huxley was an indefatigable spokesman for up-beat comprehensive "transhumanism" or "evolutionary humanism" (Julian Huxley 1957, 13–17; 279–312). Like Kant, he was keen to answer the question whether humanity was getting any better, but unlike Kant he could propose to draw on evolutionary science to answer this question squarely and affirmatively (explicitly dismissing Aldous Huxley's scepsis in the process): "progress is not myth but science, not an erroneous wish-fulfilment, but a fact" (Julian Huxley 1957, 21). The essay from which this confident statement is lifted, "A Re-Definition of Progress," has an interesting publication history that demonstrates Julian Huxley's prominent if controversial role in public discourse as "evolution's representative man" (Nys 2011).

In November 1945, following three years of meetings of the Ministers of Education of the United Nations exploring a post-war future for the allied countries, the decision was taken to establish an organisation for educational and cultural cooperation. In the run-up to this decision, the name that was originally proposed, UNECO (United Nations Educational and Cultural Organisation), was changed to UNESCO—the S for Scientific was added partly at the instigation of Julian Huxley, a member of the new organisation's Preparatory Commission. A few months later, Huxley became Secretary of the Preparatory Commission and began to draw up a pamphlet on UNESCO's purpose and philosophy, aiming for nothing less than "the beginning of a world brain" (qtd. Nys 2011, 404). Huxley borrowed the term "world brain" from H.G. Wells (1866–1946), author of science fiction classics like *The Time Machine* (1895) and *The War of the Worlds* (1898), but also one-time student of Thomas Henry Huxley and co-author, with Julian Huxley and his own son G.P. Wells, of the successful three-volume book *The Science of Life: a summary of contemporary knowledge about life and its possibilities* (1929–30).[14] Wells had developed his notion of a World Brain in a series of texts published in one volume in 1938, and it is now widely credited, alongside the work of Paul Otlet (1868–1944), as a prefiguration of the world wide web (Rayward 2008, 236; Heylighen 2011, 278). Wells and Otlet obviously could not yet think their visions of a global community of information through into the digital format so familiar to us now, and neither could Huxley—though it is worth recalling that the world wide web eventually did get started in CERN, the European Organisation for Nuclear Research established by UNESCO in 1954.

Huxley's pamphlet *Unesco: Its Purpose and Its Philosophy* was published in 1946, and it is a curious piece of internationalist evolutionary propaganda for peace. It opens by recalling the Constitution setting out UNESCO's aims, including the "noble words" of the then Prime Minister of the UK, Clement Attlee: "since wars begin in the minds of men, it is in the minds of men that the defences of peace must be constructed" (Julian Huxley 1946, 5). Having summarised the principal aims of the organisation—furthering "the democratic principles of the dignity, equality and mutual respect of men" through "the wide diffusion of culture," "the education of humanity for justice and liberty and peace," and the promotion of "the intellectual and moral solidarity of mankind"—Huxley then advances "a philosophy for Unesco": "a working hypothesis concerning human existence and *its* aims and objects" (6). What he comes up with is scientific world humanism based on "an extended or general theory of evolution which can provide the necessary intellectual scaffolding":

> It not only shows us man's place in nature and his relations to the rest of the phenomenal universe, not only gives us a description of the various types of evolution and the various trends and directions within them, but allows us to distinguish desirable and undesirable trends, and to demonstrate the existence of progress in the cosmos. And finally it shows us man as now the sole trustee of further evolutionary progress, and gives us important guidance as to the courses he should avoid and those he should pursue if he is to achieve that progress (7–8).

Huxley distinguishes three types of evolution in the universe: the very slow *inorganic* processes of physical interaction throughout the cosmos; the process of *biological* evolution based on self-reproduction with variation and natural selection in the struggle for existence—much faster than inorganic evolution but restricted as far as we know for certain to earth; and finally *human* evolution, based on cumulative tradition enabling the "social heredity by means of which human societies change and develop" in a process of "conscious selection, a struggle between ideas and values in consciousness" (9). Human evolution is much faster again than biological evolution because it "consists mainly of changes in the form of society, in tools and machines, in new ways of utilising the old innate potentialities, instead of in the nature of these potentialities" (9). As the product and the producer of this third and highest type of evolution, humankind is the "sole heir" and the "sole trustee" of evolutionary progress, and its "destiny" "may be summed up very simply: it is to realise the maximum progress in the minimum time" (12).

For Huxley, the key to human evolution is "the fact of cumulative tradition, the existence of a common pool of ideas which is self-perpetuating and itself capable of evolving," and so it is "obvious" that "the more united man's tradition becomes, the more rapid will be the possibility of progress: several separate or competing or even mutually hostile pools of tradition cannot possibly be so efficient as a single pool common to all mankind" (13). If UNESCO wants to realise this destiny, Huxley continues, it must promote "world political unity, whether through a single world government or otherwise, as the only certain means for avoiding war"—though he concedes that such world political unity "does not fall within the field of Unesco's competence" (13). Still, "in its educational programme it [UNESCO] can stress the ultimate need for world political unity and familiarise all peoples with the implications of the transfer of full sovereignty from separate nations to a world organisation" (13).

As H.G. Wells had written in the conclusion to his massive and best-selling *The Outline of History* in 1920, "the final achievement of world-wide political and social unity" in a "World State" may be envisaged, but human history at the time of writing, in the wake of the disasters of the Great War, increasingly looked like "a race between education and catastrophe" (Wells 1920, 594). Julian Huxley, writing after yet another catastrophic World War, also sought to appeal to a global cosmopolitan ideology of unity, but even the limited sample of the world represented in UNESCO was not having it.[15] The pamphlet's "universalist utopianism" and its "expansionist conception of UNESCO" did not go down well with some other members of the Preparatory Commission, so it was decided to present it as a "private" publication rather than an official policy statement (Nys 2011, 405).

We are back at the vicious problem Kant encountered in *The Conflict of Faculties* a good (or bad) two centuries before, but now on an explicitly global scale: the efficient organisation of the education of humanity requires political unity, but for political unity to be achieved the education of humanity is required. In itself this is not necessarily an objection to getting on with the job, which Huxley did as UNESCO's first Director-General in 1946–48. Yet it does call for some qualification of the assertive scientific confidence with which he tried to make his case.

For one thing, it does not necessarily follow from "the fact of cumulative tradition" that the unification of different traditions will lead more efficiently to "progress." In "A Re-Definition of Progress," which recycles a couple of pages of the UNESCO pamphlet, Huxley tries to make the same point in some more detail, but not much more convincingly, by distinguishing between "major" and "secondary" "critical points" in evolution (Huxley 1957, 36). The "origin of self-reproducing matter or life" is the major critical point in biological evolution, which has as its secondary critical point "the origin of learning—the formation of mechanisms for profiting by experience." In human evolution, the major critical point is "the origin of self-reproducing culture"; its secondary critical point "will be marked by the union of all separate traditions in a single common pool, the orchestration of human diversity from competitive discord to harmonious symphony."

> Of what future possibilities this may be the first foundation, who can say? At least it will for the first time give full scope to man's distinctive method of evolution and open the door to many human potentialities that are as yet scarcely dreamt of. Meanwhile anything that can be done to increase the interpretation of traditions and their fruitful union in a common pool will help, and is itself assuredly a prerequisite for full progress (36).

So before the harmonious symphony of full progress can commence, there is interpretation to do, and that is where Huxley's pet analogy between natural evolution and cultural evolution (or more accurately: cultural history) breaks down.

In its most succinct form, basically an attempt to build scientific credibility for the root metaphor informing words like "culture" (and indeed "propaganda"), the analogy runs as follows:

> Biological evolution depends on natural selection, which was made possible when matter became capable of self-reproduction and self-variation. Psycho-social or cultural evolution depends on cumulative tradition, which was made possible when mind and its products became capable of self-reproduction and self-variation (48).

Slightly more expanded into an explicit analogy, this becomes a just-so story:

> Just as the main method of biological evolution is the adjustment, by means of natural selection, of a mechanism of biological heredity capable of reproducing itself and any viable changes that may take place in it, so the main method of human evolution is the adjustment, by means of psycho-social selection, of a mechanism of cultural heredity, involving the cumulative transmission of tradition (105).

In "Evolution, Cultural and Biological," one of Huxley's most sustained attempts to keep this analogy up and running, he specifically turns for this purpose to the genetic uniqueness of *Homo sapiens* as an evolutionarily successful type that has not "diverged into numerous biologically separate species and lineages" (Huxley 1957, 67). There are some subspecies of modern humans resulting from initial geographic isolation, commonly referred to as races,[16] but that is where genetic divergence stopped and gave way to genetic convergence "as man's expansive or migratory urges brought previously isolated populations into contact": "Biologically, modern man has thus remained one species, a single interbreeding group." In cultural evolution, there has also been divergence, though here, too, he contends, "the same unique trend toward convergence" has occurred (68).

Huxley concedes that "the degree of unity produced by cultural convergence is still far below that reached on the genetic level" and acknowledges the difference between "physical interbreeding of divergent types" and "various forms of culture-contact and diffusion," yet his confidence in eventual cultural convergence remains unshaken. In itself, there is nothing wrong in such confidence, and the idea of humans as not only biologically but also culturally unique in their trend towards convergence may be attractive and inspiring in its own right—but even if it were unproblematically true genetically speaking (so that *Homo sapiens* is indeed biologically unique because of migratory interbreeding rather than as a result of the species' success in, directly or indirectly, driving all other contenders like *Homo neanderthalensis*, even after interbreeding with them too, to extinction [Harari 2014, 19]), it would still not add up to the scientific fact Huxley wants it to be. The reason is simple: the transmission of genetic material and the interpretation of cultural material—interbreeding and inter-reading—are very different things.

Huxley knows this, of course, and he goes out of his way to find planks for the intellectual scaffolding of his analogy between biological and human evolution, as when he turns later on in the same essay to some concepts from anthropology as would-be cultural counterparts to genes as heredity units:

> A culture consists of the self-reproducing or reproducible products of the mental activities of a group of human individuals living in a society. These can be broadly divided into artifacts—material objects created for carrying out material functions; socifacts—institutions and organizations for providing the framework of a social or political unit and for maintaining social relations between its members; and mentifacts—mental constructions which provide the psychological framework of a culture and carry out intellectual, aesthetic, spiritual, ethical or other psychological functions (79).

It is to Huxley's credit that he spoils his own argument by implicitly admitting that cultural heredity units are not just "self-reproducing" but may also be—or indeed, as the logic of "or" allows, may very well *only* be—"reproducible." For something to be reproducible, a reproducer is required. When biological organisms reproduce, the result is not helpfully called the reproducer: biological reproduction is the process whereby genetic material is transmitted from "parent" or "parents" to "offspring," and "offspring" is not usually thought of as reproducing its "parent(s)" since it was not around when the reproduction got going in the first place. It may be fun to think of children as reproducing their parents, but that is because they do not—except in the very different sense that they follow their example (if they do, or, come to think of it, do not). Whichever way we turn it, if units of cultural heredity are "reproducible," rather than just "self-reproducing," there is a rogue factor in cultural transmission critically different from genetic transcription error. The problem is not that Huxley denies this, but that he fails to acknowledge its impact on the analogy central to his evolutionary ideology of full progress.

In the conclusion to "A Re-Definition of Progress" Huxley proposes to put "the disasters and miseries of a nation, or of an entire age like our own" into perspective. Measured against the "universal scale" of progress,

> [...] these appear either as necessary destruction opening the way to new construction, or as temporary setbacks of no greater importance to the general trend of evolution than are the wavelets raised by a contrary breeze to the sweep of the incoming tide (40).

What with sea levels rising, this is probably not an image he would have used today—though we should never underestimate what a memorable image can let you get away with.

Genes, Memes, Imaging and Imagination

"Artifacts," "socifacts," "mentifacts"—no wonder they did not catch on. In fact, they are not even Huxley's, as he borrowed them, as he admits, from the anthropologist David Bidney, though in parts of the World Brain today that has been forgotten and they are credited to Huxley.[17] At any rate, they are just not very good memes. Unlike memes, which are too good for their own good.

Most digital natives today probably think of memes first as the bits of something spreading from user to user on the Internet, nowadays mainly via social media, typically for fun, fear-mongering or followship-building. That use of the term dates from the late 1990s but, as the *Oxford English Dictionary* notes, the word "meme" was coined a good two decades earlier as the name for "[a] cultural element or behavioural trait whose transmission and consequent persistence in a population, although occurring by non-genetic means (esp. imitation), is considered as analogous to the inheritance of a gene."[18] Richard Dawkins, who came up with the term in the closing chapter of the first edition of *The Selfish Gene* (1976), later lost confidence in the analogy, admitting in 2001 that he was "increasingly thinking that nothing but confusion arises from confounding genetic evolution with cultural evolution" (qtd. in Shermer 2006, 229; see also Burman 2012). But the meme was out of the bottle.

Dawkins introduces the term "meme" as "a noun that conveys the idea of a unit of cultural transmission" (Dawkins 2006, 192). His reasons for doing so are sound: he is a self-confessed "enthusiastic Darwinian," but the attempts of his "fellow-enthusiasts" to explain human behaviour with reference to "biological advantages" alone leave him "dissatisfied": "for an understanding of the evolution of modern man, we must begin by throwing out the gene as the sole basis of our ideas on evolution. [...] The gene will enter my thesis as an analogy, nothing more" (190–91). Like Julian Huxley, whom he curiously does not mention in this connection, Dawkins pitches his analogy as a just-so story:

> Examples of memes are tunes, ideas, catch-phrases, clothes fashions, ways of making pots or of building arches. Just as genes propagate themselves in the gene pool by leaping from body to body via sperms or eggs, so memes progagate themselves in the meme pool by leaping from brain to brain via a process which, in the broad sense, can be called imitation. If a scientist hears, or reads about, a good idea, he passes it on to his colleagues and students. He mentions it in his articles and his lectures. If the idea catches on, it can be said to propagate itself, spreading from brain to brain (192).

It is a vivid and arresting image, these genes and memes leaping around—a typical instance of the kind of engaging science-writing for a wide audience Dawkins has made his mission. The image of course takes some liberties, notably in the admittedly minimal personification of genes and memes as agents with a mission but, as Dawkins points out in his introduction to the 30th anniversary edition of the book, in reply to some critics who accused him of "anthropomorphic personification," "no sane person thinks DNA molecules have conscious personalities, and no sensible reader would impute such a delusion to an author" (x). Fair enough, but there is something else going on in the analogy between genetic transmission and cultural transmission which does raise relevant critical questions.

To say that genes leap from body to body via sperms or eggs is indeed unproblematic—not so much because we know they do not but because as readers of Dawkins's book (the analogy is introduced in the final chapter of the first edition) we have a fairly good understanding of how DNA *is* transmitted. Scientists may disagree with some of the details of Dawkins's account of gene replication, and indeed with the macro-narrative of evolution he derives from it, but the basic principle of "a DNA sequence that maintains an uninterrupted physical integrity in its transmission from generation to generation" is clear enough, so we can enjoy the Disney spectacle of DNA molecules piloting sperms and eggs cavorting in the gene pool (Haig 2006, 61). But to go on from this to assert that memes propagate "just as" genes do is not just another vivid image complementing the first; it is not just lively science-writing but bad science. As John Gray puts it: "the theory of memes is science only in the sense that Intelligent Design is science. Strictly speaking, it is not even a theory. Talk of memes is just the latest in a succession of ill-judged Darwinian metaphors": "a classic example of the nonsense that is spawned when Darwinian thinking is applied outside its proper sphere" (Gray 2008).

As mentioned above, Dawkins later on, in 2001, came to doubt the analogy of the meme as a replicator formed in "the soup of human culture" just as the gene is a replicator formed in the "primeval soup" of chemical materials, but already at its first introduction in 1976 he seems to have had second thoughts, as is suggested by the fact that, instead of further unpacking the analogy himself, he lets a colleague do the writing:

> As my colleague N.K. Humphrey neatly summed up an earlier draft of this chapter: "... memes should be regarded as living structures, not just metaphorically but tech-

nically. When you plant a fertile meme in my mind, you literally parasitize my brain, turning it into a vehicle for the meme's propagation in just the way that a virus may parasitize the genetic mechanism of a host cell. And this isn't just a way of talking— the meme for, say, 'belief in life after death' is actually realized physically, millions of times over, as a structure in the nervous systems of individual men the world over" (Dawkins 2006, 192).

To say that memes "should be regarded as living structures, not just metaphorically but technically" is not just wrong but *exactly* wrong, no matter how "neat" it may sound, for living structures are essentially dependent on uninterrupted *metabolic* processes (dead DNA does not leap) while human cultural transmission is distinctively dependent on *symbolic* technology overriding the flow of physical fluids.

Dawkins was smart enough to shift the blame for this piece of bad thinking to his colleague, but the temptation to rewire culture into nature proved too strong when he revisited *The Selfish Gene* for its second edition in 1989. Though here too, he revealingly takes cover by letting someone else deliver the evidence, such as it is. In a new endnote to the "not just metaphorically but technically" quotation from Humphrey, Dawkins writes:

> DNA is a self-replicating piece of hardware. Each piece has a particular structure, which is different from rival pieces of DNA. If memes in brains are analogous to genes they must be self-replicating brain structures, actual patterns of neuronal wiring-up that reconstitute themselves in one brain after another. I had always felt uneasy spelling this out aloud, because we know far less about brains than about genes, and are therefore necessarily vague about what such a brain structure might actually be. So I was relieved to receive recently a very interesting paper by Juan Delius of the University of Konstanz in Germany. Unlike me, Delius doesn't have to feel apologetic, because he is a distinguished brain scientist whereas I am not a brain scientist at all. I am delighted, therefore, that he is bold enough to ram the point home by actually publishing a detailed picture of what the neuronal hardware of a meme might look like (323).

Dawkins does not mention the title of the paper he received from Konstanz, but in all likelihood it is "Of mind memes and brain bugs," a paper delivered by Delius in

1986 at a symposium on "The nature of culture" and later published in the proceedings, which does contain a curious picture:

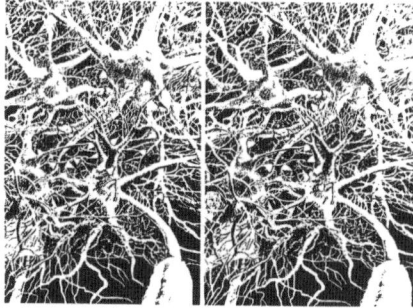

"A cultural trait encoded as a pattern of activated synapses somewhere in the brain of two different individuals (schematic)." (Delius 1989, 46)

A revised version of the paper was published two years after the second edition of *The Selfish Gene* in a volume of essays, notably co-edited by Dawkins, celebrating the work of the ethologist Niko Tinbergen, Dawkins's mentor at Oxford. It, too, contains a curious picture:

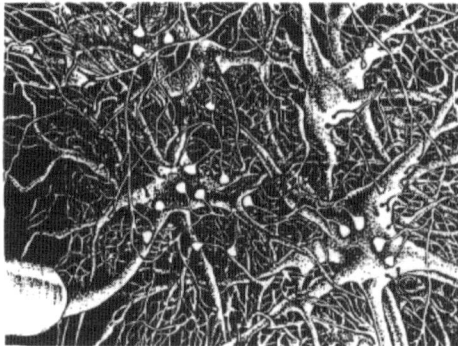

"A meme as a constellation of activated neuronal synapses lodged somewhere in the brain of an individual" (Delius 1991, 83)

It is hard to decide which of the two figures is the more ridiculous. The first one, at least, is candidly acknowledged as "schematic" only, though the suggestion that it represents the brains of two different individuals is hard to take seriously. The second picture is of slightly better quality, and drops the ludicrous pretence of presenting two different brains, but it also drops the admission that it is schematic only, thereby assuming an aura of scientific objectivity not backed up by anything like evidence. Significantly, Delius does not pay much attention to these pictures himself: his papers are largely speculative arm-chair explorations of how memes as hypothetical "constellations of activated and non-activated synapses within neural memory networks" might be said to behave on a larger scale (Delius 1989, 45).

If anybody is "ram[ming] the point home" by delightedly welcoming "a detailed picture of what the neuronal hardware of a meme might look like", it is Dawkins. Note that the point rammed home is really only a drawn image of synapses, not a picture of a meme "lodged somewhere in the brain of an individual," as the caption deceptively suggests. That the production, reception, storage and transmission of memes involves brainwork is uncontroversial, but that does not mean that a schematic representation of synapses is a meaningful representation of memes at work. Consider, in contrast, the famous diagram of DNA published by Watson and Crick in 1953.

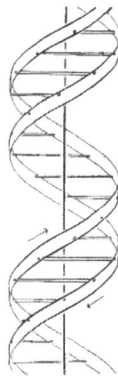

Diagram of the structure of DNA (Watson & Crick 1953, 737)

Based on an X-ray diffraction photograph (nicknamed "Photo 51"), the diagram schematically represents the structure of DNA as a double helix combining paired bases (adenine, thymine, guanine and cytosine) and phosphate-sugar chains.[19] As

Watson and Crick indicated, what this "purely diagrammatic" figure suggests is "a possible copying mechanism for the genetic material," and that turned out to be demonstrably true. Combined with an understanding of the physical properties of the chemicals involved, the double helix diagram captures the mechanism of replication necessary for genetic transmission. The "picture" of the meme, on the other hand, is still only a hand-drawn image of a bit of brain. The question is why Dawkins is so delighted by it.

To answer this question, it is useful briefly to sketch the overall set-up of *The Selfish Gene*. Its first chapter has as its title a question posed by a "curious child"—"Why are people?"—and starts out by claiming that Darwin was the first to enable us to come up with a sensible answer. "[w]e no longer have to resort to superstition when faced with the deep problems: Is there a meaning to life? What are we for? What is man?" (Dawkins 2006, 1). And Darwin does indeed deliver an answer to the question of the curious child—or at least to one inflection of it. "Why are people?" is (among other things) a multi-directional question: it can ask for an answer in terms of the past origin of human beings or in terms of the future purpose of people. Darwinian evolutionary theory offers answers only of the first kind: human beings are the biological species we are as a result of reproduction with chance mutation and natural selection. Evolutionary theorists argue about the level at which selection takes place (the species, the group, the individual organism, the gene) and about the consequences of this for the interpretation of behaviour. In *The Selfish Gene*, the principal theme in this regard is "the biology of selfishness and altruism" (1). Dawkins's overarching argument is that selection happens at the level of the gene, that the gene is essentially selfish, that this does not prevent forms of altruistic behaviour from evolving, but that there is little point in looking for "a morality based on evolution" (2).

> Be warned that if you wish, as I do, to build a society in which individuals cooperate generously and unselfishly towards a common good, you can expect little help from biological nature. Let us try to *teach* generosity and altruism, because we are born selfish. Let us understand what our selfish genes are up to, because we may then at least have the chance to upset their designs, something that no other species has ever aspired to (3).

The Selfish Gene is overwhelmingly about "what our genes are up to," not so much about a better society, which also means it offers only a very reduced retrospective version of an answer to "the deep problems." That is also its strength: by sticking to aggregated description and interpretation of the behaviour of living organisms, and ruling out "the psychology of motives" (4), it manages to construct a plausible (though not uncontested) account of all kinds of behaviour as having evolved on the basis of gene replication with chance mutation: there is a good reason for everything, though typically not a nice one, and it is good because it is coded in genes that just happened to be selected. By definition, however, this process is wholly divorced from deliberate future-oriented purpose, so the curious child is not really getting much of an answer to the second inflection of its question.

"Why are people?" The bulk of the book is not about human beings, but in the chapter on memes Dawkins sets out to acknowledge that our species is in fact "unique" (188), which suggests that people deserve a specific answer to this question. As it turns out, we are unique in at least two ways. First, we have developed memic evolution—or, rather, we have become carriers of memes replicating in our brains. All that is required for this is that "the brain should be *capable* of imitation: memes will then evolve to exploit that capacity to the full" (200). Importantly, these memes have no more "foresight" than genes and are just as "selfish," intent only on self-replication in competition with rival memes. So humans are unique in the sense that they host "a new kind of replicator" (192), but that replicator appears to behave much along the same lines as genes do. Since memes "propagate" in the brain, it is harder to factor out "the psychology of motives" than it is in the account of gene replication, but by reducing it to the "deep psychological impact" of memes (198) Dawkins manages to stick to the script: it is not so much humans consciously choosing to host a particular meme for a specific motive, but rather the successfully mutated meme forcing them to replicate it for its own survival. To clinch the analogy, it would help to have something that gives memes the demonstrable bedrock body that the double helix provided for DNA. No wonder Delius's image brought Dawkins such delight.

Such as they are, Delius's pictures of memes are of course bogus. But their enthusiastic reception by an otherwise sceptical scientist like Dawkins is instructive, in that it illustrates the image-hunger invariably induced in humans by big questions. The digital turn broadly conceived has played a major role in further whetting that appetite for images, and often in ways Dawkins may be less than happy about. Already in *The Selfish Gene* (but since then increasingly explicitly, to the point of embarrassingly), his agenda has been aggressively atheist, "the god meme" (193) and its associated "nasty" (197) memes in the "religious meme complex" (198) providing him with pet examples of memes gone bad because all too good at replicating themselves for all the wrong reasons (we will return to the issue of right and wrong reasons below). But what if there were images of brains engaged in religious practice showing real changes in the brain advanced as evidence of the positive effects of religious belief? And, importantly, what if they were better images than Delius's, in fact actual images rather than schematic drawings not showing anything much?

As one instance among many, consider what Peter Lunenfeld (2006) has called the "God scans" produced by Andrew Newberg in the early 1990s. By means of the brain imaging technology SPECT (single photon emission computed tomography), Newberg managed to measure cranial blood flow in Tibetan Buddhists and Franciscan nuns during meditation, with an atheist well versed in meditation now asked to contemplate God thrown in for good measure. Unsurprisingly to many, but to the delighted surprise of many others, there was a result: while the Buddhist and Franciscan brains showed increased activity in the frontal lobes, the atheist's frontal lobes remained neutral: "the individual was not able to activate the structures usually involved in meditation when he was focussing on a concept he did not believe in."[20] Note that these images do not prove the existence of God; they only show blood flow in the brain, and even that not directly but via computation and digital manipulation. But this does not prevent Newberg from publishing books with catchy titles like *How God Changes Your Brain: Breakthrough Findings from a Leading Neuroscientist* (2009).

We need not agree on the question whether or not God exists, but we should be clear that the images on show so far are no more a representation of specifically theist versus atheist thought than Delius's drawings are images of memes. They all show something, but no sooner are they shown than they are seen as showing much more. As Lunenfeld writes, "the rush to capture complex science in an 'irrefutable image' seems tied up with the general population's unexamined acceptance of the 'readability' of images. The grail of the image in our ocular epistemologies can trump other, less compellingly visualizable modes of inquiry and research. With the God scan, we see the democratic urge to comprehend merge with an almost transcendental desire to derive essence from the image."

More recent brain imaging experiments engage with the at first blush less divisive phenomenon of "empathy," which for our purposes here we can think of as a version of sympathy as a moral sentiment as defined by Adam Smith. Here, too, it is essentially a matter of measuring and visualising blood flow in the brain, typically by means of fMRI (functional magnetic resonance imaging). A particularly extreme example in popular science writing is Simon Baron-Cohen's *Zero Degrees of Empathy: A New Theory of Human Cruelty and Kindness* (2012).[21] Baron-Cohen's ambition is to replace "the unscientific term 'evil'" with the term "'empathy' erosion," and to make this work "empathy" must be objectively captured by science. So brain scans are produced as evidence for an Empathising Mechanism, and claims are made that by scanning the brains of the bad we can actually see nastiness at work as the empathy circuit is blocked. It is highly unlikely that these fMRI scans can be meaningfully said to represent empathy or its absence in individual humans (Scull 2012, Scull 2018), but what is arguably more important is the larger claim that they are made to support. "Empathy is like a universal solvent. Any problem immersed in empathy becomes soluble" (Baron-Cohen 2012, 132). First supposedly identified in blood flow patterns, empathy is now turned into a chemical that can dissolve all conflict. As with Dawkins's leaping memes, we know this is just a vivid image, but here too the image outstrips the evidence in ways the science cannot contain.

Baron-Cohen acknowledges the importance of cultural contingencies, but identifying malfunctioning of the empathy circuit as the necessary condition for human cruelty does suggest that if only we were true to our neuro-typical human bio-being, universal peace would reign at last. If only we could be nicer to each other. To identify bits in the brain showing higher blood traffic when humans feel kindness as they are shown a picture of a kid with a kitten is one thing; to argue that this is evidence of an empathy circuit hardwired in the brain as an evolutionary adaptation reflecting advanced prosocial predispositions in humans when compared to other primates is another; but it makes little sense to conclude from this that empathy is therefore "effective as a way of anticipating and resolving interpersonal problems, whether this is a marital conflict, an international conflict, a problem at work, difficulties in a friendship, political deadlocks, a family dispute, or a problem with the neighbour" (Baron-Cohen 2012, 132). If empathy could achieve all this, it would have done so already. Of course, we are working on it—if we were not we might not even *be*, such is the logic of natural evolution. As the final sentences of Michael Tomasello's *Natural History of Human Morality* have it: "[i]t just so happens that, on the whole, those of us who made mostly moral decisions most of the time had more babies [...] morality appears to be somehow good for our species, our cultures, and ourselves—at least so far" (Tomasello 2016, 163). A question whispers between these lines: Even *more* babies?

There is no doubt more can be done to unlock the positive potential of empathy in all manner of situations, but to image it as a *neuroscientific* answer to the challenges of 21st-century life on this planet is to commit a category mistake. If religion can sometimes mask the real contradictions of human life by appealing to an alternative order of ultimate reality and meaning, then neuroscience as image-ideology denies real-time historical disorder by gesturing towards a deep-time source of truth that will restore natural human harmony that never was.

Big Words

We are unique, Dawkins suggested, in that our brain has evolved as a medium for meme-replication. Unlike Baron-Cohen, he is not certain that we are also uniquely equipped as a species with "a capacity for genuine, disinterested, true altruism" (Dawkins 2006, 200). But he does add another "unique feature" of human beings, "which may or may not have evolved memically": our "capacity for conscious foresight" (Dawkins 2006, 200). It is a curious concession of "qualified hope," given the relentless emphasis throughout the book on evolution as "blind to the future" (8), on genes and memes as "unconscious, blind replicators"—whose "worst selfish excesses" we may be saved from after all by "our capacity to simulate the future in imagination" (200).

> We can even discuss ways of deliberately cultivating and nurturing pure, disinterested altruism—something that has no place in nature, something that has never existed before in the whole history of the world. We are built as gene machines and cultured as meme machines, but we have the power to turn against our creators. We, alone on earth, can rebel against the tyranny of the selfish replicators (200–01).

As we noted earlier, Dawkins already hinted at the need for educational efforts to counter our selfish nature in the first pages of the book, but at this stage of the argument, as he appears to acknowledge implicitly, the price to pay for this thought may well be the meme itself. For what could such rebellion against the selfish replicators be based on other than an engagement with what is neither evolutionary biology nor memes imaged as being "lodged somewhere" in mindless brain-matter? The imagination needed for such rebellion is not likely to be measurable in the brain: our brains have been engaging with thought technology producing human history for too long for that to make much sense. But we may indeed still come up with fictions of a future to keep us going, and the tools for imagining beyond imaging provided by the digital turn may help.

Among those tools today, so obvious that they may escape notice, are the various search engines that facilitate instant access to data and arguments that life in the pre-internet period of increasingly compartmentalised modernity was too short for most of us to get hold of. There are obvious restrictions to such access still, most obviously various kinds of paywalls, and a lot of what is available, even behind such paywalls, is junk. Still, particularly also in academic work this access can make a substantial difference, since it has become much easier to test scholarship within one discipline or group of related disciplines, such as the humanities, against research in other disciplines, like behavioural sciences or biology. To be sure, the massively enhanced accessibility of academic publications can also lead to comfort-zone reinforcement by biased source selection as a protection against inconvenient facts or values, but it has much more powerful bubble-bursting potential.

In 2018, the US National Academies of Sciences, Engineering, and Medicine published a consensus study report on *The Integration of the Humanities and Arts with Sciences, Engineering, and Medicine in Higher Education*. The report is less conclusive than it appears its authors would have liked it to be, since it is poor on clear causal evidence proving "that educational programs that mutually integrate learning experiences in the humanities and arts with science, technology, engineering, math, and medicine (STEMM) lead to improved educational and career outcomes for undergraduate and graduate students" (National Academies 2018, x). Yet the report does include a wealth of narrative or anecdotal evidence leading the National Academies committee to recommend in principle initiatives promoting the integration of arts and humanities in STEMM in higher education (169–80).

What is important about this for humanities scholars and students, overruling any quibbles about detail and therefore acknowledging its anecdotal quality, is that STEMM takes the initiative and invites the humanities in. It is always wise to be wary about invitations from unexpected quarters, but not to accept them is usually weak, and not to consider them is often stupid. The smart thing is not just to accept them but to reciprocate.

A recent plea for such reciprocation I want to end this part on was posted by the literary scholar Ted Underwood on a free successor to the *Berlinische Monatsschrift* Kant posted his articles in, the online magazine *Public Books*, which ever since it started in 2012 has admirably succeeded in its mission to unite "the best of the university with the openness of the internet."[22] Underwood's essay "Why an Age of Machine Learning Needs the Humanities" opens on a warning: "[i]f democracy depends on informed citizens, democracy is in trouble" (Underwood 2018). Search engine bias both generates dodgy information and is used to cast doubt on sound information, so citizens need to be trained in new ways of making up their minds: "[t]o prepare students for a world where information is filtered by computers, we will need a stronger alliance between the humanities and math. This alliance has two reciprocal parts: cultural criticism of the mathematical models shaping our world, and mathematical inquiry about culture."

As his title indicates, the example Underwood develops is machine learning, but it is important to underscore that his overall argument is that the humanities will be of any use to an age of machine learning only if they learn about statistical models themselves and apply these methods to their traditional objects of study. In the past, such application was often compromised by the lack of adequate, sufficiently fuzz-tolerant statistical modelling methods and by the lack of big enough data in formats that lend themselves to such modelling.[23] Among the major achievements of the digital turn are the prospects it has opened to remove those obstacles, and to forge new alliances between sciences and humanities: "the fuzzy, context-specific models produced by machine learning have a lot in common with the family resemblances historians glimpse in culture," so on the one digit "machine learning is turning out to be useful for cultural history," while on the other finger "helping students understand the strengths and limitations of historical knowledge can also be a way of helping them understand the strengths and limitations of machine learning."

For Underwood, this signals nothing less than "a turning point in recent intellectual history."

> New connections between disciplines won't displace the traditional strengths of history, philosophy, art, and literature, but the emerging assumption that humanists and scientists are working on a shared educational project still represents a massive change. For much of the 20th century, these parts of the university saw themselves as (civil) antagonists. The sciences taught you *how* to clone *T. Rex*, as one familiar

poster has it. The humanities taught you *why* you shouldn't. It's a clever story but one we need to get beyond. The real monster in our world is not a dinosaur we could avoid creating. It is human history, already broken loose, already ravenous and hard to predict. To understand it—to understand ourselves—we will need numbers as well as words. Humanists have a lot to contribute to this struggle, since we know the monster's past and understand its slipperiness better than anyone else. Healthy skepticism about numbers is one thing we bring to the table, but we have much more than skepticism to offer. We can also join forces with science, to show students that statistical inference and historical interpretation are allied, intertwined parts of a life committed to understanding.

Not everyone will be convinced, but this conclusion sets an agenda in big enough words to challenge us all to make up our minds.

PART TWO
Medium

3 Media Cultures

....

Just as there is no digital culture without culture, there can be no culture without media. This chapter will present and critically analyse some of the most current definitions of the concept of medium. It claims that a cultural analysis of the medium should exceed the technological definition of the medium as information channel (this is what happens in "media theory") and try instead to approach media in terms of cultural practices (this is typical of "medium theory"). We focus here on the theoretical insights elaborated by authors such as Marshall McLuhan (communication studies) and Stanley Cavell (film studies and visual analysis), while also addressing a certain number of key concepts such as remediation. Special attention will be paid to the debates on medium-specificity and essentialism as well as on the historical dimension of media evolution and the teleological or archeological takes on changes in the field.

Keywords: automatism, (media) archeology, communication, hypermediacy, intermediality, medium vs media theory, (medium) specificity, remediation, repurposing, teleology, transmediality

....

> A computer engineer can explain how digital files really are created
> and saved, but I would insist that the vernacular experience of this
> creatability and savability makes at least as much difference to the
> ongoing social definition (that is, the uses) of new, digital media.
>
> (Lisa Gitelman 2008, 20)

Medium Theory vs Media Theory

It is always good to start with a story, in this case "The Book of Sand" (1975), a short story by Jorge Luis Borges (1899–1986), a former librarian who at the end of his life, when he had become completely blind, was forced to dictate his speculations on reading and writing to his secretary and wife (a highly gendered situation to which we will return). With the help of Wikipedia, the story can be summarised as follows:

> An unnamed narrator is visited by a tall Scots Bible-seller, who presents him with a very old cloth-bound book that he bought in India from an Untouchable. The book is emblazoned with the title *Holy Writ*, below which title is emblazoned "Bombay," but is said to be called *The Book of Sand...* because neither the book nor the sand has any beginning or end. Upon opening it, he is startled to discover that the book, which is written in an unknown language and occasionally punctuated by illustrations, is in fact infinite: if one turns the pages, more pages seem to grow out of the front and back covers. He trades a month of his pension and a prized *Wiclif Bible* for *The Book of Sand* and hides it on a bookshelf behind his copy of *One Thousand and One Nights*. Over the summer, the narrator obsesses over the book, poring over it, cataloging its illustrations, and refusing to go outside for fear of its theft. In the end, realizing that the book is monstrous, he briefly considers burning it before fearing the possibility of the smoke of an infinite book suffocating the world. Instead, he goes to the National Library where he once worked (like Borges) to lose the book among the basement bookshelves, reasoning that "the best place to hide a leaf is in a forest."[1]

There are many (obvious) ways of reading this story, and we will have to come back to the similarities between this object of antiquarian connoisseurship and the properties of today's digital art, but it would be a mistake immediately to single out the hermeneutical or philosophical interpretation of this modern tale, referring for instance to the idea that the meanings of the Bible are infinite, even for an individual—and in the case of *The Book of Sand*—well-trained reader. As important as the issue of the multiple meanings is the medium of this terrifying work, not a "Bible" but a "biblon," that is a book—a medium all the more foregrounded since its content resists direct understanding (it is written in an unknown language), while strong attention is drawn to its material form (to read a book is presented first of all as turning its pages). The theological and philological dimensions of *The Book of Sand*, not to mention its properly literary stakes which have to do with the chosen genre, namely the short story,[2] can certainly be activated, if one wants, but what Borges proposes is above all a conjecture on the material properties of a medium (a book, but also a library, first a personal and then a public one), the properties of the work's meaning being nothing else than a consequence of its materiality. The medium is here, quite literally, the message, and Borges's story highlights the necessity of studying culture—be it verbal or visual (please note that *The Book of Sand* is an illustrated volume)—from a medium-oriented point of view.

Yet what is a medium? In the narrow sense of the word, a medium is a channel. In the broad sense of the word, it is a culture. Roughly speaking, the difference between the two meanings is the difference between *media theory* and *medium theory*, the former focusing on the medium as material communication channel, the latter emphasising the notion of medium as social practice. This difference is also that between the more empirical and quantitative social sciences approach of medium, more specifically of mass media, as illustrated for instance by the well-known audience and impact studies, and the more interpretive and qualitative model of the humanities, which refers to any approach of medium uses and artifacts that gives agency to the host medium and its specific material characteristics. As explained by Joshua Meyrowitz:

> A handful of scholars—mostly from fields other than communications, sociology and psychology—have tried to call attention to the potential influences of communication technologies in addition to and apart from the content they convey. I use the singular "medium theory" to describe this research tradition in order to differ-

entiate it from most other "media theory". Medium theory focuses on the particular characteristics of each individual medium or of each particular type of media. Broadly speaking, medium theorists ask: what are the relatively fixed features of each means of communicating and how do these features make the medium physically, psychologically and socially different from other media and from face-to-face interaction? Medium theory examines such variables as the senses that are required to attend to the medium, whether the communication is bi-directional or uni-directional, how quickly messages can be disseminated, whether learning to encode and decode in the medium is difficult or simple, how many people can attend to the same message at the same moment, and so forth. Medium theorists argue that such variables influence the medium's use and its social, political, and psychological impact (Meyrowitz 1994, 50).

Medium theory is thus defined in very broad terms. Its main theoretical insights have been elaborated in various disciplines: communications studies (Marshall McLuhan), film and visual arts (Stanley Cavell), semiotics (Régis Debray), book history (Roger Chartier), although there are many overlaps and hybridisations in the work of these authors as well as in the subsequent thinking they have made possible, and which have given birth to the field of media archeology (a discipline both rooted in the past and strongly looking ahead). The following paragraphs will briefly sketch the main contributions of some major figures to medium theory as a springboard to the study of current tendencies within the medium-theoretical approach of digital culture.

Marshall McLuhan (1911–1980)

A founding father of contemporary media studies (understood as electronic mass media studies), a forerunner also of the *pictorial turn* (although many elements of his theory appear to be at odds with the current almost exclusive emphasis on the image), and a prophet of the new post-Gutenberg, post-print society (with a "post" apparently less problematic than in post-modernism and other related *post-isms*), Marshall McLuhan has recently risen from the purgatory and oblivion to which the mystical turn of his late writings had suddenly condemned him. Although in some circles he continued to be seen as the brilliant spokesman of the initial years of the TV era, his own medium theory and its philosophical underpinnings hardly encountered any creative echoes in the 1980s, a decade that saw political activism starting to overtake the field of academic research on culture and thus ferociously opposing some of McLuhan's allegedly depoliticised stances. Since the emergence of digital culture in the personal sphere (the first home computers appeared in the early 1980s), his work has known a spectacular come-back and to this day he remains the key reference in any medium-theoretical approach whatever.

Continuing the efforts of the Toronto school, which was the first to explore the link between communications systems in the material sense of the word (roads, travel, commerce) and sign systems ("tele"-systems, bringing together spatially separated persons and places: telephone, telegraph, television), McLuhan's contribution to the field of medium theory cannot be overstated (Berland 2009).

First of all, he introduced a very broad definition of medium, which blurs the boundaries between sign and tool (or, if one prefers, between semiotics and technology). Ever since his first book, *The Mechanical Bride* (1951), a critical reading of the advertisement industry (the mechanical bride being the car), up to the two major works, *The Gutenberg Galaxy* (1962) and *Understanding Media* (1964), that made him into a real rock star,[3] McLuhan defines a medium as an "extension of man," either physical (clothing is thus no less a medium than the telephone, since the former protects us from the weather while the latter allows us to communicate beyond the natural range of our voice) or psychic (electronic circuitries extend the connecting capacities of our brains). Virtually anything thus becomes a medium, and reading McLuhan, always a real adventure since he is a mastermind of creative academic writing, is often a roller coaster that brings us to all aspects of society.

A medium, however, and this is a second key element of McLuhan's thinking, is not just an extension of man, it is also a message, as famously summarised in one of his apodictic slogans: "the medium is the message." The meaning of this statement is simple: it is not only the idea that the vehicle of a message counts more than the content or the form of the message itself but also the idea that the existence of a medium—certainly in the case of a "new" medium—is an event that dramatically modifies both the position of the user, whose interface with the environment is no longer the same, and the structure of a society, equally transformed by the new connections and expansions established by the medium. McLuhan has been much criticised for his somewhat abstract and definitely also somewhat naïve take on media.

One will not find in his work many remarks on the socio-political and economic aspects of media structures. Who owns the media, for instance, was not one of the most urgent questions on his agenda, and despite his concerns with "war and peace in the global village," to quote another of his catchy slogans, his media analysis was notably underpoliticised. It was however anything but deprived of a social agenda, often a very concrete one, as shown in Montreal's "1967 Expo World Fair," which is seen today as a real-life attempt to materialise McLuhan's media utopianism (Gagnon and Marchessault 2014). The claim that media do not channel messages, but are themselves messages and, conversely, the claim that meaning does not exist outside media and that something like "information" never exists as such is widely shared by all medium-theoretically oriented scholars. As Lisa Gitelman states:

> Just as it makes no sense to appreciate an artwork without attending to its medium (painted in watercolors or oils? Sculpted in granite or Styrofoam?), it makes no sense to think about "content" without attending to the medium that both communicates that content and represents or helps to set the limits of what that content can consist of. Even when the content in question is what has for the last century or so been termed "information," it cannot be considered "free of" or apart from the media that help define it. However commonplace it is to think of information as separable from, cleanly contained in, or uninformed by media, such thinking merely redoubles a structural amnesia that already pertains (2008: 7).

In the work of McLuhan, the question of "meaning" is directly related with a third dimension of his medium theory, which has to do with history. McLuhan always historicises, which means that he never examines a medium in itself, but always in relationship with a previous "old" medium that is now superseded by the "new" one. This relationship is described in technical terms: the "old" medium does not simply vanish, but becomes the content of the "new" one: photography, for instance, which takes over the reproductive capacities of painting, is itself taken over by cinema, which adds the feature of mobility to photography's fixed images, each "old" medium thus being incorporated in a "new" one that offers a larger "extension of man." Yet this relationship is not merely technical, it is also driven by a strong teleology: mankind is always looking for "better" media and the final horizon is the absolute medium, that is the medium that offers so maximal an extension that it can no longer be superseded by another medium—and that eventually produces a kind of mystical fusion of man and God (Mc Luhan calls this absolute medium "light"; it is the horizon of the electronic media that govern modern society—at that time, this meant television, certainly not the Internet). There is an explicit influence on McLuhan of Catholic thinkers like Teilhard de Chardin, who coined the notion of "noosphere" as medium-enhanced world's brain, and McLuhan's teleology sometimes has an eschatological undertone.

Fourth and last, McLuhan's historical and dynamic media analysis is far from being linear or monolithic. Indeed, media change is not only a matter of extension, enhancement, enrichment, empowerment, in short fun and progress, it can also be a source of profound trauma (and McLuhan explicitly refers to war's post-traumatic stress disorder). For not everybody is prepared to handle the new media with the necessary care and to interact with them in a fruitful way. The new is often "too" new and provokes all kinds of misunderstandings, if not real adversities. Moreover, certain media transformations are considered intrinsically problematic and harmful, such as the alphabetical revolution provoked by Gutenberg's mechanical printing process. According to McLuhan, this invention of movable type was the detonator of a process of fragmentation (the flow and freedom of living oral speech being broken up by the rigidity and normativity of individual characters) that disrupted the organic and creative interplay between individuals and communities, now divided into language groups that would become independent and competing nations (unified by grammars that were needed to make sure that words would be understood in the absence of their speakers, but always unified against their others, politically as well as religiously, the Great Schism of Christianity being one of the consequences of the introduction of print culture). The electronic "global village," which McLuhan interprets as a rebirth of oral culture and the return of face-to-face communication between people, is therefore not just a new step in the evolution of media cultures; it is also a change that is meant to cure the calamities of a previous era. On a more individual scale, and relying on the metaphorical distinction between "hot" and "cool" media, that is between media that use a channel offering either too much or too little information and therefore negatively impact the users, McLuhan observes that new media do not always deliver all the promises they theoretically hold (the generation gap, for instance, is read by him in medium terms). Yet in spite of the ambivalent position towards the immediate practical impact of many medium changes, many of them causing traumas and fragmentation (the anti-value *par excellence* in a worldview teleologically defined by the ideas of unions and fusion), there is no room for pessimism in McLuhan's thinking. A child of the 1960s, he fundamentally believes that the best is yet to come and that medium traumas can be cured through education, whose aim should be to "heat up" cold media and "cool down" hot ones.

McLuhan's techno-utopianism has been open to many debates, even in the new generations that in a very short time achieved a spectacular social and intellectual reappraisal and re-evaluation of their guru. For the agents of the digital revolution of the 1990s who consider the master of the electronic revolution the best representative of pre-cyberphilosophy, the idealistic overtone of McLuhan's work is not necessarily the most inspiring part of it. Or, as Lewis H. Lapham puts it, speaking of the mystic McLuhan: "The rhetoric falls into the rhythms of what I take to be a kind of utopian blank verse, and much of it seems [somewhat] overblown" (Lapham 1994: xviii). Yet in spite of the visionary force of most of his writing, one had to wait for the Internet, the world wide web, virtual reality and so on to grasp fully the ideas behind some of his sibylline—but indeed intriguing and exciting—formulas. As the blurb of the reprint of *The Medium is the Massage* puts it, via a quotation from Tom Wolfe: "I pay attention to every one of Marshall's [McLuhan, JB] insights, no matter how implausible they seem at the time, because he has been proven right over and over again" (McLuhan and Fiore 1996). And if the first reception of McLuhan strongly emphasised his importance for a better understanding of the electronic age, often reduced to television, the digital revolution of the 1990s has fostered a new reading that helped rediscover the relevance of his thinking for today's culture, which is a medium culture.

Stanley Cavell (1926–2018)

Like McLuhan's, Cavell's approach is fundamentally holistic. Its range and field of application, however, are less that of communication and technology than of art, more particularly visual art (painting, cinema). Its starting point is the art-historical debate on medium-specificity, as epitomised in the typically Modernist theory of Clement Greenberg, who defended the possibility of drawing sharp distinctions between different art forms as well as the necessity for each of them progressively to disclose and apply its own specific features (in the case of painting: colour and flatness, to take Greenberg's best known example, as theorised in his defence of the abstract expressionism of the 1940s and 1950s).

For Cavell, a medium is an *automatism* that links three types of elements: 1) *a host medium*, that is the material channel that circulates certain signs (for instance a sheet of paper, a DVD, a celluloid strip, a silk screen, a computer screen, the human body, etc.); 2) a *sign* or group of signs, generally organised according to criteria of sensorial perception (it should be noted that certain signs address more than one sense, for instance verbal signs, which are generally speaking both visual and oral: we "hear" the words we read, we "write" the words we hear, even if the match between the visual and the oral is never complete or perfect); 3) a certain *content*—a medium aspect or dimension that is often overlooked by other medium theories; instead Cavell insists very much on the idea that each medium has to discover or reshape its own content, which cannot freely migrate from one medium to another.

The example of the comic book immediately shows some of the basic assets of Cavell's theory. Appearing in the early 1930s (*Famous Funnies* is supposed to be the first of them; it was first published in 1933 and was initially a reprint of earlier newspaper comic strips), this medium is defined by the interplay of a specific *host medium* (small size, more or less A5, pulp magazines of a limited number of clamped pages—so no real "books" in the Unesco sense of the word[4]), a specific type of *signs* (of comic art in the form of sequential juxtaposed panels that represent individual scenes) and a specific *content* (the perception of comic books as an independent medium, different from mechanical reprints of newspaper comics, results from the "invention" of a new type of stories, superheroes comics, the most iconic example being *Superman*, appearing in the first issue of Action Comics in 1938). The comics example clearly indicates that the broader, holistic notion of medium is different from medium definitions that foreground just one of the elements under scrutiny. A medium cannot be reduced to a host medium, nor to a certain sign type or to a certain content. Comic books are different from newspaper comics—a previous form of comic art—as they will be different from graphic novels—one of its subsequent forms: all these comic forms may have something in common, but their "medium mix" (host medium, signs, and content) is radically different. One of the most direct consequences of Cavell's medium theory is thus a critique of the alleged homogeneity of most of our medium labels. If one follows Cavell, there is no reason to believe that there is something such as "cinema," for instance. One should instead accept that there are many forms of cinema, all with their own medium mix, and the same applies also to painting (canvas painting is not fresco painting, for example), photography (a daguerreotype does not represent the same medium as a calotype), or literature (oral literature is shaped differently from print-born literature). At the same time, Cavell also makes us understand that works that seem to belong to the same medium can nevertheless belong to other medium uses (as happens, for instance, in works that do not follow the complete medium mix, for instance three-dimensional comics, which may tend to sculpture or installation art, or mechanical remediations as movies seen on television, which lose certain elements of cinema while not necessarily adopting all aspects of television). In other words: Cavell's theory makes room for hybridity as it dismantles overgeneralising definitions of media. Moreover, the multiple cases of hybrid, mixed or impure media should also be taken as an invitation to abandon the study of independent or autonomous media in favour of a more realistic approach in terms of media networks or media ecologies. Some authors rely on the notion of "series" to tackle the internal and external multiplicity of any medium (Gaudreault and Marion 2015). Others formulate the same idea in more directly anti-essentialist ways:

> So it is as much a mistake to write broadly of "the telephone," "the camera" or "the computer" as it is "the media," and of—now, somehow, "the Internet" and "the Web"— naturalizing or essentializing technologies as if they were unchanging ... Instead it is better to specify telephones in 1890 in the rural United States, broadcast telephones in Budapest in the 1920s, or cellular, satellite, corded, and cordless landline telephones in North America at the beginning of the twenty-first century (Gitelman 2008, 8).

In this context, the link between medium and automatism, which counterbalances the idea that anything more or less goes, is a very interesting one. Automatism refers first of all to the fact that a medium "automatically" generates its own occurrences (media exist only to the extent that there are concrete works that represent them). Second, it designates also the fact that this creation of concrete works is performed by the medium itself (which does, of course, not mean that a medium also exists on its own; each medium is part of a broader mediascape), not by the (human or mechanical) agent that uses it (true, agents are necessary, but what they perform is what is programmed by the medium). Third, the finished work exists on its own, it is not dependent on an author's intention (which, of course, does not signify that intentions do not exist or matter, but their importance can only be relative).

This holistic and medium-specific approach, each medium being defined by its own automatism, is however not a rigid or deterministic conception. Two major reasons explain the *anti-essentialist* approach of Cavell's take on medium specificity. On the one hand, as already hinted at by the mention of hybridity, a medium is not necessarily defined by a cluster of medium-specific features or characteristics: all media can include elements from other media or mix elements from various media; what is specific to a medium is not the channel or the sign-type or the content that forms it, but a certain automatic combination of all these elements that the receiver identifies as typical of this or that medium (an idea one also finds in prototype theory in linguistics). On the other hand, all media can and do change over time, sometimes very radically, as seen for instance in the graphic novel, which is no longer a type of comic art, combining words and images, but a type of literature or verbal art, including some extreme examples of *wordless* graphic novels (Beronå 2008). In many recent art-historical debates, much attention has been paid to oblique or "cross-medium" approaches, such as those represented by Gerhard Richter, a painter who is considered to do photography, and Jeff Wall, a photographer who claims to continue the tradition of genre painting.

What all these often extremely sophisticated examples and analyses finally suggest is that a medium—and this is also what Cavell is saying—is the socially accepted idea of what a medium "is" (or is supposed to be) at a certain moment and at a certain place, and this "idea" cannot be separated from the social practices that surround it. Medium, as meaning, is use, but use can never be limited to a set of strictly technical procedures, as repeatedly argued by cultural studies since the late 1950s. For the example of television see Williams 1975, who analyses the difference between British public television and US private television—actually two different media—in terms of use and social, that is political and economic practices. Williams first presents the differences between the two systems: the British system with its clear distinction between information, instruction and entertainment, and the no less clear distinction between two different programmes; the US system which blurs the boundaries between information, instruction and entertainment and which replaces the sequence of autonomous programme units by a mechanism he calls "flow" and which refers to both that blurring of boundaries and the fact that programmes are permanently interrupted by all kind of inserts pointing at what will come next. In a second step, he explains these differences by linking them with the mission statement as well as the capital structure of the various stakeholders (public authorities in the UK, private investors in North America). In the latter case, it is crucial that the spectators are watching all the time, to make sure that a maximum of ads is being seen. In the former case, it is the clarity of the message that counts.

The shift from comics to literature, as in the case of the graphic novel, is for instance directly linked with dramatic changes in the way the medium is produced, designed, circulated, read, and eventually appropriated or continued by its readers (Baetens and Frey 2015). Graphic novels not only distinguish themselves from comics by the fact that they claim to be "serious stuff" for adult readers (as if comics were only meant for kids as mere entertainment), they are different from comics in that they are sold as culturally legitimate items in bookshops (instead of being offered for purchase in newsstands or by subscription only) and institutionally attributed to "complete authors" (that is authors that are in charge of all aspects of their work, as in *auteur* cinema, rather than anonymous employees working on the chain in corporate owned studios).

Remediation, Intermediality, Transmediality and the Others

In the wake of McLuhan and Cavell, medium has become a key notion in cultural analysis (Murphet 2016). Given the open and dynamic dimension of the debate, the field has witnessed the birth of a large number of related concepts, which aim at mapping the wide range of possible forms and uses of media structures. In this section, we will briefly present the most influential of these concepts.

Chief among them is the notion of remediation, as coined by Jay David Bolter and Richard Grusin in a book whose subtitle contains a direct reference to McLuhan: *Remediation. Understanding New Media* (Bolter and Grusin 1999; for a theoretical update see Grusin 2015). While categorically rejecting McLuhan's teleological impulse, Bolter and Grusin accept the fundamental instability of the Western mediascape (the authors explicitly limit their analysis to post-Renaissance Western culture). Medium variability is mainly the result of the gap between what users want, namely a representation as complete and transparent as possible of the world by man-made sign systems, and what media actually offer, namely a representation of the world that is not yet fully complete and transparent. Man's mimetic desire is the fuel of media evolution and transformation, as signalled by the continuous replacement of less mimetic by more mimetic media, that is by media that offer us the promise of coinciding with the very thing they represent (and by emphasising this point, Bolter and Grusin reveal that their position has inherited quite a lot from McLuhan's teleology). Obviously, such a desire always remains utopian, and history is full of backslides and anachronisms. Each time a new format of 3-D photography becomes available, the audience rapidly goes back to 2-D photography, theoretically speaking a weaker mimetic form than 3-D photography (Timby 2015). And the allegedly fatal remediation of novel by film is also a phenomenon that in practice works very differently from what might have been expected in theory, not only because people continue to read books (in certain cases even books that remediate… films; see Baetens 2018), but also because the film industry seems to be in need of literature's prestige when it comes down to producing new movies (even if nobody will ever read the novel that inspired the film, the film will be more successfully marketed when the audience is being told that it is based upon a literary work: see Murray 2011).

When the medium—or a specific type of medium use—foregrounds the sign's referent (and it should be noted that Bolter and Grusin's approach gives priority to the "host medium" definition), the mimetic logic is phrased as "immediacy," that is transparency (at the moment of *Remediation*'s publication, the then strongest form of immediacy was to be found in virtual reality). When the medium on the other hand brings to the fore not the referent of the sign but the medium itself, Bolter and Grusin introduce the notion of "hypermediacy," a mechanism that generates a totally different experience, not that of transparency but of opacity, since the users will be extremely aware of the properties of the medium itself. This experience, however, is not incompatible with the fundamental law of mimetic desire: even if immediacy remains the ideal horizon of all media, the strong hypermediatic sensation offered by the contact with a medium that resists transparency may give the illusion that the user is experiencing the world in a new and exciting way (innovations in sound technology in cinemas are a typical example of the hypermediatic effects of media innovations). In other words, the success of a new medium depends on two diametrically opposed mechanisms, which exclude each other, while pointing in the same direction, since a new medium will supersede an old one if it proves either more immediate or more hypermediate than previous ones. As *Remediation* makes very clear, however, immediacy and hypermediacy are not essential categories: as time goes by, immediate media are always in danger of becoming hypermediate (photography is a good point in case: we no longer believe that pictures are the "real thing," and the same applies to virtual reality: after the initial excitement, what we see and feel are the helmet and the gloves), whereas initially hypermediate forms can turn into more mediate forms (once we get used to a technology it may feel so natural that we forget about its materiality). Moreover, and this is perfectly in sync' with the authors' refusal of strict teleology, they also acknowledge the importance of "repurposing," that is the appropriation of features that are typical of new media in order to guarantee the survival of older media (the typography of old-fashioned newspapers in print will try to emulate, for instance, the more mosaic-like structure of digital news sites).

Among the most significant fine-tunings in the debate on medium transformation and remediation one undoubtedly finds the notion of the "double birth" of a medium, as theorised by film historians and theoreticians André Gaudreault and Philippe Marion. In various publications, most importantly in a key essay entitled *The End of Cinema?* (Gaudreault and Marion 2015), they claim that media do not appear overnight, for instance as the result of a technological invention (the "invention" as such), but that their actual birth as a socially accepted and functioning medium (the "invention" as it is made into a socially relevant tool, after changes and adaptations suggested by users) is always a process that stretches from the material appearance of the medium as a new technology to the implementation of the complete form of the medium's automatism in the available mediascape of the time. During that period, the medium adapts itself to the mediascape, in order to become acceptable as a medium that is both bringing something new to the field and offering the guarantee of being recognised by the users. Early cinema is a good example of this second birth: although the technical specificity of this new medium was immediately recognised, its first uses did not radically separate it from, among others, photography, the magic lantern and fairground magic tricks. Current film historians consider early cinema as the merger of two existing larger series, that of moving images and that of projected images, and the social importance of these two practices (movement and projection) may explain why the first contact with film was not immediately framed by all viewers in terms of "a new medium," but in terms of another variation on a set of entertainment formats that had been permanently shifting throughout the whole 19th century.

If *Remediation*'s conceptual framework is simple and easy to use, other aspects and domains of medium theory have fallen prey to terminological chaos: intermedia, multimedia, cross-media, hypermedia, polymedia, transmedia, and its countless synonyms and parasynonyms litter the field. In order to reduce crippling terminological confusion it is necessary drastically to reduce the existing terminology to a binary opposition, that between *intermedial* and *transmedial*.[5] The limitations of such a simplification are blatant, but one may hope that the practical profits of this move will be more important than its losses.[6] The question, here, is not to determine whether certain works are more or less intermedial or transmedial—both intermediality and transmediality can be key features of any form—but to develop a model as simple as possible to discuss artistic issues in the broader contemporary context of digital multimedia culture. In order to enable a correct understanding of transmedia storytelling, we will also introduce two other notions, namely *demediation* (a concept we borrow from Garrett Stewart 2010) and *serialisation* (and here we will pay tribute to the seminal work of Letourneux 2017). However, the twin notions of intermediality and transmediality are essential to the argumentation of this section.

On the one hand, each medium is directly or indirectly in contact with other media, and influenced as well as changed by them in the broader mediascape. Each medium is actually the result of a remediation due to its conflict with other media. On the other hand, each medium is also itself a blend of several media, as powerfully argued by WJT Mitchell in one of the most quoted articles in the field: "There are no visual media" (2005). Each medium is intermedial, be it in writing or visual art. In a literary text, for instance, there are visual signs as well as oral signs (as already hinted at above, we hear when we read and we see when we hear, even if orality and visuality do of course never totally coincide), but also tactile and olfactory signs (when read in print, a literary text has also a touch and feel as well as smell, and similar synesthetic phenomena also occur in non-print versions). In visual art, the blending of the optic and the haptic (that is an active way of looking, also linked with body movement and proprioception) is also a widely shared observation, and the (universal) phenomenon of synaesthesia, currently strongly debated in the field of neurology, goes in the same direction. In practice, however, the use of the term "intermediality" is restricted to these cases in which different types of signs, for instance words and images, are combined. The radical stance on intermediality that is defended here tends to claim that even monomodal signs are characterised by internal complexity.

Intermediality, in other words, is not only the general term that defines the relationships between autonomous media, it is also the term that identifies the internal plurality of each medium. The intermedial study of literature therefore refers to the study of the relationships between the literary text and its "others" (for instance the illustrations that accompany it, to give an elementary example), but it also includes the study of the literary as a heterogeneous material that conveys a more or less radical "semiotic rupture" within itself (for instance when we interpret aspects of typography, from typeface to page layout and book design, as aspects of the text's visuality—a dimension of literature that has always been at the centre of visual and experimental poetry).

As for the other term, transmediality, it refers to the fact that more and more works tend to appear in various media. The key phrase in this depiction of transmediality is "tend to": the reappearance of a work in another medium is a possibility, not a general law; moreover, its presence and impact depend on its historical context. This process is evident in, but not exclusive to, cyberculture, where a number of factors come together: massive digitising of cultural texts and global spread of new media languages; a strong competition among media entertainment corporations; the proliferation of popular culture reception and distribution platforms and the enhancement of the subjects' creative intervention in the emerging cultural land-scape. Various forms of transmediality occur in a context of increased media mobil-ity where all forms of adaptation, recycling and extension are combined. In certain periods, cultures, environments, genres, etc., transmediality will be more present than in others. In principle, however, transmediality is a universal phenomenon. As in the case of intermediality, which is both internal and external, it is necessary here to make a further distinction between two aspects, or even *phases*, of transmediality.

On the one hand, transmedialisation is the mechanism or process that adapts a work that exists in a given medium to another medium. One could call the result of these operations *snowball transmedial narrative worlds* (as for instance in many Hollywood franchises). This process, as we know, is not one-sided (a book can be adapted into a film; a film can be novelised into a book; a painting can be converted into a musical score; a musical score can become a canvas painting, etc.). However, not all adaptations are equal. Once again depending on the context, this or that type of adaptation will be more present, from a quantitative as well as from a qualitative point of view. Even if there are as many novelisations as there are filmic adaptations of books, for example, novelisations are definitely less visible, since they are consid-ered aesthetically less worthwhile than filmic adaptations (Baetens 2018). It should be stressed that transmedialisation and adaptation are in no sense synonyms: even if all transmedialisations are adaptations, not all adaptations are transmedialisations, since it is perfectly possible to adapt a work while staying within the same medium (the examples of such an internal or intramedial adaptation are countless: translations, reader's digests, rewritings, parodies, etc. are all cases of non-transmedial adaptations) and there are certainly good reasons to maintain a sharp distinction between the broad field of *adaptation*, which can be seen as part of translation theory, and the narrow field of *rewriting*.

Yet, on the other hand, there is also the fact that certain works are not first elaborated in a given medium and then adapted into other media, but produced more or less simultaneously in various media, none of them being the "source" of the other ones, by means of a multi-platform production design where a fictional/narrative world emerges through a complex planning of multiple media contributions. This second dimension or *phase* in transmediality is what Long called "hard transmedia" (2007), defined by Pratten as follows:

> "Transmedia storytelling" is telling a story across multiple media and preferably, although it doesn't always happen, with a degree of audience participation, interaction or collaboration. In transmedia storytelling, engagement with each successive media heightens the audience's understanding of, enjoyment of and affection for the story. To do this successfully, the embodiment of the story in each media needs to be satisfying in its own right while enjoyment of all the media should be greater than the sum of the parts (2011, 1).

From a theoretical point of view, it is crucial to stress the difference between these two types of transmediality, which are at the same time very comparable, since both are aspects of what Jenkins calls "convergence culture" or media collusion, and very different, since the ways in which they rely on adaptation go into different directions. If the former case exemplifies the mechanism of adaptation in a rather traditional sense (a work existing in a certain medium becomes something else in a different medium), the latter, which is of course not sourceless, starts with something that one might call "demediated content." The notion of demediation has been put forward by Garrett Stewart, yet in a more restricted and specialised sense, in the field of installation art to identify what he calls *bibliobjets*, i.e. books used as sculptural material in visual and installation art, namely the exhibition of books as purely visual/tactile objects in the art gallery and museum circuit (Stewart 2010). Stewart calls these items *nonbooks* and stresses that they are not to be confused with previous forms of book art in which the interplay of the verbal and the visual/tactile did not exclude the actual reading of the text (Stewart mentions the *livre d'artiste* tradition popularised by Picasso and

Matisse). Demediated books are, in short, books that are transformed into works of visual art by the artist's focus on the materiality of the object, at the expense of the very content and even readability of the text. Stewart finally labels this phenomenon of the non-book in more general terms as demediation: "what I am calling demediation peels away the message service, leaving only the material support" (413).

Demediation, however, is a concept that goes far beyond its mere use in the contemporary gallery and museum space. Even if the word itself does not appear directly in this context, one can find clear echoes of it in discussions on book publishing in the era of digital reproduction. As demonstrated by Thompson (2010), modern multimedia publishers and transmedia storytelling producers have replaced "text" by "content" or even "experience." More generally speaking, the idea that there are no bodies or materialities in e-space, only ideas and information (which, moreover, one wants to be "free," i.e. circulating without being encumbered by material or other obstructions), is one of the strongest myths driving the world of cyberutopia. Demediation goes into a different direction, of course. Content as being immaterial is a naïve utopia: semiotically speaking, there is no *signified* without *signifier*, no *substance* without *form*, no *interpretant* without *sign*, etc., and N. Katherine Hayles has persuasively driven home the point that the world of bits and bytes is necessarily an embodied culture, which does not dissolve issues of materiality and corporality in empty abstraction and pure idealities (Hayles 1999). It is better to use the term demediatisation to identify and name the fact that the content of a work does not have to be completely actualised in a given medium before it is possible to adapt it into other media; it has been elaborated in such a way that it can be easily elaborated in various media, without being hindered by the existence of a previously existing form.

The fundamental reason for this demediation is *not* the digitisation of all media (a point to which we will return very soon), but the shift from traditional cultural forms to cultural or creative industries, in which the exploitation of a given idea, pilot or format in as many forms and on as many platforms as possible is an economic necessity. Digitisation reinforces this tendency towards *demediation-cum-transmedialisation*, but it is certainly not the trigger or the fundamental cause of this larger change. Moreover, as convincingly shown by Matthieu Letourneux (2017) in his research on serialisation in popular culture, demediation is not just the (partial) putting between brackets of the material form of the initial content, it also involves a far-reaching redefinition of what content actually is, or rather which specific form it takes when integrated in the cultural-industrial logic of serialisation—it was not included by Jenkins among his seven principles of transmedia storytelling (2009) by chance. To think of a story as content, for instance, does not signify that one tries to invent a story that will resist its adaptation into a film, a video game, a novel, a comic, a toy, a theme park, etc. as little as possible. It will first of all refer to the shift from story (in the sense of a series of actions organised in the form of a plot) to a story world (i.e. a set of characters and a certain setting).

Although the notion of transmedia storytelling clearly covers the two aspects of transmediality (traditional adaptation on the one hand, the transmedialisation of demediated content on the other hand), the dramatic implications of this distinction for the notion of storytelling are not always acknowledged. In the former case, transmedia storytelling will be closer to story adaptation as it unfolds in traditional franchises (i.e. to the adaptation of a story that has already been embodied and materialised in a narrative discourse, hence the difficulties of adapting it easily or seamlessly into another medium). In the latter, transmedia storytelling will have more to do with adding a storyline to a story world (and here the verbal realisation of the story will be less elaborate in order to avoid problems of medium migration as much as possible).

The Digital Turn

It would be absurd to deny that the digital turn is everywhere in our culture. However, in light of the medium-theoretical issues raised above, it must be possible to address anew two of the major questions that are systematically asked in the debates on the digital. First, is the digital turn a real break with previous cultural frameworks?—and the related question: if there is indeed such a break, does this imply that the shift towards the digital has an automatic impact on culture? Second, is this digital turn the result of a teleological process?—and here a related question as well: does the shift towards the digital produce a "post-medium" condition, in which the computer (to put it very simply) is aimed at superseding all existing media, producing a medium that can be seen as the merger of all existing media? The scope and stakes of this kind of questions are huge and they obviously exceed the primarily artistic and aesthetic interrogations of this chapter. Yet the medium-theoretical framework as presented in the previous pages should enable us to make some modest contributions to the inquiry.

A positive answer on the first set of questions (is there a real digital break, and does this break encompass both form and content of culture?) would reveal a technodeterminist attitude, if not bias, à la McLuhan, which is far from being shared by all medium theoreticians. Once again, it would be absurd to try to downsize the many changes brought about by the digitisation of culture (most visibly produced, at the level of the end-user, by the introduction of the first personal computers around 1980). But for many scholars, the digital revolution was already underway before. Lev Manovich's *The Language of New Media* (2000), a study that is still considered a vital reflection on the fundamental issues, topics and techniques of digital culture, resolutely claims that the digital revolution had actually started in the field of cinema, more specifically thanks to the impact of Soviet montage techniques (on which more later in the next chapter, but it is already worth stressing that this kind of segmentation of a continuum is much older: see the Introduction to this book). It is worth quoting some fragments of this text at some length here, for it illustrates in a very challenging manner the idea of cultural continuity as it can be formulated from a medium-theoretical point of view:

> One general effect of the digital revolution is that avant-garde aesthetic strategies [the model Manovich is referring to is Vertov's *Man with a Movie Camera*, J.B.] came to be embedded in the commands and interface metaphors of computer software. In short, the avant-garde became materialized in a computer. Digital cinema technology is a case in point. The avant-garde strategy of collage reemerged as the "cut-and-paste" command, the most basic operation one can perform on digital data. The idea of painting on film became embedded in paint functions of film-editing software. The avant-garde move to combine animation, printed texts, and live-action footage is repeated in the convergence of animation, title generation paint, compositing, and editing systems into all-in-one packages (xxxi).

> I analyse the language of new media by placing it within the history of modern visual and media cultures. What are the ways in which new media rely on older cultural forms and languages, and what are the ways in which they break with them? What is unique about how new media objects create the illusion of reality, address the viewer, and represent space and time? How do conventions and techniques of old media—such as the rectangular frame, mobile viewpoint and montage—operate in new media? If we construct an archaeology connecting new computer-based techniques of media creation with previous techniques of representation and simulation, where should we locate the essential historical breaks? (8).

The digital as a new medium thus appears to be a remediation—as well as expansion, intensification, acceleration, dissemination, globalisation...—of the older medium of cinema, that is of a specific type of cinema, and as such it is perfectly possible that it will itself be remediated one day by other, newer media, yet never in a purely linear way. The same applies to the longtime hotly debated issue of digital photography. It was first seen as a disruptive medium transformation, including the moral panic that sometimes goes along with this kind of change (do editors or reporters have the right to digitally retouch a picture?), but progressively one has come to understand that digital photography is less a revolution in terms of picture-making (many previous forms of photography and photographic reproduction were just as "manipulative") than in terms of storage and dissemination as well as in terms of price and numbers (even if photography had rapidly become a democratic medium—the first Kodak was commercialised in 1888—the ease of making, archiving and circulating pictures has become such that the world of photography has entered the—metaphorically speaking—big data era). Besides, it should be stressed that the digital is never isolated from (other parts of) the mediascape. In that regard, the digital medium is not essentially different from other media—as we have seen, film is also anything but an autonomous medium—even if its impact on the larger mediascape is dramatically strong. But similar claims could be made in the case of the newspaper, for instance—definitely the dominant medium of the 19th century, to the extent that some scholars have rephrased this whole century as "the newspaper era" (Kalifa et al. 2011).

As far as the impact of the digital is concerned, the technodeterminist approach should equally be nuanced. It does not make much sense to launch general and somewhat abstract discussions on whether the digital changes culture and to what extent these changes are mechanically produced by the appearance of digital media—and one easily imagines that the very use of the plural, media instead of medium, is a partial answer to any attempt to provoke general and abstract answers. What is more interesting is the detailed analysis of impact as well as failure of impact of the digital in very specific cases, always in comparison with the larger cultural series of the medium under scrutiny.

The question of "reproduction" may be a good example of this type of question. Obviously, the reproductive possibilities of digital media are not new in themselves. Non-mechanical as well as mechanical reproduction techniques (from engravings to photographs, for instance) were widely used long before the computer gave us the impression, that is the illusion, that it would become possible to reproduce anything and to make it accessible in no time and for free. What matters here is not the question whether the digital will achieve what other reproduction techniques had started to do, but to examine the details of its impact, for instance on the way we consider artworks, for instance visual artworks (the case of literature, an allographic medium, raises completely different questions[7]). Since the publication of Walter Benjamin's article on the impact of photographic reproduction, there has been a tremendously rich and intense debate on the alleged loss of "aura" of the original (Benjamin 1969), but from a medium-theoretical point of view it may be more suggestive to turn to a less studied, although no less important, critic, André Malraux.

The inventor of the so-called "museum without walls," that is the exhibition of artworks via photographic reproductions, either in books or on the walls of a museum (in the 1950s a truly revolutionary proposal, that was part of a larger programme of cultural democratisation), Malraux (1954) has shown how the use of photography, not in general but as photography applied to art in the context of the museum without walls, has radically changed art history. On the one hand, photography has enhanced the possibility of making visible the relationships between works from different periods and cultures. On the other hand, it has also dramatically reshuffled the relationships between certain types of works and certain types of media. For not all works and media are equal in front of the photographic lens: miniatures, for instance, a traditionally "minor" art form, suddenly move to the centre of the field, since it is very rewarding to reprint them in books, where one can admire enlargements of original works; three-dimensional works like sculptures are much more difficult to reproduce, since one often has the impression that important features such as size and the ability to walk round the object are lost in a picture. The debate on the impact of the digital should be addressed in this way as well. Not: does the digital change the work of art, but: what is won and what is lost when a work of art is digitised and seen on which kind of screen (anything between the giant screen on the façade of a museum and the mini-screen of a wristwatch, if one takes "size" as the relevant feature—see Manovich 2000: 94–115, for a more encompassing reading of screen types)?

The second set of questions raised by the digital turn—is the digital the "logical" evolution of the transformations within the Western media system, and are we evolving towards a post-medium condition where the computer is taking over the role of all other media?—should also be tackled from a medium-theoretical point of view. The term "post-medium" has been coined in the field of art history to critically reframe the alleged supersession of typically Modernist debates on medium-specificity, while drawing attention to the progressive unification of all media forms and formats in contemporary digital culture (Krauss 1999). The historical dimension of many medium-theoretical studies (see below) is certainly one of the elements that encourages this kind of teleological thinking à la McLuhan, whose major representative at the turn of the 21st century was definitely Friedrich Kittler (1992, 1999). His emphasis on the convergence of all media in the computer as super-medium is reinforced by the accompanying claim of the fundamentally military- and intelligence-driven evolution of technological thinking, a point also made in the medium and technology theory of Paul Virilio, who systematically frames all media changes in light of the need of increasing speed in military applications (see Virilio 1989 and countless other publications).

Various scholars have seriously questioned the belief in the digital as epitome of the post-medium condition, mainly for three reasons. First, from an art-historical point of view, authors such as Krauss, who strongly defined the critical capacities of avant-garde work, have drawn attention to the industrial recuperation of the digital turn, more and more controlled by large conglomerates whose logic is not that of art but that of the cultural industries—always in danger of falling prey to the logic of the culture industry.[8] Second, many specialists of digital culture, both in visual studies and literary studies—a distinction that is of course less sharp than before—have made strong pleas in favour of a renewed care for the notion of medium-specificity. Lev Manovich did so at the very beginning of his seminal study on digital culture, as if he wanted to make clear that the shift from analogue to digital should not be confused with an abandonment of historically Modernist concerns. But it is N. Katherine Hayles, one of the chief theoreticians in the field of digital writing, who articulates the point with the utmost clarity. Within the broader defence of medium-specific analysis, she coins the term of *technotext*, which she defines as follows:

> When a literary work interrogates the inscription technology that produces it, it mobilizes reflexive loops between its imaginative world and the material apparatus embodying that creation as a physical presence. Not all literary works make this move, of course, but even for those that do not, my claim is that the physical form of the literary artifact always affects what the words (and other semiotic components) mean. Literary works that strengthen, foreground, and thematize the connections

between themselves as material artifacts and the imaginative realm of verbal/semi-otic signifiers they instantiate open a window on the larger connections that unite literature as a verbal art to its material forms. To name such works, I propose "tech-notexts," a term that connects the technology that produces texts to the text's verbal constructions (2002, 25–26).

Thirdly, authors such as Matthew Kirschenbaum who address not only the "surface" of digital productions but also the underlying code,[9] criticise the neglect of the "hidden" materiality of digital media, which should dispel the misconception that the digital is the somewhat miraculous merger of all possible media forms in a kind of super-medium that resists further analysis since it is both all-encompassing and supposedly "immaterial." From the very moment that one opens the black box of the digital, one immediately notices that the digital can only be thought of in the plural—but this should be no news for ordinary users struggling with compatibility problems between and within software systems. Moreover, all futurologist speculations, be they Luddite or cyber-utopian, on the gradual replacement of non-digital by digital media have proved at least incomplete. We still paint, we still read books, we still go to the theatre to see live performances, etc., even if what we paint, what we read, what we experience is no longer the same, because the digital has given a new social existence to older media (such as for instance oral literature, in the case of verbal arts, and improvising or sketching techniques, in the case of the art of drawing).

Medium Archaeology

Medium theory has a very open and dynamic approach to what a medium actually is, but all existing definitions and methods rely to a large extent on the dialectics between the old and the new, even if no theory will make essentialist statements: old and new are relative qualifiers, their position is permanently shifting, and in certain cases it can even be inverted (old media can be rediscovered and become—for a time—very new, while media that were once excitingly new can fall into complete oblivion—before a new cycle of old and new restarts). Since the historical dimension is ubiquitous, it should come as no surprise that medium theory has not only the ambition to be part of cultural theory in the broad sense of the word, but also that of elaborating a fully-fledged media history. This history, however, is not simply that of the media themselves, as proposed for instance in media theory, which is of course also interested in the historical changes of the phenomena it studies. In the specific framework of medium theory, scholars will try to understand these changes in larger cultural and contextual terms, while also taking on board the distinctive features of medium analysis as sketched above.

In many cases, medium theoreticians will enlarge the dialectics of old and new so that it becomes a "complete" history, with or without the teleological undertones one finds in the work of Marshall McLuhan, who proposed to summarise all media transformations to three major periods: oral culture, print culture (the "Gutenberg Galaxy"), and electronic culture (a phase of "reborn orality," since electronic culture helps to supersede the negative aspects of print culture—fragmentation, isolation, both individually and collectively—as well as update the positive aspect of oral culture—shared presence of producer and consumer, community, union, fusion). The underlying structure of this chronology—with a clear thesis, antithesis, and synthesis—is remarkably Hegelian, and similar ways of organising media structures can also be found, yet not always with the same teleological horizon, in the work by "mediology" specialist Régis Debray 1995, medium historian and philosopher Friedrich Kittler (1985, 1986), and philosopher of photography Vilém Flusser (2000), three authors who tend to highlight the moving relationships between the verbal and the visual, more precisely the replacement of verbal writing systems by visual writing systems, and who will prove crucial for the introduction of medium theoretical insights in art studies, beyond the mere domain of communication studies.

Flusser thus introduces a ternary structure that 1) starts with "traditional images," that is mental images created by human imagination and that can be used to interact with the world and almost magically change that world; these mental images, which can eventually be materialised, are a way of arranging the world in new ways and representing it on a two-dimensional plane; 2) continues with "texts," which are not abstractions from reality, but abstractions from images: "texts do not signify the world; they signify the images they tear up. Hence, to decode texts means to discover the images signified by them" (Flusser 2000: 11); and 3) ends with "technical images," first photographs, then digital images, that is images that are reinterpretations of texts and thus third-order abstractions. Technical images are different from traditional images since they are produced by apparatuses (a camera, a computer) and based on mathematical codes, which impose their own programme on the user. The latter will be the slave of the technical images if he or she mechanically follows the instructions of the apparatus, but will discover new forms of freedom as soon as new uses of the programme are being explored (an ambivalence reminiscent of McLuhan's thinking of either traumatising or liberating effects of the use of new media; trauma is of course also a key theme in the work of those media historians who underscore the military background of media changes such as Kittler and Virilio).

The stakes of media archeology are however higher than those of a broadened and theoretically enhanced media history. As Timothy Druckrey puts it:

> An anemic and evolutionary model has come to dominate many studies in the so-called media. Trapped in progressive trajectories, their evidence so often retrieves a technological past already incorporated into the staging of the contemporary as the mere outcome of history. [...] Ingrained in this model is a flawed notion of survivability of the fittest, the slow assimilation of the most efficient mutation, the perfectibility of the unadapted, and perhaps, a reactionary avant-gardism ("Foreword" to Zielinski 2006:vii).

Media archeology takes stock from the Foucauldian notion of the "archive," that is the underlying rules of what can be said and hence thought within a given discursive framework (and, more extensively, within a given medium), but they rethink it with the help of the equally Foucauldian concept of "archeology," which rejects the linear and rational *post hoc ergo propter hoc* chronology of traditional historical writing (often linked with the term "genealogy"). In order to make room for approaches that give full weight to gaps and counternarratives (Foucault 1982), media archeologists follow a programme that does not want to highlight history as archive, but history as archaeology. As Thomas Elsaesser states:

> Rather than pursue these aesthetic parameters, I want to sketch indeed an archaeological agenda, taken from Michel Foucault's *Archaeology of Knowledge*, which, for instance, states: "archaeology does not imply the search for a beginning, [it] questions the already-said at the level of existence [...] and it describes discourses as practices." It is easy to translate these three propositions into terms that echo the preoccupations of scholarship in early cinema: No search for beginnings: what early cinema has taught us is that the cinema has several origins, and therefore also no specific origin; in fact; at the limit, it has yet to be invented (Elsaesser 2006: 17).

The most sweeping examples of this radical agenda are probably to be found in the work by Siegfried Zielinski, who reformulates the archaeological programme in the following, highly idiosyncratic way:

> However, if we are to understand history as being present not only when it demands to be accepted as a responsibility and a heavy burden, but also when there is value in allowing it to develop as a special attraction, we will need a different perspective from that which is only able to seek the old in the new. In the latter perspective, history is the promise of continuity and a celebration of the continual march of progress in the name of humankind. [...] This view is primitive pedagogy that is boring and saps the energy to work for the changes that are so desperately needed. Now, if we deliberately alter the emphasis, turn it around, and experiment, the result is worthwhile: do not seek the old in the new, but find something new in the old (2006: 3).

A rapidly organised (sub-)discipline, media archaeology, is then both a history and theory of media, more precisely a way of doing history from a medium-theoretical point of view that tries to understand the present by an unconventional rereading of the past, with a strong focus on dead, forgotten, censored or obscured media as well as an *a priori* sympathy for the dreams and fantasies of (not necessarily successful) inventors, tinkerers and amateurs (Huthamo and Parikka 2011, Parikka 2012). Or, to put it more succinctly, media archaeology is one of the most challenging current developments of the long history of medium theory.

Important as it is for the broad cultural understanding of medium theory, media archaeology is also an approach that forces us to examine the future of media, more particularly digital media, and as well as to do it in a concrete and practical way. This is the purpose of the three following chapters, first, by offering a comparative view of some major production and reception changes in the two fields of literature and the visual arts—the two arts that are most dramatically present in today's screen culture ("Electronic Literature, Internet Art"); second, by scrutinising the actual place where these changes actually take place, for there is much more in digital culture than the computer screen and electronic hard- and software ("The Relocation of Digital Writing"); and, third, by evaluating the mechanisms of cultural value production, traditionally framed in terms of the cultural canon, a concept that digital culture does not supersede or exclude, but profoundly redefines ("The Problem of Canonization in the Digital Era").

4   Electronic Literature, Internet Art

Like most medium-specific readings, this chapter starts by distinguishing digital-borne and digital-born. The former refers to works in print—or theoretically thinkable in print—that are offered through an electronic channel. The latter refers to works that rely on the technical and creative possibilities of the digital host medium and that can no longer be appropriately realised in print form. This chapter suggests that the difference between the two regimes is vital, as shown by the notions of ergodic literature and database narrative, but not always as absolute as it is being claimed. It further presents digital-born literature from a historical point of view: we describe the various "generations" of e-writing, while putting a strong emphasis on issues such as technological obsolescence, for many forms of e-writing prove dramatically ephemeral. The chapter also stresses the profound relationships between textual and visual artistic practices, which both foreground problems of originality and appropriation.

Keywords: database narrative, digital-borne vs digital-born, ergodic literature, hypertext, interactivity, sound poetry, text generator, unoriginality, visual poetry

Digital Writing before Electronic Writing

If new media, according to Manovich, started with Soviet montage, electronic literature has a long history too. From the 1950s onwards, at least, computers have been
used for all kind of literary experiments (the best recent overview is Rettberg 2019).
The first generation of electronic literature was mainly that of the so-called text
generators, that is machines programmed to generate new texts either by applying a
certain number of rules to a given text (for instance: replacing the nouns of this text
by their corresponding definition as given in a certain dictionary) or by converting
a certain input—a list of words, a string of words, a short fragment—into a "real"
text (for instance: composing a well-formed sonnet by using the following nouns
and adjectives as rhyme words).

Primitive as these first attempts may have looked, they were in perfect synergy
with the spirit of the times, open to questioning 1) the traditional notion of individual and human authorship: electronic texts were supposed to be made by machines
only, without human interference, as had happened with the first interpretations
of photographs more than a century earlier); 2) the notion of a fixed text and the
idea that the final version of a text, as long as it had been approved by its author,
was by definition the "right" one (a stance that, from a qualitative point of view, is
highly debatable, as shown for instance by the catastrophic revision of some of the
early *Adventures of Tintin*, sometimes ridiculously weaker than their initial version):
these were the years of Umberto Eco's "open work," which theorised the work as an
open network of context-driven variations on an unstable centre (Eco 1989); and 3)
the classic hierarchy of author and reader: the idea of interactive works was already
in the air, even if the current notion of "participatory culture" was still a faraway
dream. It should be recalled however that the intertwining of "production" and
"reception," a key feature of contemporary media, is actually typical of the emerging phase of many new media, which are often created by trial and error, in direct
contact with users and consumers: "[w]hen media are new, when their protocols are
still emerging and the social, economic, and material relationships they will eventually express are still in formation, consumption and production can be notably
indistinct" (Gitelman 2008, 15).

And it was not a coincidence either that the same period also witnessed the birth
of Oulipo (*Ouvroir de littérature potentielle*, 1960–) or workshop for potential literature (Motte 1988, Bloomfield 2017). Founded by writers who were also mathe-

maticians, the initial programme of Oulipo was to replace the romantic idea of the author as individual genius and the process of writing as dependent on inspiration by a more formalist approach of "constrained," that is rule-based, writing (a classic example is of course rhyme and meter, but the field of constrained writing entails a wide range of techniques and procedures, a very popular being the "lipogram," that is the writing of a text that avoids the use of one or more letters)—later also painting, composing, drawing... Newly invented or already well-known, these rules, such as for instance the lipogram (writing a text without using this or that letter or set of letters, for instance the letter "e", the most frequently used letter in French) did away with intention as well as individuality. The trigger of the writing process is a self-imposed constraint, which can be freely used by all those who want to do so, individually or collectively. Moreover, constraints are considered productive and transformative: they disrupt what the author wants to say (they are obstacles to direct expression), but help him or her to come up with new solutions (often works that were previously unthought of; constraints are powerful writing machines). Both a think tank and a creative writing workshop, Oulipo rapidly developed an interest in electronic literature, eventually creating a branch called "Alamo" (*Atelier de Littérature Assistée par la Mathématique et les Ordinateurs*, or "computer and math enhanced literary workshop"). The fundamental link between constraint writing and computer writing has to be found in Oulipo's commitment to combinatorics, an age-old yet somewhat eccentric, if not exotic, literary practice that both Oulipo and digital culture will bring to the very heart of writing and creative art in general, as we will see when discussing database art and the aesthetic of lists and archives. Regardless of the artistic value of these first experiments—and we should recall that not all Oulipo productions were meant to be published, and that some of them were not so much considered autonomous works as exercises aimed at illustrating the very possibility of using a certain constraint—it is important to stress that electronic literature does not appear in a vacuum. From the very beginning, it interacts with existing literary and cultural practices and this interaction is always a two-way interaction, as later examples will clarify.

The second type of electronic literature to emerge, which continues to be very much alive, is visual poetry and sound poetry, two key practices of post-war avant-garde movements which had started to dismantle the mutual and exclusive relationship of text and book. Here as well, electronic literature and print literature go hand in hand, even if this back and forth movement is far from homogeneous. It occurs so much that electronic literature simply imitates established forms of literature. By doing so, it helps foreground forms of reading and writing that go beyond these forms, thus supporting the attempts of non-electronic authors to revolutionise writing in print as well.

A third step, today almost forgotten for reasons that we will examine later, is that of hypertext fiction, a genre of electronic narrative characterised by the use of hypertext links that provides a new context for non-linearity in literature and reader interaction. Directly linked to the development of software programs such as *Storyspace* and *HyperCard*, which these hypertext fictions had to "illustrate" more or less in the same way as certain Oulipo exercises were meant to demonstrate the creative possibilities of a constraint, the genre offers a non-sequentially arranged number of textual units (often called *lexias*), which the reader can explore in different ways by clicking her way through the text. Hypertext fiction may seem a totally new way of writing, but its ancestors and models in print are well present in all types of literature. The "Choose Your Own Adventure" genre, although generally restricted to children's entertainment and gamebooks, is a popular print version of it, but highbrow Modernism has frequently explored the principle of the "forking paths" (the allusion to Borges' 1941 short story[10] is of course made on purpose, although this text does not formally implement the mechanism it discusses at story level). Three works should be mentioned here, for all of them continue to inspire electronic authors in each of the specific genres—poetry, narrative fiction, historical fiction— these works illustrate. Almost a manifesto of the Oulipo aesthetic and its fascination with "combinatory literature" (that is a specific type of constrained writing based on the remix of a limited set of items or data), Raymond Queneau's *Cent mille milliards de poèmes* (1961, "One Hundred Million Million Poems"), is a book containing a set of ten sonnets printed on card with each line on a separate strip. Any lines from a sonnet can be combined with any from the nine others, allowing for 10^{14} (= 100,000,000,000,000) different poems. Julio Cortázar's *Hopscotch* (1966) is a novel that the reader is encouraged to read in alternative ways: sequentially and linearly, from A to Z; linearly but incompletely, by skipping certain chapters; non-sequentially, by intertwining chapters from the different parts of the work, following the instructions of the author; and finally in whatever order he or she chooses. Neither a poem nor a novel but a "lexicon," Milorad Pavić's *Dictionary of the Khazars* (1988) takes the form of three cross-referenced mini-encyclopaedias, sometimes contradicting each other, each compiled from the sources of one of the major Abrahamic religions (Christianity, Islam and Judaism). All these books definitely underscore the importance of the database and they remain important sources of inspiration in the electronic age, even if the actual activity of the reader, who must take as many decisions as any hyperfiction reader or videogame player, does not rely yet on electronic devices and affordances. They are considered "predigital" works, and we will discuss later on what happens to literary creations "after" the digital turn.

Digital-Borne versus Digital-Born

The first attempts to cope with the novelty as well as the stakes and challenges of electronic literature have had a strong medium-theoretical starting point. On the one hand, they have tried to define what is specific about this form of writing. On the other hand (see next section), they did not define this medium-specificity in narrowly technical terms. They instead approached it as cultural forms, looking for the message of the medium.

Most medium-specific readings logically start by distinguishing digital-borne and digital-born. The former refers to works in print—or theoretically thinkable in print—that are offered through an electronic channel, be it already existing texts that have been digitised, or texts that simply use the computer as an old-fashioned writing machine. The latter refers to works that rely on the technical and creative possibilities of the digital host medium—they are created on a computer and meant to be read on a computer—and that can no longer be appropriately realised in print form. True, almost any text, even the most traditionally printed ones, is now to a large extent digitised, but that does not dissolve the fundamental distinction between the two categories. As N. Katherine Hayles puts it:

> In the contemporary era, both print and electronic texts are deeply interpenetrated by code. Digital technologies are now so thoroughly integrated with commercial printing processes that print is more properly considered a particular output form of electronic text than an entirely separate medium. Nevertheless, electronic text remains distinct from print in that it literally cannot be accessed until it is performed by properly executed code. The immediacy of code to the text's performance is fundamental to understanding electronic literature, especially to appreciating its specificity as a literary and technical production (2008: 5).

If we follow the medium-definition as sketched above, it is possible briefly to describe electronic literature as the encounter between three elements.

First of all, a certain *host medium*: the digital software and hardware, in permanent change and dizzyingly heterogeneous. Besides, digital-born texts have to be activated by, no pun intended, active readers: if users are purely passive, as happens for instance when one is asked to tick a box or to type the digits of a credit card, one misses a vital element of the medium's creative specificity. Hence, for instance, the strategic importance given to non-trivial ("trivial" meaning here: mechanical, without any conscious decision by the user) interaction between user and interface, as theorised by Espen Aarseth under the name of "ergodic" (derived from the Greek words *ergon*, meaning "work", and *hodos*, meaning "path"):

> In ergodic literature, nontrivial effort is required to allow the reader to traverse the text. If ergodic literature is to make sense as a concept, there must also be nonergodic literature, where the effort to traverse the text is trivial, with no extranoematic responsibilities placed on the reader except (for example) eye movement and the periodic or arbitrary turning of page (1997: 1–2).

Second, a certain type of *sign*, such as letters, sounds, pictures, drawings, etc. It does of course not suffice to label the words, images and sounds on screen as digital code materialised as pixels, for instance, to understand what happens to signs in a digital context. Instead, the key element is without any doubt the increasing combination of all these signs and thus the progressive multimodalisation of what can be read, seen, heard and touched on screen (for a technical discussion on the rejection of "code" as part of a natural language sign system see Cayley 2018, who also gives examples of "real" texts written with bits and pieces of code). This very general reading can be fine-tuned with the help of some features that focus on more than one aspect of the medium. Important in this regard is certainly the notion of differential text, that is the impossibility to limit the work to just one version, be it the final version or another one, and even more importantly to maintain a strict hierarchy between the various coexisting and perhaps competing versions of a work. They are, as Marjorie Perloff explains, "*differential* texts—that is to say, texts that exist in different material forms, with no single version being the definitive one" (2006: 146).

Third, new *content matter* (digital literature has produced new genres, such as *flarf* poetry, which remixes fragments retrieved from internet searches, and dramatically reshaped existing domains such as *games*, much less open and interactive in their print or analogue form). Undoubtedly the most far-reaching medium-specific innovation of electronic media, verbal as well as visual, has been the use of the database for artistic purposes. The following quotation by Lev Manovich drives this point home in a very assertive way:

> After the novel, and subsequently cinema, privileged narrative as the key form of cultural expression of the modern age, the computer age introduces its correlate—the database. Many new media objects do not tell stories; they do not have a beginning or end; in fact, they do not have any development, thematically, formally, or otherwise that would organize their elements into a sequence. Instead, they are collections of individual items, with every item possessing the same significance as any other (2000: 218).

The database is not "a simple collection of items," but "a structured collection of data" (id.). If it is the fundamental structure of the computer age, it is because software can only work if it treats structured data: the digital and the database imply each other. And Manovich continues:

> As a cultural form, the database represents the world as a list of items, and it refuses to order this list. In contrast, a narrative creates a cause-and-effect trajectory of seemingly unordered items (events). Therefore, database and narrative are natural enemies (2000: 225).

Whatever way one interprets the database, it should be clear that, in practice, the relationship with narrative, that is the database's "other," can never be put between brackets. This is the ecumenical position defended by N. Katherine Hayles (2007), who presents narrative and database as "symbionts." The expression "database narrative" does not make sense if one defines it as non-narrative or anti-narrative. It is a new form of telling that includes narrative aspects, just as modern narrative tends to include database aspects.

As in all other cases of old versus new media, digital literature displays a wide range of occurrences, some of which are more medium-specific than others. In principle, and this is also in line with the "double birth" theory by Gaudreault and Marion, the difference between digital-borne and digital-born, between less medium-specific and more medium-specific, has a strong temporal dimension. The automatism is almost never produced overnight, since each new medium has to find its own place within an already well-structured mediascape. To quote Hayles:

> When literature leaps from one medium to another—from orality to writing, from manuscript codex to printed book, from mechanically generated print to electronic textuality—it does not leave behind the accumulated knowledge embedded in genres, poetic conventions, narrative structures, figurative tropes, and so forth. Rather, this knowledge is carried forward into the new medium typically by trying to replicate the earlier medium's effects within the new medium's specificities. Thus written manuscripts were first conceived as a visual continuity of connected marks reminiscent of the continuous analogue flow of speech; only gradually were such innovations as spacing between words and indentations for paragraphs introduced. A similar pattern of initial replication and subsequent transformation can be seen with electronic literature (2008: 58–59).

The gradual adaptation to new automatisms concerns not only the words of the text. As seen in the previous quotation, punctuation is no less concerned. A suggestive example of the move from one medium to another has been analysed by Jeff Scheible (2015), who offers a both historical and cultural reading of the changes in punctuation. On the one hand, Scheible notices that in the history of writing punctuation has not always been present. One might say it is a typical, although not exclusive, feature of print culture, and as such it is not unthinkable that it will disappear again in the always newer forms of machine reading and writing that are currently taking over the role and function of traditional print, introducing new forms of punctuation that are at odds with the automatisms of print. On the other hand, Scheible also approaches punctuation from a cultural, quasi-philosophical point of view, for the way we punctuate (or not) reveals a hidden cultural logic that exceeds the mere domain of writing and printing, and touches upon long-term shifts in the relationships between sign, communication and meaning. Typographical marks, of which punctuation signs are one of the most interesting categories, can therefore be seen as shortcuts to cultural changes that are so general that they escape ordinary attention. Scheible illustrates this thesis with the help of three exemplary signs: the *period* (a traditional sign, but whose function is now changing), the *parenthesis* (an equally classic sign, whose traditionally spare use has been replaced by a much more active and diverse use in recent history), and the *hashtag* (a sign that can be considered radically new, even if as a form it already existed before).

As far as the period is concerned, Scheible observes that in digital culture this punctuation mark is no longer (only) used to signify the end of a sentence (a specific use of the period that Scheible tends to foreground at the expense of other uses, well presented in the history of Western writing, which he seems to leave aside), but that different uses tend to come to the fore, such as the one we observe in email addresses (first name + period + family name, for instance) or in domain names (noun + period + com, .edu, .net, and so on). This change is not a detail: it signifies the shift from a semantic use of the period (and of punctuation as a whole) to a syntactic use. Typography ceases to underline the logical structure of the meaning of a sentence, a paragraph, a text, and instead displays the way in which the strings of letters and words in electronic environments have to be structured in order to be recognisable for the encoding and decoding machines behind and below our texts. The period becomes a dot, and that is something completely different. Regarding the parentheses, Scheible examines not only the increasing presence of a typographical sign that was not really appreciated in traditional typography (although the Victorian era may offer a good counter-example), for it was seen as something that interrupted or deviated from the logical structure of the sentence, he also scrutinises the stakes of its prominence in modern typography, where it often appears as a sign *per se*, i.e. without any specific "content" inside (information presented between parentheses is not necessarily parenthetical any more; the punctuation is no longer there for purely cognitive or structural reasons). Scheible argues that the sudden manifestation of the parenthesis can be understood in light of a larger crisis of all forms of monolithic and orthodox thinking that are now challenged by the open and more participatory aspects of the internet and digital culture, making room for what is now moving from the outside to the inside, as if the boundaries between the dominant sentence and its margins were no longer there. Frequently quoting from filmic examples, such as the romantic comedy "500 Days of Summer" (dir. Marc Webb, 2009), which structures its mosaic composition with the help of parenthesised intertitles such as "DAY (8)," Scheible analyses the ubiquity of these parentheses as follows:

> Parentheses would seem to be in the most obvious sense of the term floating signifiers, helping to both manage and complicate information, alternately evoking

an air of distinction, an independent quirk, the banal, or the cute, along with the gimmicky aesthetics that sometimes accompany these features at the same time [...] (2015, 74).

In his reading of the hashtag Scheible notes that this sign has become the contemporary equivalent of the typical post-modern typographical mark, namely quotation marks (as a sign of irony and distance). He emphasises the fact that this sign illustrates the mutation of a symbol (namely the "number sign") into a typographical sign (the first meaning of the hashtag is no longer "number sign"; the hashtag refers instead to the way in which digital signs are related to each other when we start combining messages from different sources).

More generally speaking, the changes studied by Scheible disclose a fundamental transformation of what punctuation is or, more precisely, what it actually does. Rather than structuring the meaning of independent sentences, texts and meanings, typography is now a way of organising the relationship between textual occurrences and underlying digital codes and databases. The notion of meaning is then no longer taken care of by punctuation, but is left to the agency of who is combining textual material on the screen. This "who" can be a person or a machine or rather both, since the machine is now writing for us (think of the spelling checker) and we are writing for the machine (think of the ways in which we have to correct the autocorrection that is part of any writing software today).

As already suggested as well, the idea of a single digital medium and thus a single medium-specificity would be absurd. Just as there is not just one type of cinema or one type of painting, there is not one type of electronic literature, but a wide array of partially overlapping automatisms. These automatisms have many elements in common.

The Digital as Cultural Form

The examples above—database as competitor of the novel, the metamorphoses of punctuation in the internet era, the concern for interaction and participatory creation, and so forth—have already touched upon a second aspect of the medium-theoretical approach, where the study of electronic medium-specificity tips over towards the study of the cultural meaning, or if you prefer the "meaning" of the new media (for, once again, to address electronic writing or electronic art in singular would be an essentialist misunderstanding of the vast array of materialities and technotexts that define the new mediascape).

This cultural perspective was present from the very start. One of the first in-depth attempts to delineate the meaning of new media in the field of writing was George Landow's *Hypertext* (Landow 2006). First published in 1992, this book is still considered a landmark in the academic study of electronic writing systems. Although subsequent editions of this work have slightly downsized the radical claims of this work and reframed the scope in order to take into account broader issues of globalisation, Landow's basic stance has always been that the practice of electronic writing materialises and implements the theoretical claims made by critical theory (in this regard, the changing subtitle of the book, initially "The Convergence of Contemporary Literary Theory and Technology" and currently "Critical Theory and New Media in an Era of Gobalization," unquestionably exposes a shift of priorities, while reaffirming the central position of post-structuralism). The critique of any form of fixed or essentialist meaning, the belief in a subject in full control of what he or she is expressing through signs, the trust in linear and monodirectional structure of communicating messages from sender to receiver, the acceptance of the closed and homogeneous character of a work, formally as well as semantically, and the conviction that writing and reading are necessarily different activities, all these themes and issues had been heavily discussed in post-structuralism and deconstruction, but always in direct relationship with the Western canon (philosophical as well as literary). Electronic writing and literature, for Landow, is critical theory come alive. Most parts of the book have a title that starts with "reconfiguring," and what is being reconfigured are the key notions of post-structuralism as a new grand theory: the text, the author, writing, narrative, literary education. Some family resemblances between electronic literature and critical (post-structural, deconstructionist) theory are undeniable. At the same time, however, it rapidly appeared that certain claims made by Landow or, perhaps more precisely, the followers of his highly influential study proved too optimistic—provided of course one accepts the idea that digital culture is a positive good that should undo as soon as possible the classic state of the art in the field of writing and culture—and in certain cases also somewhat over-generalising.

Interactivity is a good case in point. The notion is systematically used when it comes down to circumscribing the medium-specificity of digital writing as well as the social impact, that is the "meaning," of these practices. Landow himself is critical of the concept:

> Readers may have noticed that in the preceding discussions of electronic media I have not employed the words *interactive* and *interactivity*. As many commentators during the past decade and a half [that is, between the first publication of *Hypertext* and the publication of *Hypertext 3.0* we are quoting here, J.B.] have observed, these words have been used so often and so badly that they have little exact meaning anymore. Just as chlorophyll was used to sell toothpaste in the 1950s and aloe was used to sell hand lotion and other cosmetic products in the 1970s and 1980s, interactive has been used to sell anything to do with computing, and the word certainly played a supporting role in all the hype that led to the dotcom bust (2006: 41–42).

Yet rather than trying to avoid the term, as Landow does, or to replace it with a better alternative, and here Aarseth's *ergodic* immediately comes to mind, it may make sense to try to specify the notion of interactivity, by elaborating a new definition not of what it is, but of the various forms it can take, and thus creating the possibility of implementing it in the analysis of medium-specific technotexts. An interesting example is given by Jean-Paul Fourmentraux, a specialist of (visual) internet art who introduces the following typology, applicable to verbal as well as visual arts (summarised from Fourmentraux 2005: 90–107[11]).

–   *Exploratory* interaction: based on the principle of navigation and aiming at experiencing the work.
–   *Contributing* interaction: based on the principle of execution of commands and aiming at an activation of the application.
–   *Alterating* interaction: based on the possibility of changing the work, yet always within the rules and procedures as programmed by the work itself, and aiming at either making transformations or adding new materials.
–   *Alteracting* interaction: based on the principle of communication between all those who collaborate in the making of the work, and foregrounding alteraction, that is the reaction in real time to the action of other agents.

Similar caution has been urged concerning agency and the possibility of "freeing" the information circulating on the internet. If the developers of the first home computers had their roots in the radical-liberal DIY movement of the counterculture, the same cannot be said of the big conglomerates—the GAFAs (Google Apple Facebook Amazon) or MAFiAAs (Microsoft, Apple, Facebook, Amazon, Alphabet) of this world. The digital turn may have been experienced in the beginning as a major leap into the direction of personal freedom, sharing of information, surpassing of the difference between producers and consumers (readers and writers, now all "wreaders", artists and public, now all co-creating in participative forms outside the traditional institutions of museum, gallery, arthouse, university, and so forth), in short: total democracy. Yet reality did not evolve the same way, although the myth of freedom (political, legal and economic), personal development, community building is still there, as shown for instance by the ideology of "open access" in academic publishing (actually all too often a new business model imposed by extremely profitable trusts to have the publishing and distribution costs paid by the author rather than by the reader). To put it very simply, we are allowed to buy an iPad, but not to open the device in order to have a look at the code—as was still the case for the first Apple computers.[12] Moreover, as hinted at in the taxonomy proposed by Fourmentraux, not all forms of interactivity allow a real exchange between the positions of those who make and those who "consume" (not to speak of all the intermediary positions that are inevitably involved in the production, dissemination and exhibition of a digital artwork, as will be detailed later on).

If the digital turn is not the complete disruption it was promised or feared to be, its large-scale cultural effects are indisputably there and perfectly visible. Yet rather than analysing them in axiological terms—is the digital turn "good" or "bad" for arts and culture?—it is vital to circumscribe these effects in order to disclose their meaning, once again in the medium-theoretical sense of the word. In that perspective, we would like to highlight four major transformations in the field of digital literature as well as digital visual art.

First, the *complexification of the sign*. Digital works do of course continue to work with specific signs of types—mainly words, images, and sounds—but the merger of these signs has become a reality. It suffices to visit any "literary" website whatsoever to notice immediately that a literary production is no longer a words-only product, for instance. Besides, the signs in question are no longer just the signs of the work itself. The material aspects of the interface and the hardware are often part of the work as well and the user is no longer supposed to ignore them (interface ergonomics in videogames are a key aspect of the work, which thus implements an important haptic dimension). This complexification of the sign also has a strong temporal aspect, given the fact that signs both move (digital texts are capable of animating formerly fixed letters) and remain open to change (texts can be modified in real time—provided the program allows one to do so, which is of course far from being always the case, most forms of interactivity being cases of "exploratory" interactivity). Notice however that the importance given to the complexification of the signs seems to draw the reader away from the traditional "unit" of a literary work—most traditionally speaking the book, that is a book-length publication accessible in one or more volumes. Digital texts tend to be fragmentary, not only because we live in a zapping culture which deeply affects our attention span (Waters 2004)—as can be observed also in the different reading patterns of texts in print and on screen, but also because works themselves are becoming as open and boundless and permanently shifting as the signs they use, which of course makes less relevant, if not impossible, the reading of a "complete" work. Whether this situation is "new" or nothing more than a return to older forms of reading, publishing and writing remains an open question, which certain authors are more than willing to answer in a dedramatising way (Gardner 2012a and b, Henkin 2018).

Second, the dynamic turn of signs and works or, more precisely, the *shift from objects to practices*. Digital works are still objects, obviously, but to a certain extent the focus of digital writing shifts from the object (which, as we have seen, is never totally finished, at least in theory) to a more process-oriented approach of its making and experiencing. Instead of focusing on "just works," digital writing focuses on "doing things with works"—and this applies to the various aspects of this doing: making, editing, publishing, disseminating, exhibiting, experiencing (to follow the classic temporal logic that is dramatically reshuffled by digital art). Writing is no longer aligning words, making sentences, composing chapters and books; it has become text-processing, that is the copying and editing of already existing texts, a fundamental move that Kenneth Goldsmith has compared with the introduction of photography in the visual arts:

> With the rise of the Web, writing has met its photography. By that, I mean that writing has encountered a situation similar to that of painting upon the invention of photography, a technology so much better at doing what the art form had been trying to do that, to survive, the field had to alter its course radically. [...] What we're dealing with here is a basic change in the operating system of how we write at the

root level. The results might not look different, and they might not feel different, but the underlying ethos and modes of writing have been permanently changed. If painting reacted to photography by moving toward abstraction, it seems unlikely that writing is doing the same in relation to the Internet. It appears that writing's response will be mimetic and replicative, involving notions of distribution while proposing new platforms of receiverships. Words very well might be written not to be read but rather to be shred, moved, and manipulated. Books, electronic and otherwise, will continue to flourish. Although the new writing will have an electronic gleam in its eyes, its consequences will be distinctly analog (Goldsmith 2011: xvii and xxi).

In this context, the fading of the distinction between reading and writing—two sides of the same artistic coin, but in the predigital era less automatically intertwined—becomes very clear. Yet the smooth transitions of reading and writing, initially theorised as an important breakthrough in the overturning of traditional—supposedly non-democratic or unequal—forms of literature, engender new questions and problems that also have a strong medium-theoretical component (see below, point 3).

The transition from item to practice is even more visible in the case of digital visual art works. Starting from the actor-network theory and thus the mutual involvement of objects, human agents, and machines and institutions, Fourmentraux has elaborated the various steps between the initial concept of a project—a concept that is of course from the very beginning shaped by the technical possibilities and limitations of a given software and hardware, on the one hand, and the commands and expectations of the funding bodies, on the other hand—and the final experience of the work by its user—which is not a neutral moment either, given the strongly ritualised character of our contact with art works. This trajectory reframes the work as a moving object involving a huge number of steps (each of them with overlapping and feedback moments) as well as agents (and here it is not only the distinction between man and machine or between maker and audience that is being blurred, but also that between the traditional instances of an artwork—maker, work, receiver—and the permanently growing network of intermediary instances, agents, bodies and structures[13]). A digital artwork is definitely "work", but this word has to be seen as a verb, not as a noun. To study such a work, ideally as a technotext, necessarily implies that one addresses the full range of operations and mechanisms that "are" the work as well.

Third, a series of mutually related shifts that restructure the institutional field of writing: from an aesthetics of *originality* to an aesthetics of the *unoriginal*; from a poetics of *scarcity* to a poetics of information *overload*; and from a situation of *secured* copyright to a situation of *contested* copyright. We will briefly sketch the essentials of these moves, before illustrating their convergence in the work of digital artist Kenneth Goldsmith (who, by the way, started his career as a sculptor, following thus a career path that is the opposite of that taken by Marcel Broodthaers who, after an unsuccessful start as a poet, decided to become an "artist," that is, one supposes, to start making money).

If writing has become a form of text-processing, it is no longer possible to rely on the longtime hegemonic value of "originality," either to define or to judge the work of the author. Already challenged in the post-modernist yet still predigital years, the stereotypically Modernist value given to novelty and originality has come under pressure in the digital era. Internet culture has made copy and paste, remix, sampling and so forth, in short all kinds of modern-day versions of imitation, fashionable once again. However, the success of this way of writing should not prevent us from seeing that serious and deliberate imitation always involves a high degree of admiration and awe, but not fear. Not all forms of copying are the same, and most of them are perfectly compatible with new forms of authenticity and originality that Marjorie Perloff has dubbed "unoriginal genius" (Perloff 2010)—the montage- and collage-driven writing and composing techniques that, according to her (very convincing) analysis, represent the major cultural form of the 20th century, the most inspiring example being, of course, Walter Benjamin's (unfinished) *Arcades Project*, actually a summarily edited mosaic of quotations, on city life in Paris in the years of Charles Baudelaire (Benjamin 2002).[14] In digital culture, the (qualitative) debate on originality cannot be separated from the (quantitative) debate on information overload, actually an age-old problem (from the very first years of the invention of the modern printing press readers were complaining about the sheer number of publications), but a problem that the extreme ease and speed of copying and disseminating texts on the net have only exacerbated. Books, texts and images are no longer just "out there" in incredible and totally unmanageable numbers, they have above all become (more or less) immediately and (often, but not always) freely available: the world's library is only one click away, and the immediate accessibility of so many words and images of course puts even more pressure on the ideological claims of originality and authenticity, which we now see as Modernist myths and no longer pursue as enviable qualities. What is valued today is the capacity to make it new by reusing the old, rather than to try to put forward something that has never been said or thought. Information overload, contrary to what one might fear at first sight, does not appear as an obstacle to literary and, more specifically, poetic creation. In an information-saturated culture, where the sheer number of available data and the ubiquity as well as the instantaneous reproduction and dissemination of these data is already beyond human imagination (and perhaps also beyond human control), there may be good reasons to think that poetry is no longer a relevant way of using language. The concrete situation of the genre is, however, a little different, not only because poetry does not disappear at all (its very resistance can be seen as the symptom of its lasting and stubborn social significance), but also because the poetic medium, at least in its most ambitious and avant-garde forms, helps to develop new strategies to counter the bureaucratic and depersonalised management of data, language, and eventually people (see Stephens 2015 for a good overview of the ongoing dialogue between poetry and information overload).

On top of that, the move from writing to copying and from publishing to making available—if one wants crudely to summarise the two previous shifts—cannot but have severe consequences for our traditional use and notion of ownership, of which the various copyright systems we know are both an illustration and a warrant.[15] How to claim ownership of a copy? And how to protect the ownership of something that can be copied and reused for free by virtually anyone? Digital culture is not paradoxical in this regard, but highly and often painfully ambivalent: the easier it becomes, from a technical point of view, to beg, steal and borrow—a move that is ideologically backed, if not stimulated, by certain artists, even when applied to their own work—the more difficult it becomes to obtain the authorisation to do so, certainly in the field of the image, where there are countless ways to get round the notion of "public domain": rights vary from country to country, more and more artworks are trade-marked (which allows for a theoretically infinite extension in time of intellectual rights), rights are not only those of the author, but also those of all the intermediaries that one needs to get a copy (for instance the photographer of a 17th Century painting, if the museum does not grant the authorisation to visitors to make pictures), fair use regulations for quotations are applied in arbitrary ways, etc. Whatever the concrete situation may be—and it cannot be denied that the situation is incomparably more complex for images than for texts—the increasing tension between what one can do and what one is allowed to do has to be taken into account in the analysis of digital artworks.

In "Being Boring" (n.d.), looking back on his most recent book, *Day*, "in which [he] retyped a day's copy of the *New York Times* and published it as a 900 page book," Kenneth Goldsmith provocatively writes:

> I am the most boring writer that has ever lived. If there were an Olympic sport for extreme boredom, I would get a gold medal. My books are impossible to read straight through. In fact, every time I have to proofread them before sending them off to the publisher, I fall asleep repeatedly. You really don't need to read my books to get the idea of what they're like; you just need to know the general concept.
>
> Over the past ten years, my practice today has boiled down to simply retyping exist-ing texts. I've thought about my practice in relation to Borges's Pierre Menard, but even Menard was more original than I am: he, independent of any knowledge of *Don Quixote,* reinvented Cervantes' masterpiece word for word. By contrast, I don't invent anything. I just keep rewriting the same book. I sympathize with the protag-onist of a cartoon claiming to have transferred x amount of megabytes, physically exhausted after a day of downloading. The simple act of moving information from one place to another today constitutes a significant cultural act in and of itself. I think it's fair to say that most of us spend hours each day shifting content into differ-ent containers. Some of us call this writing (n.d.).

Goldsmith's *Uncreative Writing* (2012), a book that is at the same time a manifesto, a handbook, a literary history and a collection of essays helps one to see this singular poetics in a different frame. Indeed, the notion of copying ceases to be presented in a purely mechanical way. It is approached instead in relationship with the key issue of selection, that is of responsible and relevant choice: for what is being cop-ied is not "anything goes," but a meaningful chunk of information—for instance the live report on the assassination of JFK on a local radio station in Dallas, whose exhaustive transcription discloses a kind of "collective voice" that is a profoundly disturbing robot photo of the Deep South (Goldsmith 2015b). Besides, the many examples of *Uncreative Writing* also demonstrate how creative the mechanical act of copying inevitably is and what an incredible number of decisions one always has to take while "just copying." In spite of the many differences between uncreative composition and the poetics of the ready-made, which focuses on isolated objects, not on large archives, and polemically foregrounds "futile" objects, not socially significant messages, there is a strong Duchampian dimension in Goldsmith's art, the common feature being the importance of both selection and presentation.

Perhaps the term that summarises best the many changes of the digital in cultural terms is *relocation* (I am borrowing it here from an article on literary databases by Joe Tabbi, the founding editor of *ebr/electronic book review:* see Tabbi 2017). Digital writing, but also visual digital art, can no longer be studied within the traditional limits of these practices: the studio of the painter, the table of the author, the bookshop or the library, the gallery or the museum, the canvassed image, the bound pages. Digital writing and digital arts function in a different environment, which will be examined in the next chapter.

Digital Culture and "Performation"

A more general take on the shift from work to process should not be considered from the viewpoint of one specific medium and type of practice such as reading and writing. Even when the observations that apply to writing may apply to digital arts and culture in general—and there is no reason to doubt that the database model, for instance, can be found in visual arts as well, as demonstrated by the frequent use of archive-based or archive-oriented productions and presentations (found footage aesthetic, vernacular photography, simulated archive presentations, etc.)—there is always the danger of a disciplinary bias. Hence the necessity of complementing the notions and mechanisms already addressed by the study of key concepts and practices that have emerged in different sectors of digital culture. In this regard, the notion of "performation" is a good candidate for further analysing the user's or participatory dimension of the digital.

This is how Samuel Bianchini introduces the concept and practice of "performation":

> Interactivity is a vital supplementary dimension of 21st-century media, as was the adding of movement to photography at the appearance of cinema. Contemporary modes of representation ask for the active participation of their audience in order to achieve the full range of their realisation, for instance playing at a videogame, dancing on an interactive system, geolocalising on a map, dwelling in *Second Life*[16]

> [...] This involvement of the audience takes place according to various modalities which increasingly imply a bodily involvement. [I would like to propose here a general hypothesis:] Isn't there a particular type of human action that is appearing in this context: "performation"? (2012, 137–38; my translation).

According to Bianchini, performation should be seen at the intersection of three other notions, each of them belonging to a different discipline:

– automated information management ("informatique") and man-machine interaction;
– performance, in the artistic sense of the word coined in the 1960s, that is a unique and unrepeatable event or situation that involves four basic elements: 1) time, 2) space, 3) the performer's body, or presence in a medium, and 4) a relationship between performer and audience (this kind of interaction can already be linked with the "demo or die" principle we will introduce in the next chapter, although the artistic dimension is there far from always being part of the game);
– performativity, in the linguistic and pragmatic sense defined by philosophers such as J.L. Austin, for whom "saying is doing" (*How to Do Things with Words* is the title of his best known publication).

Together with the concept of the database, which is not a static but an active model, that is a model of information management, retrieval and presentation, but also production (by interactive users, be they senders or receivers), the general concept of performation is dramatically useful to seize the transformations of media culture in the digital age. It is not only much broader than the (equally very useful) concept of the "ergodic," but it is also much more precise than the vague and over-used notion of interaction or interactivity. In addition, it gives insight into the near-systematic presence of performance aspects in the visual arts and the role played by installation art in this domain as well at the renewed actuality of dance as an artistic practice, both as a separate discipline and as part of installation art. Finally, it strongly underscores the bodily dimension of digital culture, which continues to be associated with immateriality, if not spirituality—perhaps in the wake of certain wild speculations of McLuhan, happily echoed by the information and communication industry. Today, however, it should no longer be possible to claim, as did an AT&T advertisement about the Internet from 1996–1997: "There is no race, there is no gender, there are no infirmities..."

5   The Relocation of Digital Writing

....

This chapter asks a very simple question: where does digital art actually take place and how can we make sense of the open and permanent distribution and transformation of ephemeral and collectively appropriated artefacts? We clam that digital culture is not the return of the oral after print, it is instead a new step in the continuing complexification and diversification of concurrently interacting, interplaying, and competing media and art forms. A central concept in this regard is that of the expanded form and space of artistic works and practices. The chapter highlights the importance of the performative dimension of the work of art, be it a text, an image, a sound, etc., while also examining the key role of the archive (as a form of database art). However, it equally underlines the importance of nostalgia and the many attempts to discover new forms and uses as well as define new stakes for allegedly old media and media practices.

Keywords: artist, community, differential (text or image), expanded art, institution, network, nostalgia, (reborn) orality, performance

....

Expanding and Relocation

The digital turn has dramatically changed the very form and content of the artistic sign: for instance, texts have become "differential" (Perloff), fixed units have become mobile, words and images are not only increasingly combined in multimodal groupings, their very difference becomes open to debate. In addition, these signs have moved to screens, which also allow for new approaches of authors and audiences, while further exploring the fundamental move from object to practice, from (un)finished work to "doing something" with a work, which is no longer the sole horizon of participatory creation. However, it would be a mistake to believe that the new location of the digital is the screen, that is: "just" the screen. True, the screen as a host medium is a key to the digital, but it is far from the only one, and the message of the new medium has to be examined as well in light of the larger mediascape it transforms. This chapter aims at addressing having to do with the place where reading and writing digital texts or creating and watching digital visual art is taking place. Digital culture pushes the boundaries of the traditional places where we make and receive signs: we are now working in expanded places and spaces, and the place we do so is permanently relocated.

Digital literature is here, once again, a perfect case in point. In spite of the initial panic raised by the appearance of writing on screen and other forms of electronic writing and by the seemingly limitless possibilities of the e-book (Nunberg 1996), writing in print has not vanished. "The book, Umberto Eco famously stated in *This Is Not the End of the Book*, is like the spoon, scissors, the hammer, the wheel. Once invented, it cannot be improved" (Eco and Carrière 2012, 19). Both printed and digital texts continue to proliferate, and if certain domains certainly move towards the digital (the example of scientific journals comes to mind here), the paperless office remains a futurological gimmick, graphic novelists and their readers stubbornly stick to ink and print (even if the authors produce with the help of digital tools and their books are digitally printed), many other forms of literature remain strongly paper-bound, book art is a hype in visual arts, as demonstrated by the countless examples of "demediation," and even digital-born creations can be remediated in print. Yet this "survival" does not mean "business as usual": literature in print, as we will see later, is no longer the same. The most important feature of the new writing (and artistic) environment might be defined as "relocation": writing is no longer taking place in the spaces and places we usually associate with it; it has been relocated to new and other constellations, such as "networks, knowledge bases, global systems, material, and mental environments" (Tabbi 2017). The notion of "relocation" should be preferred to that, often used in art-historical settings, of the "expanded field" (Krauss 1979), strictly related to the contextualisation of one single discipline or art practice. The concept of "expanded field"[17] is undoubtedly a powerful tool to challenge relationally narrow definitions of medium-specificity, but it remains somewhat limited when it comes down to displaying broader relationships (which would then have to be seen as overlapping tensions between expanded fields). In other words: whereas the notion of expanded field paradoxically remains centripetal, for the expansion continues to be seen as that of a no longer existing homogeneous centre, that of relocation emphasises the polycentrality of the new environment, which makes more room for the centrifugal powers at work.

The most general approach of the newly relocated digital writing environment is that of "reborn orality," a metaphor already very active in McLuhan's thinking and frequently addressed since then, yet never without nuances, certainly when one addresses the equally McLuhanian connection between reborn orality and the global village (Appadurai 1996). It is too easy, however, to discard the reference to orality—in the sense of a pre- or post-print culture in which sender and receiver are simultaneously present and collaborate in ways that make their respective positions perfectly interchangeable—as simplistic. This may be the case—and in the previous chapter we already hinted at the partial myth of interactivity in digital culture—but at the same time this metaphor helps to disclose certain basic elements of digital culture, both in literature and in the visual arts.

The most salient of these features is certainly the link between digital production and performance culture. Digital works, be they textual or visual creations (provided one wants to keep that distinction here), exist only if they "work," that is if all technical and cognitive conditions are gathered to make the work accessible. In an early but still very sharp reflection on digital art, Peter Lunenfeld has called this the "demo or die" principle:

> The demonstration, or "demo," has become the defining moment of the digital artist's practice at the turn of the millennium. For artists and designers who work with technology, no amount of talent, no ground-breaking aesthetic, no astonishing insight makes up for an inability to demonstrate their work on a computer in real time in front of an audience. The demo, as immortalized in the MIT Media Lab's credo

"Demo or Die," is now at the heart of the professional imagemaker's life. Artists and their machines are on display. This does not simply presage the artist as cyborg; it also augurs the transformation of digital presentation into live performance (2001, 13).

Digital works, in other words, strangely often require the presence of the artist, which transforms the actual displaying of the work into a kind of performance. More generally, and beyond the very specific example highlighted by Peter Lunen-feld, one easily observes that the rise of digital culture, which is (falsely) associated with the idea of disembodiment and immateriality, has given birth to a strong return of art forms and art experiences that emphasise not only the body and the materi-ality of creation, but the very interplay between the artist and a physically present audience. Something like the "artist talk" or the "artist conference," which has now almost become an art form in itself, would have been unthinkable during the hey-days of the Modernist "white cube" model, in which the work was supposed to speak for itself, without any practical or contextual interference (the "untitled" fad is another aspect of this ideology, which tended to scrape away all that was not the work itself—except of course the (invisible but extremely present) price tag. Dig-ital works, which seem over-determined by immaterial logarithms and impersonal machines, in practice repeatedly function in tandem with some live performance. More in general, the digital era displays an impressive return of art forms that prior-itise the physical presence of the body of the artist and the unique performance of her work. Is this a symptom of digital culture as reborn orality? Yes and no.

Yes, because the idea of performance is definitely closer to oral culture than to print culture. In one of the founding texts of modern narratology, *Simple Forms* by André Jolles (first edition 1930), the author addresses at great length the Romantic debate on the transcription of fairy tales, that is of the fixation in print of anony-mous oral stories, and the features he ascribes to this oral production—mobility, generality, and plurality (or "pluricity," to follow the English translation)—could be extremely relevant to define many digital creations:

What we are saying here about fairy tales and novellas can however be generalized: it is the difference between simple forms and literary forms. That is also the difference that Jacob Grimm was talking about. Where we approach the world with a form, reach constructively into it, render concise a part of it that seems coherent thanks to some common attribute, Grimm speaks of *concoction*; conversely, where we allow the world to enter into a form that has evolved according to a principle prevailing solely within and determining only this form, and where the now transforms itself in accord with this form, there he calls it a *spontaneous self-generation*. We recognize with him the basic difference of structuring laws—but we do not agree that the one form belongs to a past time, the other to the present. [...] Our opinion is that both are always and everywhere active, and that observing them in their disparity and in their relationships is one of the basic tasks of literary criticism.

If we pursue for a moment the trajectories of the novella and the fairy tale, we can say this: what is crucial for the novella [...] is that everything it includes in this concise completion must have a *solid*, *particular*, and *singular* shape; in the fairy tale, on the other hand [...] the world retains its *mobility*, its *generality* and what I will call its *pluricity* (Jolles 2017, 189, emphasis added).

True, a fairy tale (as an example of a spontaneously generated simple form) should not be compared with a digital art work, even if, strangely enough, the imaginary of many of these works, for instance in the sphere of the videogame, relies on fantasy structures (for a "pre-database" discussion of this strange encounter see Murray 1997). But "mobility" (fairy tales do not have a fixed structure), "generality" (they do not belong to specific speakers or groups) and "pluricity" (they change at each occurrence) are characteristics that are often attributed to co-created and open digital works, and this family resemblance may give some credit to the hypothesis of digital art as reborn orality—not at the level of the material devices used for the work, but at that of its underlying logic.

But the answer is also no, and this no should not be masked by the emphasis on mobility, generality and pluricity, because these forms of reborn orality do not replace other art forms—print as well as post-print—but complement them, in a way that the notion of relocation, with all it implies in terms of simultaneity and decentring, appropriately evokes. Digital culture is not the return of the oral after print, it is a new step in the continuing complexification and diversification of concurrently interacting, interplaying, and competing media and art forms. In that sense, the link between digital culture and performance is one of the many forms taken by the phenomenon of the differential work presented above, no longer within a single medium (as the initial meaning of "differential text" implies) but among media in the larger mediascape, in which orality, traditional print, life performance, networked structures and digital writing spaces interact in multiple ways.

New = Neo?

If the digital "message" implies a change of existing media—or a rediscovery of forgotten or obfuscated ones, as media archeologists would hasten to specify—these changes must be visible in the way literature is being written—and not only printed—today. And even if, at first sight, one may have the impression that books still look the same and that they still follow the same genre norms and models, the impact of the digital turn has been dramatic.

The most important change may seem invisible, but invisible does not mean unproductive. Since texts can easily be copied and distributed, often illegally, via digital means, on the one hand, and since texts can now no less easily be self-published by authors without the help of printers and publishers,[18] on the other hand, the traditional position of the author, that is the privileged position of the one who survived the (severe) selection process between conception and publication, has been disrupted. On top of that, there is also *the slow but undeniable erosion of the traditional retail circuit*—books may be sold everywhere, but the traditional bookshop is disappearing, and this is exactly the venue where "good" books are being sold—and the crisis of both the traditional canon and the prestige of literary critics as gatekeepers of literary taste— a phenomenon Jim Collins attributes to the double influence of digital participatory culture and the waning modelling influence of elite culture in post-modern societies (Collins 2010) and also a topic on which we will further reflect in the next chapter. Finally, contemporary media culture is a personality, read: celeb culture. Mass media promote media figures and lifestyles, much less "content," the traditional "unique selling point" of literature.

As a result of these transformations in the field, writers are now forced to take up more than one role. Their job is no longer limited to writing texts; they also have to make sure, in the absence of no longer influential gatekeepers and taste shapers, that this writing finds an audience. As noted above, the shift towards performance is probably the most important one—next of course to the participation, willingly or not, of authors in today's media celeb culture. In this regard, the institutionalisation of the *public reading*—as such not a new phenomenon at all, but currently trivialised to incredible and sometimes laughable proportions (Baetens 2016)—deserves to be underlined. The public reading is not only an illustration of the "demo or die" principle, it also reflects the institutional pressure on the writer to promote the work that publishers, critics, booksellers, librarians and teachers are no longer capable of supporting—not lack of channels, but lack of the prestige that is needed to convince readers.

A similar tendency, which frequently includes the practice of public reading, is the integration of writers in new forms of institutional support that are no longer private sponsorship but public institutions, which want a kind of "return on investment," mainly via two elements: first, the commitment to producing a piece of writing, online or offline, that can be linked to the funding institution—and used for instance as a tool of city marketing; second, the active participation of the writer in the life of the community, for instance through meet and greet sessions in bookshops, lectures in schools, supervision of creative writing workshops, and so forth. Gilles Bonnet's field survey has shown that authors who receive this kind of grant in France today are supposed to spend an average of 30 per cent of their working time on this kind of activity (Bonnet 2017, 176). One of the most fascinating aspects that this study brings to the fore is the growing imbrication and interweaving of writing as a "pure" art form and all kinds of secondary activities (it would probably be impolite, if not incorrect, to use the word "instrumentalisation"). In certain cases, the latter may become as important, that is, time-consuming, as the former, and one can reasonably suppose that this new situation also affects the form and content of what is actually being produced. Poets will start writing texts that can easily be read aloud (as we know, an important strand of 20th-century poetry strongly resists this domination of the oral: see for instance Christin 1995 and 2009). Novelists will start writing texts on "fundable" subjects, for instance those that can be used in the heritage industry or the city marketing competition (true, these constraints can prove very productive, but they definitely imply a watershed change in the way authors conceive of their work—at the same time, however, it is also possible to argue that this change is actually a return to older forms of sponsorship, which go back to the historical figure of Maecenas).

The most interesting phenomenon however, next to the spread of public readings and new forms of community-oriented activities, is the emergence of new networked forms of both producing and disseminating writing that are somewhat misleadingly called "literature outside the book" or "non-book literature," an umbrella term that refers to ways of writing that either experiment with the book as a host medium (many forms of experimental typography and book design fall into this category) or try to get round the book or complement it with other forms and media (oral literature, literature in the public sphere, intermedial collaborative projects, for instance). In this case, it may perhaps be preferable to use the concept of "the book in the expanded field," for in most cases print is still active and present and remains clearly the heart of most practices, in spite of the quite cheap and opportunistic critique of book and print as solid, particular and singular (read: not only as incompatible with digital media structures and ways of doing and thinking, but also with the democratising claims of participatory culture—probably a bad joke in the case of both literary and visual arts, where massive concentrations of power and no less massive movements of capitalisation can be observed: the more we all participate, the more the only winner takes all).

"Expanded literature," that is the combination of various host media, various medium-specificities, various distribution systems, and various ways of interacting with readers and audiences, has become a distinctive feature of contemporary writing (for a good overview see Mougin 2016, who focuses on the interaction between literary writing and the gallery space). In certain cases, however, the intermedial and network logic of relocation goes beyond the contextual expansion of literature as a given discipline (be it print-based, oral, or purely digital-born). The notion of *neoliterature*, as coined by Magali Nachtergael, may offer a useful label to identify what are currently the most frequent ways of materialising the general logic of relocation, which produces a shift from independent works (texts in print, to simplify) to works combining different media and produced as well as performed in specific contexts (also to simplify, of course). As Nachtergael puts it, in a particularly flowery style:

> The plastic forms of literature and, reciprocally, the literary forms of contemporary plastic works shape a recent corpus at the intersection of the arts. The notion of neo-literature tends to disclose an epistemological stake: what if we consider these two sides of intersemiotic culture as an independent literary-visual form, remediating the well-established tradition of the visual poem. The text, or the fixed form of the text in a book, is then no more than a transitory and ephemeral element that is part of a polyexpressive whole (n.p.).

The merger of writing and visual expression is of course not the only example of neoliterature, which may also entail new "genres" such as the book on display, either in a gallery or online (Reverseau 2016–), a structure that blurs the boundaries between writer and curator, or, on a more general level, the elaboration of events and festivals that function as the large-scale equivalent of unique neoliterary performances.[19] If the term "neoliterature" still suggests a kind of literary imperialism—in other words, neoliterature as a term masking the disciplinary roots of literature in the expanded field and surreptitiously annexing the adjacent domains of the visual arts, in an updated form of the *paragone* (the debate from the Italian Renaissance in which one form of art is championed as superior to all others)—one should note that exactly the same is going on in the visual field, where authors such as Pascal Mougin have described the fusion of word and image, not in terms of the becoming visual of the text, but in terms of "temptation" of the image by the word (Mougin 2016; various authors and topics of this book are also discussed in the collection that contains the essay by Magali Nachtergael quoted above, which further proves the intersection of the fields). Regardless of the terminology being used, all these examples and debates lay bare the direct or indirect impact of the digital turn on the arts, which are relocalised in various ways.

No Medium, a collection of essays by Craig Dworkin on media art (2013), is a key example in the hybridising tendencies that are characteristic of the digital era. In this book Dworkin studies a vast array of vital works of modern and digital art from all kinds of media and formats (texts, images, sounds). Yet the internal consistency of the corpus, ironically tied together by the privative value of the book's title, is very strong. At a practical level, first, since all the works under scrutiny are "blank, erased, clear, or silent" (Dworkin 2018, back cover), from a fictional collection of poems in Jean Cocteau's *Orphée* to the actual publication of a ream of typing paper as a book of poetry or from Robert Rauschenberg's *Erased De Kooning Drawing* to John Cage's "silent" 4'33" and many others. But also at a theoretical level, for Dworkin's ambition is to show that the apparent absence of the medium is precisely what helps us see the meaning and importance of it: "Dworkin argues that we should understand media not as blank, base things but as social events, and that there is no medium, understood in isolation, but only and always a plurality of media" (id.). This is exactly what the reading of artworks as media constructions and practices is about.

New Media Writing: Return to Medium-Specificity

The impact of changing host media has been widely studied, including for the new media (see for instance the pioneering study of Perloff 1994; more specifically on digital literature see, next to the already mentioned Hayles 2002, Portela 2013, Gitelman 2014 and Emerson 2014, specialised sites such as *electronic book review* or *Leonardo Reviews Online*). It should come as no surprise that the most interesting examples of this medium-informed or medium-determined way of making art are not only digital-borne but digital-born; we will come back in the next chapter to the "anthologies" published by the leading professional organisation in the field).

Yet the "digital" is not an essentialist or dehistoricised notion. As already indicated in the short presentation of the first types of electronic literature, it is clear that their successive forms are directly related to the gradual arrival and development of new medium affordances: text generators were simply the most fitting creative reply to the then available automation formulas; the appropriation of visual poetry in the digital realm was accelerated by the entry of the WYSIWYG interface and the increasing possibilities of intermedially combining words and images; hyperfiction was explicitly elaborated in order to test and market programs such as StorySpace. The fact that the general form of the database was successfully theorised as the hegemonic structure of the new digital era, as a polemical counterweight to the outworn ideology of the individual genius (in the post-Romantic European tradition) or creative writing (as practised, on a nearly industrial level, in the US), does of course not signify that the database model as described by Manovich did not evolve over time. Today's internet is no longer that of the turn of the century, and the effects of this evolution are clearly reflected—yet not mechanically, medium-specificity not being a technodeterminist phenomenon—in more recent ways of writing, online as well as in print.

An excellent presentation of these issues is given by Craig Dworkin (2018), one of the major theoreticians of "conceptual writing," a somewhat confusing label that refers to avant-garde forms of procedural or constraint-based writing, often in combination with the aesthetic of the ready-made and the database. Dworkin's analysis starts from the major differences between two structures: on the one hand, the state of the internet as it was when the first wave of conceptual poetry became famous, in the first years of the 21st century, and on the other hand the environment that we associate with the so-called web 2.0: "[i]n the broadest terms, the Web has become less static and humanly curated and less focused on discretely structured databases" (676). Less of this means more of that: more automation, more linked data, and the transformation of user-generated material into raw data data-mined and eventually sold by the providers—or, if one prefers, less database dreams, more social media pressure.

Using the notion of "reflexivity" as a stand-in for "technotextuality" or "medium-specificity," Dworkin then identifies three "areas in which technological, economic, and literary trends overlap: affect, junkspace, and platform" (680). Having to do with the Web 2.0's attempt to draw as much personal and individual information from its users as possible and the interface's tendency towards customised presentation of materials, the upsurge of affect in electronic communication translates into the treatment of more affectively coloured material as treated by conceptual poetic constraints (for instance the endless, monotonous and deliberately boring selection of facebook messages emphasising the extreme loneliness of facebook addicts). The notion of junkspace has to do with the persistence on the Web of countless sites and messages that are "dead," for any reason whatsoever, from technical obsolescence to the actual decease of the users (the 2.0 constraints, so to speak, will no longer just focus on the selection and treatment of "relevant" material, as seen in the Goldsmith examples given above, but aggressively foreground the dead ends and "junkspaces" of the Internet as it is today). Third, the notion of platform hints at the mutual sharing and embedding of all kinds of formats and platforms, which one can see as the technological expansion as well as necessary condition of the tendency towards neoliterature or literarily tempted visual art (in digital writing, this tendency produces unseen proportions of medium- and sign-blending, while at the same time raising serious difficulties in terms of remediation in print form—hence the strictly electronic format in which this material is being made, distributed and consumed).

However, Dworkin's analysis goes much further than the mere description of electronic conceptual writing's answers to the changes in its technological and economic environment. He stresses the necessity to contextualise what is at stake in the various forms of conceptualism. In the first phase, there was not only the (negative) ambition to parody the literary and ideological illusions of creative writing, a type of writing that, in spite of its belief in originality and personal expression, proved capable only of endless repetition and hollow subjectivism, but also the (positive) hope of finding "unoriginal" ways of originally addressing repetition. In the second phase—and one can easily imagine that a third, a fourth, etc. phase are already on their way—the negative ambition is still there, even if the target is no longer creative writing but heavily commercialised internet culture, but what seems to be missing—or what may not be clearly visible—is the positive ambition, which the readers may judge the same as in the first phrase, with all the misunderstandings and frustrations such a transfer may imply, for according to Dworkin this conceptualism 2.0 no longer wants to follow the path of unoriginal originality and its texts can no longer be read in that perspective.

Back to Print: Still Making Books Thanks to the Digital Turn

The digital turn has not only produced many new forms of digital writing, some of them more medium-specific than others, it has also to a large extent taken over the whole cultural industry of publishing (Hayles 2008). However, the "message" of the new digital medium cannot be narrowed down to a new case of the supersession of the old (print) by the new (electronic publishing). At the same time, the continued presence of print is much more than just an example of the survival or resilience of older media (such as the vinyl record for music recording or black and white pictures after the commercialisation of colour photography). The books that continue to be written and printed—and from a medium-theoretical and historical point of view it is capital to stress the intertwining of both activities—are no longer the same as the ones that were made before the digital revolution. Roughly speaking, one can distinguish four types of "new" uses of the "old" print medium (by analogy with the concept of "newborn orality," we might call this "newborn print"). We will briefly present the first two types, and then exemplify in more detail the two last cases, which can be linked with the notion of expanded or relocated digital field—not that of writing itself, but that of publishing.

The first category might be called the vintage or nostalgia type, that is the type of print that strongly emphasises the most traditional aspects of print and bookmaking, which the shift from print to digital has made unmanageable in the trade circuit, but which remain very attractive to bibliophiles and other amateurs of rare and unique objects: books printed on handmade paper, in small print runs, composed with movable letters, and containing original illustrations, etc., cater to the needs of a (wealthy) public eager to buy publications that combine scarcity and craft, but that also attract a new group of writers and artists seduced by the material qualities and challenges that commercial trade publishing is not capable—and has never been capable—of giving. To a certain extent, this form of bibliophilia is part of the larger return to "life" event and bodily presence in performance and other artistic and non-artistic situations that is one of the many flipsides of digital culture, which many people fantasise as disembodied. Print, here, is clearly a compensation for a perceived lack of materiality (whether this lack is imaginary or not is another question).

A second category would fall into the category of what Bolter and Grusin call "repurposing," namely the attempt of an old medium under pressure to maintain itself, not by imitating in its own way what the new competing media are doing, but by accentuating what the old medium can do and the new ones cannot. This special type of remediation is not nostalgic, as was the first category of traditional—but thriving—bibliophilia; it is instead very forward-looking and tries to anticipate new niche markets for book printing that electronic publishing may prove unwilling or unable to explore (or to maintain). The fad of unusual sizes in book publishing is a good example of this strategy. Contrary to the computer screen, which reduces all texts and images to the same format (zooming in and zooming out may have reduced the problem, but the material limits of the reading screen are in principle not extensible, and the current tendency towards miniaturization—soon we will be watching films on wristwatches—does, of course, not help). One of the features that the graphic novel genre most actively uses in its resistance to digitisation is certainly that of size, which is often totally unpredictable (in contrast to the implicit anti-model of the graphic novel, that is the comic book, highly standardised in this regard and thus more vulnerable to digital remediation).

The third category is that of book publishing that goes towards "blended" forms of publishing, more precisely of forms that refuse the false dichotomy of print and digital and try to combine the best of both worlds. The default option of this category is, of course, the book-cum-website solution, and although there is nothing wrong with this solution, the mere combination of both host media does not guarantee that each of them is used in a medium-specific way. Hence the interest of a series such as MIT's "Mediaworks Pamphlets," a short-lived but still exceptional effort to invent in some of its titles a new type of publishing that intertwines the medium-specificities of print and digital. On the MIT website, the series is presented this way:

> The *Mediawork Pamphlets* series pairs authors with graphic designers to produce intellectually sophisticated, visually compelling, inexpensively priced short works. The pamphlets take up the themes of art, design, technology, and market economies. Series editor director Peter Lunenfeld calls them "'zines for grownups." (https:// mitpress.mit.edu/books/series/mediaworks-pamphlets)

The volume that best presents the "ideal" of the merger of book and web is probably the already mentioned volume *Writing Machines*, N. Katherine Hayles' brilliant defence and illustration of material textualism (later expanded in Hayles and Pressman 2013). Besides offering great theoretical insights, *Writing Machines* also has a strong "ars poetica" dimension: the book not only says what it does, but also does what it says. This autoreferential dimension, which one can only read as a supplementary proof of the exactness of the author's theses, appears on two dimensions. The first one can be seen on the level of its global composition. Indeed, after the general theoretical comments on technotextuality (which alternate with semi-autobiographic fragments, embodied by a persona "Kaye," on the progressive discovery of cyberculture by a book-lover oscillating between science and literature), Hayles proposes a triple illustration of her theory through three exciting close readings, first of Talan Memmott's *Lexia to Perplexia*, then of Tom Philips's *A Humument*, finally of Mark Z. Danielewski's *House of Leaves*. The essential feature to note here is the order in which these texts are placed under scrutiny, since the author does not start with a printed novel, continuing with an artist book and stopping with a web hypertext. Hayles follows the opposite itinerary, from web hypertext to print novel via artist book, in a very "anti-chronological" move that perfectly suits the demonstration: the "new" medium does not simply succeed the old; it does not simply "remediate"; it paradoxically "precedes" it, and helps to disclose the unsuspected possibilities of the old medium, which may continue to surprise and challenge us (an issue to which we will come back in the next chapter on the "canon").

The second level of the "ars poetica" mechanism has to do with the design of the book, which has been made by Ann Burdick, the house designer of *electronic book review*, one of the publications defining the standards of outstanding web design in the humanities. What is most surprising is the relative minimalism of Burdick's approach. First of all, Burdick and Peter Lunenfeld, the series editor, have decided to split Hayles's work radically, not in two parts, but in two worlds: that of print culture and that of cyberculture. The book, whose structure is amazingly linear (one really has to read it from A to Z, and there is nothing except the illustrated and finely designed text), is indeed completed by a website offering a beautifully conceived survey of the academic background of the work (one finds in it a list of errata, an index, several bibliographies, a set of excerpts from the novels analysed, and so forth—if I'm not mistaken, this site is no longer online, a problem that will be discussed in the next chapter). The surprises of the book itself have to be discovered slowly by the reader during his journey through the pages. It is a pleasure to see how Burdick avoids gadget-like use of modern technology, in order to make a theoretical statement through her design increasing the impact of Hayles's theory. The work on the 3-D aspects of the book is a good example of this (every good book designer knows that a book is not a stack of flat pages, but a volume in space that can be elaborated like a sculpture). Burdick focuses, for instance, on the edges of the object, which are not banally gilt-edged, but offer the reader not only a supplementary message, but a double message, one to be read forwards and one to be read backwards (when you curve the book slightly backwards, the word "WRITING" appears on the edge; when you curve it slightly forwards, it is the second word of the title that becomes visible). The same compliments should be given to the way the book includes its quotations: instead of being reworked in order to fit the all-over typographical design of the host medium, their original form is maintained and it is with those quotations of textual *images* that *Writing Machines* establishes a new kind of dialogue.

Fourth and finally, there is the category of publishing in print that addresses the problem of book printing in the digital era head-on. It is not a type of book that tries to offer an alternative, as to a certain extent the three previous types are all doing—and that is fine, of course—but whose ambition is to print the internet. Not by simply copy-pasting on paper the pages (?) that can be found on the Web, but by developing new projects that look for the paper equivalent of the web's creativity.

The limits of the former practice, the print remediation of a digital performance, can be seen in Mark Amerika's *remixthebook* (Amerika 2011). A co-founder of *electronic book review*, Amerika is a key artist, novelist, media theorist, and VJ artist who explores a literary version of the mash-up in various media formats: a book (print and e-book), a video trailer of the book, a blog, a website, a live performance and online exhibition. remixthebook is an all the more fascinating experience since the comparison of various formats immediately shows the thresholds of print as the remediating format of a multi-media performance, which loses much of its creativity and dynamics in the fixed form of the book, which in turn cannot stand up against the medium-specific experiments of visual writing in print.

> https://www.upress.umn.edu/book-division/books/remixthebook (publisher's website)
> http://www.remixthebook.com/ (website of the project)
> https://vimeo.com/27204611 (extended play remix)
> https://vimeo.com/27221889 (remix of Mark Amerika's book by philosopher David Gunkel)

An inspiring example of the latter practice is *Jean Boîte Editions*, a Paris-based internationally publishing company, whose programme is not that of simply hosting or remediating fragments or items of digital post-print culture, but of elaborating new projects that are no longer "only medium-specific" but that try to reinvent in the sphere of print, ink, paper and books unoriginal complements of the new digital formats (https://www.jean-boite.fr/). The catalogue of this company is thus inspired by digital-born projects and productions, but rethinks them in such a way that print appears as an added value (hence the principal role played by the various book designers, who are less subcontractors than co-creators). Take, for instance, *Triste Tropique* by Damien Rudd and Cécile Coulon (2018), a "post-Instagram" project which the website of the publisher presents as follows:

> *Triste Tropique, Topographies of Sadness* is the first atlas that matches our darkest feelings. Started on the hugely popular Instagram account Sad Topographies, that spread sadness worldwide, this 89 maps collection—all inspired by the maps service of a famous search engine—finally turns into a book to take place in our bookshelves. Depression Pond, Miserable Lake, Agony Island, Road to Nowhere and all the places featured in this [sic] maps have been gathered by Damien Rudd with a scientific precision. The work also offers the exact scales and localizations useful to each place, as well as a sad index. This graphical set is enhanced with a text commissioned from French rising star author Cécile Coulon, for whom the geography forms the raw material of the inspiration, and which here gives short comments for each map, sometimes illuminating, sometimes desperate.

6 The Problem of Canonisation in the Digital Era

This chapter deals with one of the fundamental dimensions of culture as a living and collaborative practice: the non-biological transmission of works, values, questions, and ways of doing as well as living. Digital culture is often seen as a danger to this kind of transmission and the overwhelming amount of items as well as their permanently changing nature tend to produce various forms of cultural panic. In this chapter, we study the reasons why there may be a conflict between the digital turn and the maintenance of cultural memory, before analysing in more detail the ways in which digital culture tries to make sense of a new cultural context that is at odds with culture in the traditional sense of the word. The creation of a new canon but also the attempts to use the cultural archive in radically new ways are key elements in the emergence of new forms of typically digital culture.

Keywords: appropriation, archive, canon, decay, memory, oblivion, obsolescence, remix, rogue (archive), selection

No Place for Canons in Digital Times?

No other issue in digital culture is so fraught with anxiety as that of loss of memory. And the vanishing canon is perhaps the (ideological) tip of this iceberg. The context of this debate is well known. For several decades the canon has been under fire. First of all, for political reasons: the very existence of a selection of "the best that has been thought and said" (Matthew Arnold) is accused of being a mechanism of political conformism, manipulated by those in power to disempower all groups and individuals that are not. Second, for aesthetic reasons: the canon is said to present a selection of works from elite or "high" culture, with no room whatsoever for "low-brow" productions, be they from folk culture or from modern mass media culture. And third, also for art-sociological reasons: the canon is blamed for giving priority to art forms such as literature that are no longer at the heart of today's cultural practices, where reading—at least, reading of "high literature"—is becoming increasingly marginalised (thanks to visual art's links to mass tourism and city marketing, on the one hand, and the smoother transition between traditional painting and modern visual culture, the canonical situations of high literature and high visual arts are not easy to compare). Obviously, these three reasons overlap and reinforce each other, creating a situation in which the fading of the canon is felt both as a liberation—and a chance for many new opportunities—and a lack which is all the more problematic since it touches upon the very basis of culture, which the Tartu school of cultural semiotics defines as "non-hereditary memory" (Lotman and Uspensky, 1978). Nostalgia is not a new phenomenon; it is the flipside of any novelty-driven Modernism, but the current heritage hype is undoubtedly a symptom of a civilisational memory issue. As the rest of this chapter will make clear, however, the notion of canon is far from being just a relic of the past. Canons are still there (and the plural is what matters), and the same goes for our attitudes towards these canons (which we despise less than we may think).

A society like ours, which attaches so much importance to innovation for economic rather than cultural reasons, is inevitably led to burn its history. We are in fact not focused on the contemporary, which no longer suffices, but on "the next big thing," and this paradigm has imposed a new perception of time, radically disconnected from the past. Add to this the ever more rapid acceleration of the lifecycles of products as well as cultural oeuvres while, tragically, the life of humans elongates and more and more people survive rather than live. In a modern society, the important thing is no longer to have experience, that is, to lean on a lived past, but to follow developments, which is to say to orient oneself on the future. This rupture is shown in the disillusioned observations of Henry de Montherlant, who observed in one of his notebooks:

> One cannot imagine for a moment Tacitus or Montaigne wishing to be read primarily by young people, or Pascal writing with young people in mind, or Racine seeking their approval foremost. The very thought of those whom we consider geniuses writing for boys and girls of twenty years old makes one laugh (1975, 18–19; transl. Ben de Bruyn).

Digital culture has added new aspects to the canon issue, and it does so at a moment in history in which the very making of the canon has become anything but easy or self-evident (Baetens and de Bruyn 2018). True, most of these phenomena are not entirely new and digital culture has only accelerated them. Every technological revolution that facilitates and hence expands access to reading and culture engenders these types of canon questions. New printing techniques that, around 1830, led to the split in the book market between a restricted market and a market of large-scale production, that of "industrial literature" (Sainte-Beuve 1839), provide a textbook example. The same might be said about the introduction to the paperback, violently attacked in the 1950s and 1960s by left-wing authors who feared a "conditioning" of the reader—not by the old-fashioned canon but by its very absence!—and an unacceptable intrusion of the cultural industries in the life of the spirit (Baetens 2017).

What is particular to digital culture and the canon questions it raises is mainly related to the following elements, which refer either to the objects themselves (the works) or the way we process them (reading, watching).

On the one hand, the sheer amount of material that is being produced, stored and disseminated, although not with legal and commercial barriers and thresholds, is so massive that the traditional, that is human-made ways of making a selection and shaping a canon are no longer possible. This does, of course, not mean that selection and canons no longer exist, but they are now automatically generated by datamining search engines (the best sales on Amazon, the most frequently looked-at pages, etc.), which then customise them to the equally data-mined individual tastes of the user looking for information on the Web. This digital idea of a community-built and community-representative canon is very different from what a traditional canon is (this "business" version of the canon may seem frightening, but at the same time its very visibility is also a sobering experience, which makes old-fashioned gatekeepers aware of the world out there). In addition to this question of information overload, which machines are managing in our place, there is also the problem of technological obsolescence, which jeopardizes the very accessibility of the material. The Web is not only stuffed with junkspots (see above); digital culture is also an environment where works come and go without any possibility for secure, that is stable and accessible, storage (the last paragraph of this section will go more deeply into this issue).

On the other hand, digital culture also affects our way of processing the material and, thus, perhaps, the very need to have a canon, which cannot be dissociated from the traditional practices of (trained and specialised) close-reading and close-watching. As already hinted at before, for instance in the discussion of the "boredom" of reading certain types of digital texts or watching endless lists of user-generated images, digital culture not only asks questions regarding technical and psychological readability (can we actually read the infinite number of data available? and when we do so, do we get any pleasure or reward from it?), it also invites us to reflect on the very meaning of "reading," which shifts from reading in the traditional sense of the word, be it *close* reading or *distant* reading (automated and machine-enhanced processing of large amounts of text and, increasingly, images: see Moretti 2013 and Underwood 2017), to a sense of reading that shifts from "deciphering" to "processing": instead of reading them, we "do" something with texts and images, we manipulate them on screen in certain ways that may seem to bear little relation with classic ways of reading and looking and which therefore may give the impression that a canon is no longer needed. Digital literacy, in that sense, can do perfectly without any canon—or even selection—for what matters is no longer the works, but what one does with them. Yet this is not, perhaps paradoxically, what is going on today.

The Archival Impulse

First of all, it should be noted that—at least in the domain of electronic literature—there exists something like a canon, and even a very traditional one, that is a rather selective list of works chosen and approved by official gatekeepers, in this case the most important professional and scholarly organisation in the field, ELO/Electronic Literature Organization (https://eliterature.org/), and the project leaders designated by ELO to compose this anthology (currently the anthology has been enlarged and consists of three volumes, and there is a willingness to open the project to languages other than English—key work in Catalan has been done by Laura Borràs, in Portuguese by Rui Torres, in Spanish by Domingo Sánchez-Mesa, always among others of course). As the ELO website specifies: "Each volume of the *Electronic Literature Collection* is published on the Web and as a physical version. The physical publication of the ELC3 is forthcoming. Libraries, educators, and individuals may request a free copy of the volume 1 and 2 USB by mail."

The selection is wide, more or less fifty works per volume, but not exceptionally wide, for we all know that anthologies of contemporary works tend to be less selective than those of previous periods (not only because we cannot rely yet on earlier canonising experiences, but also because the quantity of works being produced, in whatever artistic field they may appear, continues to increase exponentially). Yet the canonising policy is unquestionably there. Other organisations, such as the French-Canadian NT2 (the research centre on "hypermedia" literature hosted by UQAM or Université du Québec à Montréal), give priority to the archival dimension of a repository,[20] which also exist on the ELO website[21]). The third major player in this kind of work, the University of Bergen (Norway) based ELMCIP, also combines archival and anthological ambitions, in this case with a strong European dimension:

> The *ELMCIP Anthology of European Electronic Literature* edited by Maria Engberg, Talan Memmott, and David Prater, is now online. The anthology is intended to provide educators, students and the general public with a free curricular resource of electronic literary works produced in Europe. The works were selected, after an open call, based on four main criteria: European diversity, Formal diversity, Historical relevance, and Pedagogical relevance. The anthology includes 18 works of electronic literature, pedagogical materials, cross-links to relevant materials in the ELMCIP Knowledge Base, and video presentations. The anthology is available both online and in a USB edition available for libraries and institutions.[22]

In other words, the very fact of establishing a canon is not contested and the procedures that are followed to establish it have very traditional goals: there is a clear concern for tradition as well as pedagogy, and these are exactly the two basic features of any canon-making in a cultural-semiotic sense: taking care of a (selected) past and its transmission to future generations. That the leading organisations in the field, all deeply rooted in academic contexts and thus interweaving research and teaching, all endorse this policy should come as no surprise. The overwhelming number of digital works, on the one hand, and, on the other hand, the many difficulties of actually reading them (and, perhaps more basically, the very difficulty of beginning to think about these often strange and disquieting objects: is it "art"? is it "something else"? what "is" it?) explain that there is a real need to be guided in the digital jungle (or desert, which is perhaps even more disorienting than the jungle). At the same time, the lack of an older digital canon, which might have filtered and biased the initial entry to the field, means that there is no need to dismiss this canon in order to replace it with another one or to reject any canonisation effort whatsoever. Moreover, as already suggested by the self-presentation of the ELM-CIP anthology where the key word is "diversity", the anthologising policies of most stakeholders do not start from an initial programme or manifesto, as anthologies often do (this is what electronic literature should be and these are the works that best exemplify our claims), but try to offer well-balanced overviews of what is actually going on in the field, provided they are both representative of a certain tendency and relevant as far as their own merits are concerned. Hence the strong presence of, for instance, works that readers with a classic literary background would label as "visual art" and—unless I am mistaken—the widespread acceptance of a selection that highlights the contribution of what cultural studies would call "minorities" or "marginalised" voices (a good discussion on gender and canonisation can be read in Moulthrop and Grigar 2017, 227–37).

Yet this is not the most important aspect that explains the highly pacified and ecumenical approach of canon issues in digital culture (although one easily imagines that a further institutionalisation of the field will inevitably lead to new canon wars, but currently this is not the case). For next to the institutional enhancement of the archival and canonising impulse, there is also the fact that the field itself is "essentially" archive-driven. As already mentioned, the dominant general structure of digital culture is the database, and the very development of digital culture is systematically intertwined with the production of archives and databases, which are of course the necessary raw data of any anthologising gesture. The elaboration and implementation of digital culture is not only reflected in the high number of databases. It is not false to argue that the latter are part of the basis of the former, although it is probably more appropriate to say that it does not make much sense to maintain the distinction between digital culture (as a general phenomenon) and databases (as a concrete phenomenon). Cavell's medium theory helps us to understand why, since one of its major claims is that media only exist once there are concrete works that materialise it. This is what happens with digital art and the database (even if this does not involve the fact that databases are the only concrete materialisation in the case).

The best known of these archives is still UbuWeb,[23] "a large web-based educational resource for avant-garde material available on the internet, founded in 1996 by poet Kenneth Goldsmith [that] offers visual, concrete and sound poetry, expanding to include film and sound art mp3 archives" (wikipedia). When entering the site, which hosts thousands of items, the reader first discovers the following message,

> It's amazing to me that UbuWeb, after fifteen years, is still going. Run with no money, Ubu has succeeded by breaking all the rules, by going about things the wrong way. UbuWeb can be construed as the Robin Hood of the avant-garde, but instead of taking from one and giving to the other, we feel that in the end, we're giving to all. UbuWeb is as much about the legal and social ramifications of its self-created distribution and archiving system as it is about the content hosted on the site. In a sense, the content takes care of itself; but keeping it up there has proved to be a trickier proposition. The socio-political maintenance of keeping free server space with unlimited bandwidth is a complicated dance, often interfered with by darts thrown at us by individuals calling foul-play on copyright infringement. Undeterred, we keep on: after fifteen years, we're still going strong. We're lab rats under a microscope: in exchange for the big-ticket bandwidth, we've consented to be objects of university research in the ideology and practice of radical distribution.
>
> But by the time you read this, UbuWeb may be gone. Cobbled together, operating on no money and an all-volunteer staff, UbuWeb has become the unlikely definitive source for all things avant-garde on the internet. Never meant to be a permanent archive, Ubu could vanish for any number of reasons: our ISP pulls the plug, our university support dries up, or we simply grow tired of it. Acquisition by a larger entity is impossible: nothing is for sale. We don't touch money. In fact, what we host has never made money. Instead, the site is filled with the detritus and ephemera of great artists—the music of Jean Dubuffet, the poetry of Dan Graham, Julian

Schnabel's country music, the punk rock of Martin Kippenberger, the diaries of John Lennon, the rants of Karen Finley, and pop songs by Joseph Beuys—all of which was originally put out in tiny editions and vanished quickly.

The ambivalent position of UbuWeb, both inside and outside the "system," goes beyond the strategic complicity of bottom-up creativity and DIY philosophy, on the one hand, and institutional backing and support, on the other hand. The counter-cultural dimension of the project is not only linked to the non-mainstream character of (some of the) works gathered on the site; it also and perhaps most importantly depends on the radical use of the digital tools and infrastructures that have become available: UbuWeb is "for free"—and hence extremely vulnerable to community and volunteering support—but it is also a structure that copy-pastes (some would say "steals") what circulates on the Web. UbuWeb does not ask for authorisations, it applies the fundamental principle of "writing as copying" (but not remixing, unless, of course, at the level of the database, which provokes all kinds of unforeseen encounters) and combines with the "fair use" policy digital culture, that is copyright holders of digitised materials, is often struggling with (hence of course the emphasis on the pedagogical function of content-sharing).

Abigail De Kosnik's study of "rogue archives" (1996) helps to reframe positions such as UbuWeb, whose scholarly and didactic dimension remains vital, in the larger context of digital fandom culture. The book's originality is not only derived from the particular corpus that the author examines (mainly fan fiction archives created and managed by minority groups—in this case female, feminist, global-South and queer groups), but also from the theoretical framework that she develops for the study of what she calls "rogue" archives—a type of archive that is much more than just a digital or a digitised archive, but that exemplifies and implements several of the new opportunities disclosed by the digital turn.

For De Kosnik, whose book is based on an oral history project at Berkeley and interviews with some fifty "rogue" archivists in the domain of fan fic archives, a "rogue archive" (the metaphor is borrowed from the work by Jacques Derrida, who establishes a strong link between the figure of the rogue and radical democracy) is very different from a traditional archive, where the preservation, organisation and presentation of certain types of documents of the past produces an official interpretation for present use that also aims at maintaining itself in the future. Rogue archives are created bottom-up, by sometimes untrained and generally unpaid amateurs and volunteers sharing a special interest in a certain, often marginal or marginalised field, and whose ambition is less to transmit a certain idea of things past to future generations in a well-structured and tightly controlled way than to make possible the very survival of ignored or censored experiences as well as to generate a community life around an archive where all roles and functions become and remain blurred. Rogue archivists are almost always activists, and the driving force of their work is passion and commitment. Rogue archivists are in many cases not interested at all in technical or scientific standards and reliability, and ignore or willfully break the current rules of copyright and intellectual property rights (examples of rogue archives are therefore not YouTube channels or Facebook groups, even if a lot of rogue archiving work can be done in these digital environments, but the commercial interests of these platforms are in direct contradiction with the basic "no rules, no restrictions" spirit of the real rogue archive).

De Kosnik's book, which does not hide its sympathy for the anti-canonical and politically inspired approach of rogue archivists, is an important contribution to a better understanding of the stakes of digital culture in general. First of all, the book offers a clear and well-informed state of the art of many smaller and larger debates on the issue of digital archives (in that sense, it is almost tailor-made for classroom use—after all, the oral history project was executed with the help of MA students, and one feels throughout the whole book the strong commitment of the author to the intertwining of teaching and research). Second, and this is of course what stands out most, *Rogue Archives* is also an attempt to sketch a theoretical framework for the study of the countless grassroots initiatives that represent a huge percentage of the archival work that is being done online (the final chapter of the book proposes a big data analysis of the production as well as the reception of these online archives, and the quantitative figures are absolutely dizzying). De Kosnik does so by emphasising the notion of archival "style" (see also Kelsey 2007, for historical examples of photographic archives). Three types come to the fore here: 1) the *universal* archive (some rogue archives want to digitise theoretically everything—at least in a given field— and De Kosnik analyses the consequences of the refusal to distinguish between what is worth keeping and what is, according to non-rogues, not worth keeping at all); 2) the *community* archive (many rogue archives are made by minority groups or communities of affinity, and the long-term preservation of material that would otherwise be lost is here an absolute priority); 3) *alternative* archives, which may overlap with the second category (here the idea of user-generated content is taken in a much more radical sense than usually known: the ambition is not to complete information that is incomplete or missing in official archives, for instance with the help of crowdsourcing mechanisms, but to generate "different" content and stories, that is content and stories that are not allowed to appear in traditional archives or that are simply ignored or discarded elsewhere).

De Kosnik rightly insists on the necessity to think the relationship between the two archival categories—the canonical ones and the rogue ones—in terms of creative interaction, not of *a priori* antagonism. After all, it may happen that rogue archives are integrated into canonical archives, while the latter should also understand that the only way to have a real future is to adopt certain aspects of the former's creativity and dynamism. De Kosnik's book is an invitation to rethink the meaning of an under-studied but key cultural practice, while making us aware of the dangers of its smooth institutionalisation, which would involve the inevitable loss of what makes rogue archives essential to an open and democratic society. Here as well, if we consider databases and archives as media, we should always stick to the necessity of interlacing the technical and historical descriptions of a given medium-specificity (and as shown by De Kosnik's example, there is not one single type of archive and none of the possible types can resist change) and the cultural debate on the meaning, that is the impact of a medium on the larger mediascape and thus on society at large. Rogue archives are not "primitive" or "amateur" archives, they are "other" archives and accessing, using and making them is both an opportunity and a threat to canonical archives and thus to the very notion of canon itself. In that sense, a study like that of De Kosnik is an absolutely necessary instrument to question the apparent acceptance of new canons in digital art that opened this paragraph.

Saving the Canon

Criticising the canon is one thing; reinventing and reshaping the canon is another. But what is to be done when the actual works and the practices that accompany them—after all, electronic literature is ergodic (in the sense coined by Espen Aarseth), and digital visual arts also include many forms of non-trivial interaction which are part of the works as well—no longer exist, not because they have been forgotten, but because they have been destroyed (deleted, in the digital arts jargon) or because they have become once and for all inaccessible (due to technological obsolescence, although obsolescence, infamously known for "programmed obsolescence" production models in the industry, is definitely not the all-encompassing rule of the game: after all, companies also have interest in keeping works alive, and the example of YouTube demonstrates the possibility of reintroducing many works that we thought "lost"). To a certain extent, the question of non-retrievability of digital material repeats, at the other end of the temporal arc, the "demo or die" principle that pops up at the launch of a work or item. First one has to make sure that it can be shared with an audience, then one must take care of its dissemination, and finally one is inevitably confronted with the problem of sustainable storage.

In digital culture, littered with junkspaces and characterised by the increasingly accelerating obsolescence of software and hardware, sustainability is an issue that multiplies the proliferating problems of information overload and readability problems. But here again, digital culture is only the magnifying glass of what exists in culture at large. It is a principal concern in all modern heritage industry, where there is a maddening race between two antagonistic forces, that of innovation (that is creative destruction) and that of freezing (or, if one prefers, saving the past). There is a general agreement, however, that today the traditional preservationist and humanist paradigm no longer works: it has become impossible to give a lasting form to what is going away as well as man's refusal to accept the vanishing of "the stuff of our lives."[24] On the one hand, it becomes clear that preservation is becoming more and more difficult, from a material as well as financial point of view: There are simply too many books to be archived, too many paintings to be stored, too many buildings and built environments to be protected, restored and managed (and their number is increasing day after day), and the costs of this operation are so high that it becomes inevitable to make choices—painful choices, since in the humanist preservationist paradigm the loss of a thing, be it an object or a building, is experienced as the loss of one's own identity. On the other hand, preservation heritage clashes with other priorities, no less important, even from a classic humanist point of view, than that of the material maintenance of man-made things: in the case of architectural heritage, one may think of wildlife, plants, animals, biodiversity, for instance; in the case of digital art works, one may think of the massive investments in expensive restoration projects and their crippling effects on creation (for restoration tends to focus on canonical work and tends to condemn to further oblivion less generally appreciated works), but also on participation (it is well known that the parietal paintings one visits in Lascaux are a simulacrum; the real caves are now closed to the public whose very presence damages the original works). Finally, it also appears that preservation does not necessarily produce or enhance what is the essential motivation of heritage, namely the establishment of a deep relationship with the past (or rather with time, for the perception of the past cannot be separated from an anticipated connection with the future).

To these problems various answers have been given, and one of them is occupying a central place in the theory and practice of digital art heritage. But let us start with some other answers, not answers based on the letting go of the past, active or passive, whatever the reasons for this vanishing may be: ignorance, indifference, vandalism, censorship, lack of funding and resources to keep the past alive, and so forth, but answers that directly tackle the issue of material disappearance.

A first answer is "curated decay," as addressed in an important book by Caitlin DeSilvey (2017). Focusing on built environments such as deserted homesteads, abandoned industrial plants, harbours imperiled by sea storms and climate change, empty Cold War test sites, her study makes a plea for a different take on heritage. This take is *post-humanist* because it looks for a new balance between the needs of man and those of non-human beings (plants, animals, buildings, environments), thus putting an end to human exceptionalism. It is also *post-preservationist* since it tries to make room for the creation of new relationships with the past through the (curated) use of decay, that is of vanishing and death, addressing things no longer just as "things," capable of being kept outside the cycle of life and death, but as "processes," that is as beings and structures having, just like human beings, their own life and death. Heritage beyond saving, to quote the book's subtitle, is then the search for a new form of heritage that does not reject preservation but that tries to broaden and deepen it, first by proposing forms of curating heritage that stop seeing integral material maintenance as an absolute ideal; second by stressing the productive values of decay, which may prove much stronger instruments to give meaning and value to the past than the classic preservationist paradigm. In that regard, the positive reinterpretation of decay and entropy, the two principal notions defining what the classic paradigm wants to fight at all cost, comes as no surprise. In the experimental heritage policy defended by DeSilvey, decay and entropy are not synonymous of destruction and loss; they open instead the possibility of seeing loss and destruction as the beginning of something new, not only in the material sense of the word but also in the cultural sense, provided people manage to develop new ways of living the permanent change of things in relationship with their own transience and mortality (non-Western cultures, which often have a different approach of change and impermanence, may provide useful examples in this regard).

Curated decay is also a big issue in photography, a medium that proves to be dramatically decay-sensitive, certainly when artists start painting on photographic pictures. A Dutch research project, "Photographs & Preservation. How to save photographic artworks for the future?"[25] and the concluding conference, "The Materiality of Photographs,"[26] gave the opportunity to discuss the aesthetic and medium conflict between two extreme stances—and the whole gamut between them: that of non-intervention, mainly in the name of artistic authenticity and originality, and that of digital restoration, if not complete reconstruction—a second major answer to the problem of vanishing heritage which we will discuss below.

The issue of remaking the vanishing (or lost) original seems more controversial in the case of visual arts than in that of verbal arts, given the difference between the autographic and allographic nature of their respective productions. The differences however become very thin from the very moment that one addresses not only "texts," which are allographic, but also "manuscripts," be they old or modern, which are autographic. More generally, however, the very distinction between autographic and allographic works cannot be understood without taking into account the typically Western adoration of the aura of uniqueness, originality and authenticity: autography automatically ceases to be a value if the "origin" is not fetishised. A question mark after "typically Western" is however necessary, for we may too rapidly suppose that non-Western cultures are completely different in this regard, while not all Western heritage workers feel the need to idolise the original. In this regard, why not quote together Simon Leys's analysis of the paradoxical convergence of China's worship of the past and the systematic return of material destruction (Leys 2018)[27] with the following quotations by the Romantic fairy tale anthologiser, Achim von Arnim, as quoted by André Jolles:

> For Arnim, the significance of the *Märchen* lies in this inspiration to invention. If it does not inspire us, if it does not show how to tell stories, the ancient tale loses its value and its charm. The point is sharply emphasized: "Fixed *Märchen* will be the death of the whole world of *Märchen*." The value of old things is in their capacity to inspire new things and take them further—"poetry is neither young nor old and has no history at all". (Jolles 2017, 180).

Simulation and reproduction provoke less resistance in the case of completely vanished works, that is of works that cannot be revivified through restoration but which have to be rebuilt from scratch. An interesting example is Expo 67, Montreal's 1967 world fair, a landmark exhibition in praise of the technological and humanist optimism displayed by its unifying theme (man as creator of his own environment and builder of a community that embraces the whole world) as well as a new step in the gradual transformation of the fair into a total experience in which the boundaries between man, machine and city were meant to disappear. Expo 67 did not just show new artefacts, new technological achievements, new architecture; it was itself a kind of techno-determined *Gesamtkunstwerk* enabling the visitor to get the feeling of what modern life was making possible—and the major source of inspiration of the event was unquestionably the work of McLuhan, then at the zenith of his career. Among the most salient features of Expo 67 were its multiple cinematographic shows. Most pavilions entailed one or more shows of moving images, most of them experimenting with the then revolutionary notions of immersive and participatory cinema, blurring the boundaries between film-making and film-going. Yet the rapid dismantling of the site, the poorly documented events and exhibits, and the many failures and lacunas of subsequent archiving have turned Expo 67 into a myth, whose actual forms can now only be—approximatively—suggested via indirect reconstructions, that is reconstructions that discuss and explain the event instead of recreating it in such a way that certain forms of re-enactment become possible. In other words, such a simulation and reproduction then take the form of a book (Gagnon and Marchessault 2014), which wins in reflexivity and critical contextualisation what it may lose in directness—but what do we win if the directness in question is that of the simulacrum, which fakes the real rather than rebuilding it?

Relocating the Digital Void

Digital art is confronted with issues of storage, access, preservation and restoration, in unprecedented ways, given the explosive mix of ever more rapid obsolescence and equally proliferating quantities of data. A key intervention in this regard is Stuart Moulthrop and Dene Grigar's *Traversals* (2017), a book on the use of preservation in the digital era. Although focusing on a literary corpus, which, as one imagines, is largely intermedial, this study perfectly applies to the digital afterlife of visual art works as well. Moulthrop and Grigar take as their starting point the observation that the life span of digital works no longer depends on their inherent qualities ("good" works having more chances to survive than "bad" works, at least in general), but merely on that of the life span of the technology that made them possible—and that they helped to explore and develop at the same time (Eastgate System, Inc.'s Storyspace is a good example of the simultaneous and reciprocal development of a writing space software and the actual production of real works, in this case the perhaps bizarrely named "serious hyperfiction").

The first question that pops up then is that of the very sense of trying to keep alive what one knows is no longer there. If one decides that just moving ahead in order not to miss the next new thing and that just forgetting about the past is what matters, then technical obsolescence is not a problem. But if one believes instead that "we must struggle never to forget" (237, last words of the text), then the situation becomes quite different. The keyword of this book's subtitle is therefore twofold: it is about preservation, but even more about the *use* of preservation, a way of saying that it should be read as a double warning: first, against the illusion of the very possibility of such an enterprise (nothing can be "really" preserved—what is being preserved is always only a certain form or version of it); second, against the confusion between material conservation (which is a necessary step in the larger process but nothing more) and preservation in the broader sense of the word (which refers to the need to make meaning of the object of preservation, here and now but also in the future).

Traversals is the answer that two pioneering creators and scholars in the field of electronic literature, Stuart Moulthrop and Dene Grigar, offer to the most urgent practical and theoretical debates on how and why to preserve works that can no longer be read. The authors address the issue in two ways since their book tackles a wide range of theoretical (and political) questions, while at the same time elaborating and exemplifying a real method. To distinguish between the two is not easy since all theoretical stances are inextricably linked with methodological choices and vice versa, but for the didactic sake of this review, it may make sense to try to see what belongs to the method and what can be reframed in more general and theoretical terms.

First of all, Moulthrop and Gregar insist on the fact that to preserve implies first of all to select, that is to decide which kind of works can be considered worth preserving. In other words, *Traversals* is a book that unashamedly makes a plea for canonisation. Moulthrop and Grigar discuss four case studies (Judy Malloy's *Uncle Roger*, John McDaid's *Uncle Buddy's Phantom Funhouse*, Shelley Jackson's *Patchwork Girl* and Bill Bly's *We Descend*), which all belong to the pre-web era, a period of exceptional creative freedom and bottom-up research by independent artists. They also discuss the tactical omission of the best-known and still much debated work of that period (Michael Joyce's *afternoon: a story*) and list other possible case studies, while strongly emphasising the necessity of limiting the number of cases in order to enhance the quality of the reading.

Second, they also accentuate that to preserve should not be confused with to archive and emulate. It is of course crucial that the work should be kept materially alive, that is accessible, or in certain cases reconstructed in order to re-experience it with other means. But, time and again the authors stress the fact that it is not enough to guarantee the material availability of the work, which is only one of the conditions that make possible what really counts, namely the reading of the work. If "to preserve" means to preserve in order to be read, this reading can be organised in two steps, respectively called "Pathfinders" methodology and "Traversals" process in the authors' project funded by the US National Endowment for the Humanities' Office of Digital Humanities. First, during the Pathfinder stage, the creator of the work (but it is perfectly possible to replace the author with a knowing and informed reader) is invited to "[work] through the possibilities of these multifarious works" (5). These "demonstrations performed on historically appropriate platforms" (ibid.), which contain the comments given by the creator who speaks aloud what she or he is doing, are video-taped and are one of the materials studied in the second step, called Traversal. This second step—the results of which can be read in this book—is defined as "a reflective encounter with a digital text in which the possibilities of that text are explored in a way that indicates its key features, capabilities, and themes" (7). More concretely, reading is a creative intervention that combines two different orientations. On the one hand, a Traversal tries to analyse the internal structure of the work, both at surface level (what is the actual text that appears on screen) and at "deep" level (that is at the level of the underlying code). On the other hand, it also aims at understanding the contextual (historical, cultural, social, political, etc.) aspects of the work, of its production as well as its reception.

Finally (but this enumeration is certainly not exhaustive), Moulthrop and Grigar underline the collaborative and interdisciplinary dimension of the preservation of electronic work, and this at all possible levels and steps of the process.

The result of this two-step methodology is impressive. First of all, it produces a reconstruction of lost works that is at the same time very modest (the authors acknowledge that the outcome of a Traversal is not the work "as such," but the thick description of an encounter with it) and highly informative, since it analyses not only the surface of the work but also its relationships with the underlying and always determining code. The text under scrutiny is always a double, if not triple, text: the text as it can be seen and retold, often in its successive and sometimes quite different versions; the "hidden" codes of the text; the interplay between surface and deep structure. Second, the chosen method also discloses that the work as it appears thanks to the Traversal is a richer, more detailed, more complex and differently framed work than the one that readers and even specialists thought they knew. The Traversal of Malloy's work demonstrates, for instance, the progressive downsizing of the graphic style of the initial version, which the attempt to reach a broader audience had to soften (at least in this regard). That of Bly's *We Descend* clearly highlights the fact that this work, as was said from the beginning, was not a quite weak illustration of the narrative possibilities of Storyspace, but an example of a non-narrative use of the programme. Bly's interest was less in storytelling than in building an archive, and this new perspective helps one to understand what makes this work so challenging.

Method and concrete analyses can however not be separated from the powerful theoretical reflection on preservation that is another key aspect of this book (here as well, the medium-specific orientation of the research ties in with a cultural reflection on the "meaning" of the medium). The most striking features of this theoretical work can be found in the first and last chapters of *Traversals*, which raise fundamental questions on, first, the definition of electronic literature and, second, the larger horizon of the preservation of this kind of writing.

For Moulthrop and Grigar, the definition of electronic is actually just the starting point of a broader reflection on a set of key elements such as digital-born and digitally borne, open and closed forms of writing, or reading and writing. In this book, the debate on the definition of electronic literature is also meant to make room for new debates on the definition of literature itself. More concretely, this debate is repositioned in the larger context on the relationship between work and medium, the authors of *Traversals* making a strong case for the medium-specific or medium-sensitive materialist textualism of scholars such as N. Katherine Hayles or Matthew Kirschenbaum for whom code is anything but abstract and immaterial.

As far as the second question, that of the long-term use-value or impact of electronic preservation and the textual materialism that accompanies it, is concerned the authors make a very convincing claim for the cultural and political value of memory. Their metaphor of the "Sappho syndrome," that is "the disappearance of literary works to the extent that all that remains are fragments and references to them by others" (230), liberates us from certain forms of technological naïveté or hubris, which may make us believe that machines will allow us to preserve everything while discharging us from the obligation to commit ourselves truly to their (inescapably partial and eventually ephemeral) preservation. Moreover, the Sappho metaphor is also a great tool in correcting the systematic omission of female creators, certainly in a field that is almost automatically associated with masculinity.

Traversals is a crucial publication in the history of scholarly thinking on electronic literature. It is also a substantial demonstration of the necessity to always link theory and practice. Finally, it is also a brilliant example of the way scholars and creators can sketch new ways for socially and politically inspired and inspiring work that does not betray the heart of their own profession.

PART THREE

Community

7 Digital Politics

This chapter addresses the impact that digital media have on politics, particularly on activism. While the cyber-optimists celebrate the affordances of digital media as a privileged tool to improve democracy, the cyber-sceptics emphasise digital media's ineffectiveness when it comes to producing significant political change. Going beyond this dichotomy, the chapter critically analyses core traits that distinguish contemporary activism: first, a shift from traditional ideology-driven politics to a new kind of issue-based participatory politics; second, the logic of connective action that underpins current mobilisations; third, the processes of personalisation —or customisation — of content; and, lastly, the extent to which contentious politics has become a normal practice of contemporary politics. It furthers deals with new social movements, interrogating how their decentralised structure is intrinsically arranged according to the ontology of digital media. Lastly, we present the position of cyber-sceptics: for whom digital practices are not only ineffective politically speaking but can be counterproductive.

Keywords: politics, (digital) activism, cyber-optimists, cyber-sceptics, global civil society, new social movements, contentious politics, issue-based participatory politics, connective action, slacktivism.

On 8 February 1996, in the early days of the digital, John Perry Barlow wrote a short and controversial text entitled "A Declaration of the Independence of Cyberspace." The text was a response to the new Telecommunication Reform Act, through which the US government intended to sanction the circulation of indecent and obscene material on the internet. Considering the Act to be an illegitimate imposition of power, Barlow's performative text—in the sense that it produces the independence it declares, as Vlavo highlights (2018, 23)—describes the internet as a place of absolute freedom, a kind of updated utopia. In Barlow's words:

> We have no elected government, nor are we likely to have one, so I address you with no greater authority than that with which liberty itself always speaks. I declare the global social space we are building to be naturally independent of the tyrannies you seek to impose on us. You have no moral right to rule us nor do you possess any methods of enforcement we have true reason to fear. ... You do not know our culture, our ethics, or the unwritten codes that already provide our society more order than could be obtained by any of your impositions. ... We are forming our own Social Contract. This governance will arise according to the conditions of our world, not yours. Our world is different ... We are creating a world where anyone, anywhere may express his or her beliefs, no matter how singular, without fear of being coerced into silence or conformity.
> We will create a civilization of the Mind in Cyberspace. May it be more humane and fair than the world your governments have made before (Barlow 1996).

Barlow's text might seem to describe an outdated vision of the internet, from a time when it was conceived as a separate *virtual* world. However, this is a seminal text because it contributed to forging an imaginary that has persisted. As Papacharissi asserts, "it is not the nature of technologies themselves, but rather, the discourse that surrounds them, that guides how technologies are appropriated by a society" (2009, 230). This imaginary is, in fact, a dual one: on the one hand, as Barlow describes, the internet is a space outside—or at least capable of challenging—the established powers, a territory in which citizens can create the laws that govern them and enjoy a freedom to express themselves that is lacking in the "off-line" world. According to the view at the other extreme, represented here by the Act proposed by the US government, not only is the internet far from control-free, digital media actually afford new forms of control in more rigid, obscure and effective ways than those of the analogue era. Roughly speaking, these two positions correspond to the *cyber-optimists* versus the *cyber-sceptics*. While the cyber-optimists celebrate the affordances of digital media as a privileged tool to improve democracy, the cyber-sceptics emphasise the darker side of digital media, or, in a less apocalyptic approach, digital media's ineffectiveness when it comes to producing significant political change. No matter which labels are used, current academic debate is still engaged in the exploration of these two themes (Vromen 2017; Yates 2016). Since these early texts either celebrating the transformative and disruptive potential of digital media or warning against the potential for digital media to foster conflict, the tension between cyber-optimists and cyber-sceptics has remained one of the core debates regarding the impact of digital media on political participation.

In a similar vein, Simeon Yates (2016) labels this tension as a conflict around the *ideologies* and *utopias* of digital politics. Drawing on Mannheim's (1936) foundational sociological work "Ideology and utopia," Yates highlights that ideologies and utopias are "ideas" held by different social groups—ways of seeing the world or how the world could be. While ideologies function predominantly to explain, justify or reinforce present social and political structures, utopian positions are the forward looking "hoped for" visions of a society that has changed or transcended current form (Yates 2016, x). Put differently, utopias and ideologies could be described as forces acting on the voices of both those who use and those who study digital political media. These may be either centripetal—seeking to expand beyond existing norms— or centrifugal—seeking to maintain or reinforce the established norms. Considering both the political and digital realms, Yates maps the diverse practices carried out by political actors—citizens, activists and politicians—in the contemporary landscape:

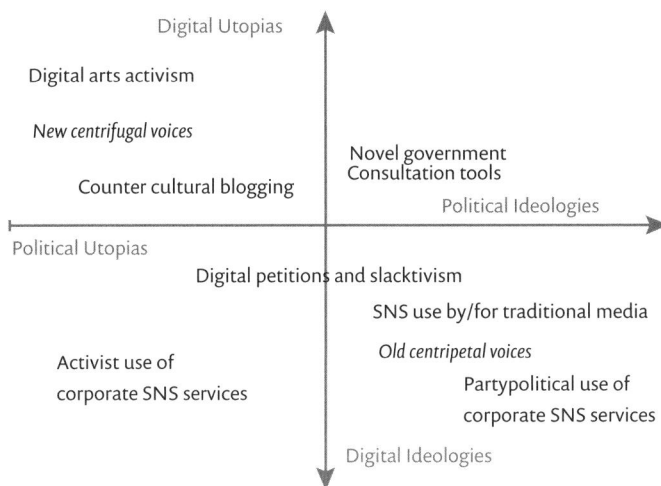

A model of digital and political spaces of action (Yates 2016, xii)

As the above figure shows, the realities of day-to-day uses of digital media in the realm of politics are far more diverse and nuanced than the dichotomy of good versus bad presupposes. Today, understanding digital politics goes beyond the celebratory or apocalyptic approach, although, as Yates warns, "we need to keep an eye to how claims about the impacts of digital media on politics and political action are themselves 'ideological' and/or 'utopian' assertions about what politics or the digital should or can do" (Yates 2016, xi). Instead of relying on dichotomist approaches— such as celebratory versus dismissive, old versus new—the digital is addressed in its hybrid character (Chadwick 2013) as well as from an ecological perspective (Miller *et al.* 2016). As Ariadne Vromen highlights:

> The trade-off in debate is not any longer between outmoded arguments about individualised clicktivism on the one hand and utopian views on movement driven, horizontal, online mobilisation on the other (e.g. Castells 2012). Instead, the more complex analysis is about how new kinds of internet-enabled organisations and movements emerge and how they operate within a largely corporatised and marketised sphere of social media platforms (Vromen 2017, 65–66).

Two remarks: Although it might seem obvious, our vision of digital politics—the positive or negative impact that digital media have on politics—is infused by our ideas of what the political or politics is or should be. We refer here to the distinction made by Chantal Mouffe, where *the political* refers to the dimension of antagonism that is inherent in all human society, while *politics* refers to "the ensemble of practices, discourses and institutions that seek to establish a certain order and to organize human coexistence in conditions that are always potentially conflictual because they are affected by the dimension of 'the political'" (Mouffe 1999, 754). Both are involved in the way we assess digital practices and their effects on the improvement of democracy. If we believe, for example, that political engagement means bodies gathering to make a claim in public space and facing the dangers which this implies, such as the threat of police repression, we would probably be very inclined to dismiss the signing of a petition or a tweet in which we voice political opinion as simple "slacktivism." So, in analysing the impact of digital media upon politics, it is always necessary to consider what we mean by politics—what conception of politics underlies the arguments as well as to what extent politics as a social system determines the implementation and uses of technologies (Yates 2016, xi).

Second, when reading the literature on new media and political participation—especially on the topics of global civil society, transnational activism or networked social movements, which will be at the centre of this chapter—it seems that digital media represent a fundamental change regarding political engagement not only in terms of the way they work but also by enabling an increase in participation. In other words, the advent of digital media implies that the majority of the population is involved in politics in an active way. This is also one of the core debates in the field of internet politics: to what extent the emergence of digital citizenship is changing—or has changed—political engagement.

The temptation to respond affirmatively arises when considering the extent of global mobilizations in the last decade, with one of its peaks in 2011, when the Arab Spring, Occupy Wall Street and the *Indignados* unfolded in the same year. People from all over the world became implicated in these movements, even if that involvement only meant using a hashtag to retweet information about the protest. This has to do with the new ways in which digital media enable people to participate politically—from voicing political opinions on Facebook to signing an on-line petition. Such participation embraces people who would probably not get involved in a traditional form of politics—for example, by joining a political party. Naturally, if we are interested in this topic we tend to focus upon phenomena of political significance (such as social movements, the work of transnational advocacy networks or the uses of social media by politicians), but it does not mean that (more) "ordinary" people in their everyday life are only interested or involved in politics because digital media provide more accessible forms of participation.

Other scholars are critical regarding the increase in the participation of people in politics due to digital media affordances. Recent studies such as that carried out by the "Why We Post" project, found that politics has a much lower profile on social media than expected. Taking an anthropological point of view, this project conducted research in nine field sites (including industrial and rural China, Chile, India, UK, Brazil, Trinidad, Turkey and Italy) that were chosen primarily for reasons that have nothing to do with politics. They hoped this would provide a balance to the majority of discussions on this subject, which are based on research in places where politics was of particular significance (Miller *et al.* 2016, 153). "Why We Post" found that, in general, politics was not a primary concern in social media (social media here encompass all kinds of platforms, including the most popular ones such as Facebook, Twitter, QQ, LinkedIn) and this for several reasons, among them that the main purpose of social media is to cultivate personal relationships that could potentially be damaged by the intrusion of politics:

> Personal relationships are the key influence that shapes online political engagement and action. People's primary concern is how their postings will impact upon their family and friendships. In several of our field sites people felt that expressing political views and opinions could result in antagonism or conflict; as a result, politics remains invisible and discussion is reserved for private spaces among one's closest friends and family (Miller *et al*. 2016, 153).

If politics is present, it is often in the form of passive participation, "referring to the tendency to criticize things in a more resigned way ... In a similar way to 'older' media, social media [are] mainly used by ordinary people to 'watch' politics, even as spectators watch a football match, rather than to 'do' politics" (Miller *et al*. 2016, 152–53), an observation that certainly contradicts the insistence with which new media has been obsessively defined as "participatory." Politics is also seen as a source of entertainment, something that provides a common spectacle, rather than a serious issue to engage with. In contradiction to the imaginary of digital media as an inherently disruptive medium, Miller *et al*. point out that social media in general have become a highly conservative place, reflecting the strategies of political debate and silence that were developed in the offline world (2016, 145–47).

Although we use the term "politics" in the singular, this can be misleading as it might suggest that politics is a single phenomenon. Politics—and therefore digital politics—encompasses a broad range of topics or themes. A possible articulation of this diversity is that proposed by John Postill (2012), who distinguishes between four broad topics or lines of debate regarding the relationship between digital media and politics:

– *Digital Government* (Executives and Bureaucracies), referring to the adoption of Internet technologies to improve the functioning of government agencies.
– *Digital Democracy* (Community, Deliberation, Participation), which concerns the debates around the concept of "public sphere"—used both as a "rhetorical token" and as a normative notion—as well as the potential or failure of the digital to enhance democracy.

- *Digital Campaigning* (Parties, Candidates, Elections), which deals with the role of digital media in election campaigns.
- *Digital Mobilisation* (Interest Groups and Social Movements) that addresses the forms of activism, social protest and mobilisation guided by emergent networking logics and practices (Postill 2012, 165–69).

Although all these topics are equally important in apprehending the functioning of digital politics, in what follows we will focus on *digital mobilisation* and *digital democracy*, paying attention to the way in which digital media foster citizen participation. Political participation has always been considered to be central in the definition of democracy, since in the absence of participation in civic life there is no democracy. Huntington and Nelson defined political participation as any "activity by private citizens designed to influence government decision-making" (quoted in Lilleker 2016, 109). Though there are many possible categories to list forms of political participation, they can be roughly grouped into four types: voting, campaigning, contacting elected representatives, or protesting (Lilleker 2016, 109). Some forms have been more affected by digital media than others. The practice of voting, for example, is still much the same, while other forms of citizen engagement have changed substantially. On the other hand, the perspective of governance and the uses of digital media made by politicians tend to be more aligned with existing political practices—their use of digital media aims at reinforcing a "business-as-usual" mode rather than exploring new forms of participation. For instance, Twitter is often used by politicians following the broadcast/one-to-many model of communication despite the interactivity that the platform affords (Di Fraia and Missaglia 2016). In what follows we delineate the main traits that help to capture the particularities of political participation in a digital age.

Digital Mobilisation

The discussion on mobilisation or digital activism—the way digital media create new forms of political participation—is inextricably linked to the emergence and consolidation of global politics and what has been termed the *global civil society*.

In 1989, an era began that can best be described as the entrance of politics onto the global scene. As Kaldor (2011) states, this is the result of diverse factors. On one hand, in 1989 the global conflict of the Cold War came to a halt. The dissolution of blocks and the waning of the privileged use of ideology to hush dissident voices meant an opening up from nation-states. This receptiveness to citizens' claims went beyond established structures. On the other hand, social movements fighting for democracy or human rights during the Cold War benefitted from this new opening, as their claims became legitimate due to the new language of the global civil society. A new actor emerged: "…at the heart of this process of change has appeared a new actor, an actor whose precise shape and contours may be indeterminate and disputed, but whose presence is not: global civil society" (Chandler 2004, 1).

This new actor is in reality many actors or, better put, a constellation of non-state actors. Not all are new as such, but their constellation and the specific frame in which globalisation situates them are. There are multiple ways of addressing these non-state actors. They have been called: "global social movements," "international NGOs (INGOs)," "transnational advocacy networks," "civil society organizations," "new social movements," without forgetting the umbrella term of "contentious politics." The term "global civil society" is proposed to include these multiplicities, encompassing not only the actors but also the values and spaces these actors create, as well as their practices. In this sense, Jordan points out that:

> Civil society has been defined in at least three ways: as the *forms* of associational life, such as NGOs, labor unions, social movements, and churches (Edwards 2009; Salamon 2004); as the *norms* of the good society, defined by values such as cooperation, nonviolence, and tolerance (Keane 2003); and as an *arena for public deliberation*, consisting of spaces that are relatively autonomous from both states and markets (Scholte 2000) (Jordan 2011, 94).

Although the norms and the spaces for deliberation are constitutive of the global civil society, the extensive bibliography on the subject has often focused on analysing the actors that make it up, with a special emphasis on NGOs and social movements. One of the clearest typologies is the one proposed by Mary Kaldor (2003), who also suggests a chronology to situate their emergence in time. This typology is useful as it allows one to identify the movement that emerges in the 1990s, commonly known as anti-globalisation or alter-globalisation, although, as we will discuss, Kaldor herself prefers the term "New Anti-Capitalist movement" (2003, 89).

This movement is key as it has become the common reference of the vast majority of theory elaborating on digital activism.

For Kaldor (2003), there are six actors that make up civil society: Old (pre-1970) and New (c. 1970 and 1980) Social Movements, understood as the modern form of contentious politics; NGOs (c. late 1980 and 1990) which, compared to social movements, are institutional and generally professional; Transnational Civic Networks (late 1980 and 1990), networks that connect INGOs, social movements and grass roots organisations, as well as individuals to specific issues and campaigns; New Nationalist and Fundamentalist Movements (1990s); and finally the New Anti-capitalist Movement (c. late 1990s and 2000s).

As Kaldor explains, the new anti-capitalist movement—often referred to as the anti-globalisation movement—burst onto the streets of Seattle and Prague at the end of 1990. She prefers to use the term "anti-capitalist" "since most of those engaged in the movement oppose the unregulated spread of capitalism and the growing power of the market over every aspect of life, and since it represents, in some respects, a revival of the great anti-capitalist movement of the late nineteenth century and early twentieth century" (2003, 101). The movement brings together "elements of the 'new' social movements and their 'tamed' successors—INGOs, networks and movements concerned with women's issues, the environment, or indigenous people's rights" (2003, 102) and includes a wide range of positions including those who want to reverse globalisation and return to the old world of nation-states, reformers who want to "democratise" globalisation, and those who want to abolish current global institutions and construct alternatives (2003, 102). Movements such as Occupy Wall Street, *Indignados,* the protests around the many G20 summits or the political actions that have been grouped under the Arab Spring could be included in this new anti-capitalist movement. These are the common references when we speak about the role of new media in digital activism, and though these movements obviously are not reducible to new media, they could not be understood without it.

The consensus suggests that since the late 20th century political engagement has declined in post-industrial societies. The number of people who come to vote has decreased. The political parties have seen the number of their members diminish, either because of a general loss in interest in joining traditional parties or because the electorate has become more unstable, opting for new parties instead of maintaining lifetime loyalties as in the past. Due to many factors, such as flexible labour markets and changing class structures, Union membership has also dropped. Traditional institutions and community associations, like the Church, which used to congregate and mobilise civil society, have lost their appeal. In sum, people have expressed an increased scepticism regarding the institutions of representative government, resulting in a growing cynicism about politics.

Nevertheless, and despite the amount of evidence supporting this view, alternative perspectives have pointed in a different direction, highlighting that citizens, especially young people, participate as much as in the past but in new ways. As Russell Dalton asserts:

> Citizens are less likely to be passive subjects and more likely to demand a say in the decisions affecting their lives. The new style of citizens politics reflects a more active involvement in the democratic process (Dalton 2014, 10).

In *Democratic Phoenix: Reinventing Political Activism*, Pippa Norris also goes against the conventional perspective that traditional political activities have waned in popularity since the post-war era. For her, what we are witnessing is a change in traditional forms or participation and, as she points out, "it is all too easy to equate change with decline" (2002, xi). Beyond providing evidence against some of the established assumptions—for example, demonstrating that voting participation has been stable in established democracies since the post-war era and has even increased in developing societies—Norris focuses on the rise of alternative avenues, "multiple newer channels of civic engagement, mobilization, and expression that are rapidly emerging in post-industrial societies to supplement traditional modes" (2002, 4). These channels include new social movements, such as environmental activism, human rights advocates and women's groups; transnational policy networks; and internet activism. For her, what happens to forms of participation in the digital age has more to do with *a production of variety* than with an *unproductiveness* of political assets:

> Political participation is evolving and diversifying in terms of the *who* (the *agencies* or collective organizations), *what* (the *repertoires* of actions commonly used for political expression), and *where* (the *targets* that participants seek to influence) (Norris 2002, 4).

In sum, "indicators point more strongly toward the evolution, transformation, and reinvention of civic engagement than to its premature death" (2002, 4). This transformation of civic engagement has been analysed in the last decades in alignment with the affordances of digital media, an alliance that needs to be understood not in terms of "technological determinism" (Yates 2016, xi) but as developing according to a common historical, social and cultural milieu.

In order to understand what is new in digital mobilisation, in the following pages we will focus upon core traits that distinguish contemporary activism (Vromen 2017): first, a shift from traditional ideology-driven politics to a new kind of issue-based participatory politics; second, the logic of connective action that underpins current mobilisations; third, the processes of personalisation—or customisation—of content; and, lastly, the extent to which contentious politics has become a normal practice of contemporary politics—the way in which citizens make visible their grievances and their criticisms, even if they are not clearly unified in common demands.

From Ideology to Issue-based Participatory Politics

Ideology—understood as a coherent system of ideas that rely on a few basic assumptions about reality—has traditionally been the foundation of political action. Ideology long provided the unifying prism that allowed us to diagnose political problems, explain their causes, and find the solutions. Ideology is not an essential entity that remains untouched across time and space; quite the contrary, it is an object of diverse interpretations that have given birth to the many regional and historical variants that almost every ideology has produced. To give just one example: the single ideology "anarchism" is far from singular. It encompasses classical, post-classical and contemporary variants, such as individual anarchism, egoist anarchism, anarcho-syndicalism, mutualism, illegalism, anarcho-pacifism, communalism, panarchism, platformism, black anarchism, crypto-anarchism, anarco-transhumanism, queer anarchism, communalism, anarcho-capitalism, post-left anarchism, to name just a few. To these temporal variants we have to add regional developments, considering, for example, how anarchism developed in different countries and regions—from Africa and Argentina to the United States of America and Korea. Finally, anarchism has been modified in combination with religious ideologies, leading to Buddhist anarchism, the Tolstoyan movement, and Islamic and Jewish anarchism. The same is true of other ideologies, such as feminism and identity politics, liberalism and environmentalism.

Beyond these differences, nevertheless, ideology provides coherence in dealing with the potential diversity of the grievances that need to be addressed. As a coherent system of ideas, ideologies possess all-encompassing goals—how society should work—and methods—the most appropriate ways to achieve the ideal arrangement. Beyond providing an epistemological and affective foundation for action, ideology functions as an essential component of collective identity which, for many scholars, particularly those who dismiss the effectiveness of contemporary activism, is the key to the success of any political mobilisation. Those who belong to a group—women, labourers, communists, right-wing supporters—share something in common that binds them together in the present and, more importantly, in the future to come.

Beliefs and values are usually institutionalised in diverse ways, providing people who share the same ideology with the space and the structure to organise their political actions in a meaningful and effective way. Traditionally, political activity has been channelled through political parties. Political parties have a hierarchical structure; this can be more or less rigid according to the organisations, but, in principle, political parties do not foster a kind of de-centred or leaderless institutional form. On the other hand, political parties rely on the logic of representation, in which the members delegate decision-making, the management of resources and choices regarding forms of mobilisation to the leaders.

The last decades have witnessed a turn to a new kind of issue-based participatory politics and a move away from traditional ideologically driven politics and linkages. During this period the importance of traditional organisations—political parties, unions and churches—has significantly diminished. Many factors converged to produce this change, such as changes in the structure of politics (the decentring of the state, corporate globalisation), post-industrial changes in society (higher levels of education, the expanded middle class, new other-oriented values), new information technology (the internet and now social media), and new political problem complexes (globalised environmental destruction, human rights harms) (Micheletti 2003).

In her book *Political virtue and shopping: Individuals, consumerism and collective action* (2003), Michele Micheletti stresses that a new form of politics has emerged, contrasting *collectivist collective action* with a new *individualised collective action*. Drawing on Micheletti, Ariadna Vromen resumes this new form of politics as follows:

In the traditional collectivist approach ideals of liberal, representative democracy underscore how we understand and experience participation. Citizens delegate their political voice to leaders or elected representatives within parties, unions, interest groups and other civic associations: "citizens are encouraged even pressured to craft and construct their political preferences to these [existing] structures. They become socialized in these organized settings" (Micheletti 2003, pp. 26–8). Thus, membership means agreeing to support organisational agendas and assumes that citizens both understand and will acquiesce to the norms, values, and rules of these organisations. Formal hierarchy and order are important to traditional political organisations, and while an activist membership may have some say on campaign directions, the majority are passive in their support and primarily have only a financial involvement (Vromen 2017, 23).

In contrast, the emergence of individualised collective action leads citizens to create new spaces for political action and engagement that are driven by issues and causes:

> individual citizens do not need to join and show loyalty towards interest articulating structures to become involved in what they deem are urgent issues of politics and society. They can become involved outside these structures by showing commitment to causes and assuming responsibility in a more hands-on way (Micheletti 2003, 28).

If ideology offers a coherent guide for political action in terms of transformative goals, single issues, on the contrary, are based on one essential policy area or idea in isolation—e.g. abortion, opposition to the European integration, or the defence of human rights violations in a Latin American country. To support a cause, citizens do not need to be part of a political party; they can tweet for or against abortion, sign a petition to support the cause, or, as Micheletti analyses in what she calls "consumerism politics," citizens can opt to express their political view by choosing what to consume—i.e. buying a fair-trade coffee. In this case, the political agency is "rooted in the integration of citizens concerns with consumer choices" (Micheletti 2003, 18), allowing citizen-consumer to work on political causes in the marketplace. The political consumer—as conceptualized here—becomes "a responsibility-taking actor who sees market transactions as having interesting political potential" (Micheletti 2003, 18).

Issue-based participatory politics is part of the phenomenon of *individualis-ation*. Anthony Giddens (1991) referred to this process as the turn from emanci-patory movements to a sort of *life politics*, which "does not primarily concern the conditions which liberate us in order to make choices: it is a politics of choice" (quoted in Vromen 2017, 21). Giddens also points out how globalising influences intrude deeply into the reflexive project of the self, and how, conversely, these pro-cesses of self-realisation influence global strategies. In a similar vein, Ulrich Beck and Elisabeth Beck-Gernsheim link the processes of individualisation with the loss of the pre-eminence of the nation-state as the space of political action, a space that is no longer closed and self-contained. "Society and the public realm are constituted out of conflictual spaces that are at once individualized, transnationally open and defined in opposition to one another. It is in these spaces that each cultural group tests and lives out its hybrid" (quoted in Vromen 2017, 22).

The politics of choice (Giddens 1991), consumerism politics (Micheletti 2003) and sub-politics (Beck and Beck-Gernsheim 2001) all allude to this erosion of the social-structural conditions of political consensus that until recently have made collective action possible, as well as allowing it to be replaced by an individualised collective action that makes *ad hoc* choices on single issues.

Obviously, the emphasis on issue-based politics does not mean that ideology and established organisations have disappeared from the political scene. As we mentioned before, the most important movements in contentious politics of the last decades—from the *Zapatistas*, to Occupy Wall Street, to *Indignados*, not to mention paradigmatic activist groups like Anonymous—can be said to share an anti-capitalist ideology (Kaldor 2003). Rather than disappearing, ideology has become more diffuse. On the one hand, citizens can support one essential policy area of an idea without subscribing to the whole set of values and norms that an ide-ology defines. On the other, the way in which citizens engage in politics is increas-ingly personalised, that is, they adapt or customise their support by linking it to their specific circumstances and needs. This, in a certain sense, is intrinsically linked to the role digital media play in facilitating loose networks that replace collective action by connective action.

The Logic of Connective Action

If politics can be defined as collective action, the importance of the title of the book by Bennett and Segerberg, *The Logic of Connective Action: Digital Media and the Personalization of Contentious Politics* (2013), in which "collective" is replaced by "connective," rapidly becomes clear.[1]

Bennett and Segerberg seek to understand how connective action is organised and how it differs from conventionally "organized collective action that builds on strong leadership, brokered coalitions among formal organizations, and action frames that draw on ideology or group (class, race, gender, nationality) identity" (2013, 2). Their point of departure is the protests that emerged following the global financial crisis that erupted in 2008. During this crisis, millions of people lost their jobs and homes and took to the streets as well as to the internet to voice their demands. These kinds of mobilisations can be traced back as far as the "Battle of Seattle" in 1999, or, for some scholars, even to the *Zapatista* uprising in 1994, the *Zapatistas* being the first group that visibly and ostensibly used digital media—a rather antiquated form of digital media compared to that of the present—to generate international solidarity and gain global support for its cause. These protests shared an "ethos of diversity and inclusiveness," addressing an array of issues "including economic injustice and unfair trade practices in the global south, climate and environmental degradation worldwide, unstainable energy and resource management ... *and all of these in a single event*" (Bennett and Segerberg 2013, 4–5).

In their book, Bennett and Segerberg take as one of their case studies the protests that took place in London in 2009 on the occasion of the G20 summit. The various planned protests occurred on two days: 28 March and 1 April. The mobilisation on 28 March was organized by Put People First (PPF), a coalition of more than 160 NGOs, trade unions and environmental groups. Its march gathered more than 35,000 people. On the other hand, the activities planned for 1 April, which included the Stop the War coalition and an Alternative London Summit, were organised by G20 Meltdown, an anti-capitalist group that brought together diverse organisations, including the Anarchist Federation or the Socialist Workers' Party. The march organised by G20 Meltdown—which converged on the Bank of England from four directions, each led by a differently coloured horseman of the apocalypse—included an estimated 5,000 protestors.

In Bennett and Segerberg's analysis, these two coalitions represent two different logics of political organisation: PPF represents the hybrid type of connective organisation, while Meltdown represents the more conventional model of organisationally brokered collective action (2013, 63). The differences between the two are observed in two aspects that are crucial to understanding the way in which digital media shape contemporary activism.

The first aspect concerns the personalisation of communication ("personalised communication") (Bennett and Segerberg 2013, 64). Bennett and Segerberg focus their analysis on websites of both coalitions: these function, as has been the case in other movements such as the *Indignados*, as the organisation's self and not as its tool. Bennett and Segerberg underline two ways in which an organisation can customise the communication: 1) their framing of protest themes; and 2) the opportunities they offer to site visitors to use technology for interactive communication (2013, 64).

"Framing" refers to how the topic is represented or, to put it simply, what words are used to describe it. Although, in this case, both coalitions were referring to a similar state of affairs—the global economic crisis—they did it in a different way. A content analysis shows that the most prominent words in Put People First's website are "people" and "crisis." Details about causes and solutions are kept in the background. The reader is encouraged to acknowledge the economic crisis but the website does not label this a result of one economic system over another. "The presentation instead emphasizes the detrimental consequences of the status quo for 'people,' letting readers identify the message and action that they wish to endorse as long as it amounts to 'putting people first'" (Bennett and Segerberg 2013, 64–65). This was reinforced by a slogan that became viral and condenses PPF's stance: "Send your message to the G20" (the slogan and a picture of a megaphone appears at the centre of the page), which invited people to express their own perspectives about the crisis and to communicate their personal stance to the world leaders. (Another clear example of personalisation from a different movement is the slogan "We are the 99 %" used by participants in the Occupy Movement, that refers to the concentration of wealth among the top 1 % of income earners compared to the other 99 %. Participants appropriated the slogan by sharing their own stories on social media, holding banners in which we can read "After suffering through nearly 3 years of underemployment my lifelong dream of returning to school was crushed by a 60K medical bill. I AM THE 99" or "In 3 hours my CEO makes more than I do in a YEAR! I am the 99%, you are the 99%, WE are the 99%").

In contrast, on the G20 Meltdown's website the crisis is defined narrowly. It has a very concrete source—capitalism—and therefore a logical solution—"overthrow capitalism." As Bennett and Segerberg emphasise, "while the PPF requires only that the reader recognize the existence of an economic crisis, Meltdown insists that the reader recognize it as a *capitalist* crisis. The goal of 'overthrow capitalism' points both to the source of the crisis ('the dominance of finance capitalism is the problem') and a drastic solution" (2013, 66).

We also find differences in the way in which each coalition site offered individuals interactive affordances—"the type of action or a characteristic of actions that a technology enables through its design" (Earl and Kimport 2011, 10)—to engage with on their own terms. Interactive affordances encompass a broad spectrum of means that enable individuals to make choices about how to participate. This includes, for example, general affordances such as signing a petition; donating money; adding content to the communication network by posting videos, text, photos or comments; Twitter and RSS feeds; calendars. It also includes unique affordances, such as buying a T-shirt or, as happened in the Obama 2008 campaign, the possibility of "Obama-ising" your own photo by transforming it to look like the iconic Obama photo by US street artist Shepard Fairey. It is not surprising to find that, in line with the personalisation of content observed regarding their framing, the PPF site offered several means to interact, ranging from providing different channels to receive information—email alerts, RRS feeds or a calendar—to using the #G20rally Twitter hashtag or installing PPF widgets on blogs or Facebook pages (Bennett and Segerberg 2013, 70–71). By contrast, the Meltdown site gave only six means of interaction which, we could add, were very standard. This strategy indicates that the main goal of the Meltdown site was not to foster personal ways of engaging with the protest but to present information unilaterally to the visitor, who can either accept or reject the message but not customise it in line with their own concerns.

The two features that define the kind of personalised communication that is central to large-scale connective action formations are thus:

> (1) Political content in the form of easily personalized ideas such as PPF in the London 2009 protests, or 'we are the 99 per cent' in the later *occupy* protests. These frames require little in the way of persuasion, reason, or reframing to bridge differences with how others may feel about a common problem. *These personal action*

frames are inclusive of different personal reasons for contesting a situation that needs to be changed.

(2) Various personal communication technologies that enable these themes to be shared. Whether through texts, tweets, social network sharing,or posting YouTube mashups, the communication process itself often involves further personalisation through the spreading of digital connections among friends or trusted others. Some more sophisticated custom coordinating platforms can resemble organisations that exist more online than off (Bennett and Segerberg 2012, 744–45).

The second feature that characterises digitally enabled connective action is the role of communication, functioning not as a tool to transmit a message but as integral to political participation and mobilisation. To put it simply, the website of a movement is not just a tool to communicate the actions organised or coordinated elsewhere; rather, it plays the role of a virtual political organisation. It is part of what makes the movement possible, what constitutes it. For example, the anti-austerity movement *Indignados* in Spain—also referred to as the 15-M for the date of the mass mobilisations that took place in more than 60 cities across Spain on 15 May 2011—gathered millions of demonstrators to protest against welfare cuts, the political system and capitalism, calling for the protection of basic rights that the current political system was failing to protect. The sustained cycle of protests delineated the movement as one not affiliated with any political party, union or any other powerful political organisation; although many civil society organisations supported the 15-M, they were kept in the background. The face of the movement was, conversely, the millions of ordinary people affected by the economic crisis. The core of the movement, in the case of *Indignados,* was the digital platform *Democracia Real YA!* (DRY, Spanish for *Real Democracy NOW!*), created by users of Spanish social media and forums. *Democracia Real YA!* was the physical and symbolic site where the connective actions originated and were sustained. As Bennett and Segerberg affirm, "on the one hand, *Democracia real YA!* seemed to be a website and on the other, it was a densely populated and effective organization. It makes sense to think of the core organization of the *Indignados* as both of these and more, revealing the hybrid nature of digitally mediated organization (Chadwick 2011)" (Bennett and Segerberg 2012, 741). Based on these distinctive features, Bennett and Segerberg outline a three-part typology of large-scale actions that feature prominently in contemporary contentious politics. These three logics of action are conceived of as ideal types; in practice, they overlap and change over time. The two extremes in the figure represent the opposite poles of *organisationally brokered collective action*—wherein coordination relies on brokering organisations, frames are collective, and the use of social technologies does not invite personalised interpretations of problems and action—and *crowd-enabled connective action*—the traits of which are the opposite of those described above. In the middle, *organisationally enabled networks* describe a hybrid type that lies between the two, pointing to "loosely tied networks sponsoring actions and causes around a general set of issues" or "hybrid online campaigning organizations such as *GetUp, 38 Degrees, Avaaz and MoveOn*" (Vromen 2017, 66) that invite followers to personalise their engagement.

These different logics follow a gradation in their use of digital media: from the more restricted usage made by traditional collective action, which aims at reducing the costs of coordination without structurally changing the logic of action, to a crowd-enabled connective action in which digital media platforms functions as organisational hubs. The hybrid type in between is composed of established organisations that give followers a prominent space to personalise their engagement, fostering, through the use of technology, a displacement of agency from the organisation to the participants. The following figure summarises the main traits of each framework:

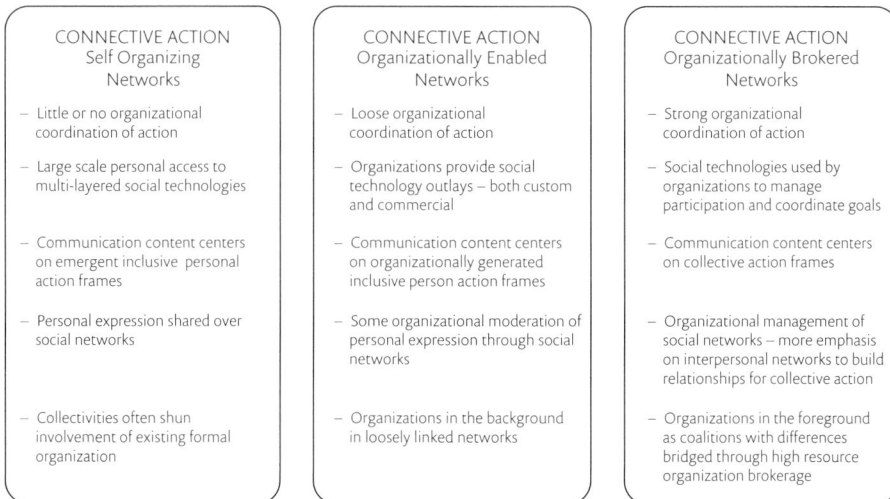

CONNECTIVE ACTION Self Organizing Networks	CONNECTIVE ACTION Organizationally Enabled Networks	CONNECTIVE ACTION Organizationally Brokered Networks
– Little or no organizational coordination of action	– Loose organizational coordination of action	– Strong organizational coordination of action
– Large scale personal access to multi-layered social technologies	– Organizations provide social technology outlays – both custom and commercial	– Social technologies used by organizations to manage participation and coordinate goals
– Communication content centers on emergent inclusive personal action frames	– Communication content centers on organizationally generated inclusive person action frames	– Communication content centers on collective action frames
– Personal expression shared over social networks	– Some organizational moderation of personal expression through social networks	– Organizational management of social networks – more emphasis on interpersonal networks to build relationships for collective action
– Collectivities often shun involvement of existing formal organization	– Organizations in the background in loosely linked networks	– Organizations in the foreground as coalitions with differences bridged through high resource organization brokerage

Elements of connective and collective action networks (Bennett and Segerberg 2012, 756)

Digital Activism and Social Movements

Over the past few years we have seen a vast increase in protests across the world. Citizens in distant countries such as Egypt, Iceland, Peru, Russia, Spain, the US, Mexico and Turkey have taken to the streets in massive numbers to challenge power and advocate for basic rights. The growth of these large-scale movements has been accompanied by a general increase in small demonstrations over schools, neighbourhood issues and other specific concerns (Dalton 2014). In addition, more ephemeral engagements, such as distributed denial of service (DDoS) or viral campaigns, have been building an alternative model of protest power. All these disparate—though related—forms of protests fall under the umbrella of the term "contentious politics" (Tarrow 2015), marking a shift to "social movement societies" (Meyer and Tarrow 1998). According to Meyer and Tarrow, forms of collective action that were popular in the 1960s became institutionalised by the end of the 20th century. First, protests have become more frequent, becoming "a perpetual element in modern life" (Meyer and Tarrow 1998, 4); second, the range of organisations involved as well as the issues addressed are more diverse; third, and perhaps most importantly, the professionalisation or institutionalisation of social movements may have changed them "into an instrument within the realm of conventional politics" (Meyer and Tarrow 1998, 4). Writing in 1998, they also contend that, in comparison to the past, contemporary mobilisations were less violent, due in part to a sort of normalisation—as demonstrations turned into a standard practice the police learned how to deal with them, exercising control without (necessarily) repressing the marchers. A recent update of Meyer and Tarrow's book—Howard Ramos and Kathleen Rodgers' *Protest and Politics: The Promise of Social Movement Societies* (2015)—seems to confirm their hypotheses about the centrality of social movements in contemporary societies. In their volume, Ramos and Rodgers take the Arab Spring, Quebec's Student Strike, Greek and Spanish anti-austerity protests, the Occupy Movement and Idle No More as examples of "the spread of contention and politics by [non-electoral] means around the world" (Ramos and Rodgers, 2015, 3, 13), highlighting the diffusion of movements and strategies fuelled by digital media.

If digital activism is essential for understanding new social movements, since it is one of their main components, it is nevertheless not restricted to them. Digital activism covers all instances of social and political campaigning practices that use digital network infrastructure (Joyce 2010a, viii).[2] In this sense, ephemeral—and very contested—practices such as "slacktivism" are also part of digital activism, although the relationship with social movements is debatable.

How have digital media modified the functioning of social movements? Before addressing the question, it is important to underscore that although it is possible to establish tendencies, point out general characteristics and identify common elements, the relationship between social movements and digital technologies is a complex one. Not only because each participant within a social movement relates differently to technology, which also requires varying levels of expertise, but because technology evolves constantly. In fact, one of the major challenges for researchers is the rapid and continual evolution that typifies the emergent digital ecology as an environment. Moreover, collective action uses digital tools in multiple ways for a variety of purposes that can range from the construction or consolidation of communities to the coordination and distribution of information (Kavada 2010, 102). The variety of purposes, the different levels of expertise, and the constant evolution of technologies help to explain the conflicting voices of the cyber-optimists and the cyber-sceptics mentioned in the introduction with regard to the use of digital technology for political mobilisation.

As previously mentioned, within Bennett and Segerberg's model new social movements are conceived as "networks of informal interactions" which have a "loose, flexible and decentralized" structure. Based on Luther Gerlach and Virgine Hine (1970), Anastasia Kavada points out how a decentralised structure of social movements follows the SPIN model:

> Segmented, meaning that social movements comprise numerous smaller groups (or, in the language of networks, "nodes") whose participation in the movement may wax and wane as new members join while others withdraw to focus on different interests.
> Polycentric, meaning that they have multiple centres and leaders whose influence tends to be temporary.
> INtegrated, meaning that these multiple segments and hubs are connected to each other through interpersonal relationships between activists or through a common identity and a shared set of beliefs (Kavada 2010, 104).

This decentralised structure is intrinsically arranged according to the ontology of digital media. On one hand, media substantially reduce the cost of coordinating actions, while on the other, multimodal, transnational and asynchronous communication make possible the existence of a structure that does not require a physical or communicational centre.

Among the many required activities for the constitution and sustenance of a social movement, the internet plays a key role in the following (Kavada 2010, 109–113):

> Access to information: the internet provides greater and easier access to relevant information (publications, reports, online newspapers, citizen journalism). It is not only the fact of having access to more information, but also the fact that this increased access to information includes censored information (the clearest example is here WikiLeaks). Moreover, the internet helps to monitor and visualize information.
>
> Dissemination of information: in addition to greater access to information, digital media allows activists to disseminate information about their cause through, for example, the creation of a website (whether for a campaign or for specific events), alternative media (such as Indymedia), or the widespread use of social networks (Twitter, Facebook, YouTube, Flickr). This propagation allows the 'viralization' of information, key to the visibility of the movement.
>
> Coordinating and decision-making: social movements have traditionally operated in regard to an informal form of membership. Digital media promotes this informal subscription by allowing anyone to join the movement, for example, by joining a Facebook group. At the same time, social media offers a space for discussion that enables participants to make decisions in a unified way, to establish schedules for events such as protests, or to coordinate the activities they will carry out. This process of exchange through social media contributes to creating an identity for the movement (Kavada 2010, 109–113).

If cyber-optimists have not ceased to venerate the role of digital media in global civil society as a force capable of organising and bolstering marginal populations or issues such as climate change and the increase in poverty, the cyber-sceptics, for their part, have unceasingly criticised the digital practices that lie in the connective action itself. The terms "slacktivism" and "clicktivism" refer to these ephemeral engagements, "such as massive online petition drives, e-mail campaigns, distributed denial of service (DDoS) attacks (when a server is rendered inoperable by flooding it with requests), and viral campaigns" (Earl *et al.* 2015). Through a single click, easy and instantaneous, those who sign a petition can feel satisfied at having acted politically, even though in real life they are not willing to compromise themselves beyond that ephemeral click. According to critics of slacktivism, it is not only ineffective politically speaking—especially if it becomes a common practice that results in the homogenising of the value judgements behind, for instance, supporting poor children in Africa and saving a white whale in the South Atlantic—but moreover it can be counterproductive. If such media did not exist, participants would become involved in costlier forms of participation such as offline protests. Those who defend, for example, "flash activism" insist it is effective, but its effectiveness lies not in its durability but in its intensity:

> Whereas power from social movements traditionally comes from sustained and persistent activism by a smaller but dedicated core of activists, this model uses a "flash flood" model of power in which short, massive bursts of activity by loosely (and even temporarily) engaged participants create pressure on targets (Bennett and Fielding 1999). Just as a flash flood can be devastating despite rapidly abating water levels, we expect that flash activism influences policy makers, public opinion, and subsequent media coverage by showcasing massive mobilizations and attracting widespread attention (Earl *et al.* 2015).

The effectiveness of these actions is in their amassment and not in the intrinsic value of the isolated practice. Each action in itself may lack impact but, when taken together, supposing the number of participants is significant, the culmination of actions may have an impact, for example, when defining an agenda or when establishing the position of one issue in regard to another. Beyond celebrating or rejecting these practices altogether, what is at stake, as Earl and Kimport (2011) point out, is an evaluation of how the circumstances of such activism can be tactically useful to the movements. Moreover, to condemn slacktivism requires referring to false or at least disputable statements; for example, the claim that only long-lasting activism can be politically effective, which is not demonstrated in literature. Another example is the claim that these more ephemeral practices are always easy and risk-free. This may be true in democratic countries, but the same argument cannot be applied to authoritarian contexts in which even ephemeral practices may actually involve danger (Earl *et al.* 2015).

If the stance of cyber-optimists thus supports this kind of ephemeral engagement, cyber-sceptics are openly critical of it. Two clear positions that represent the cyber-sceptic point of view are those of Malcolm Gladwell (2010) and Evgeny Morozov (2009). Gladwell's article, "Small Change: Why the revolution will not be tweeted," published in *The New Yorker,* opens with a description of the well-known sit-in at the Woolworth's store in Greensboro on 1 February 1960 in which four black students—Ezell A. Blair, David Richmond, Joseph McNeil and Franklin McCain—sat down at the segregated lunch counter to protest against Woolworth's policy of excluding African American from being served food there. In remembering this sit-in, Gladwell emphasises that activism *always* involves risk and also remarks that a key reason people are willing to take risks is the personal relationships that links activists. Without this support, it is more difficult for people to be willing to take risks, and without assuming at least a certain degree of risk there is no possible political effect. It is precisely this that people engaging through digital media are not willing to do. Digital media can be useful for other purposes but not for activism because you can only expect people to participate as long as it does not require much from them. As Gladwell affirms,

> That's the only way you can get someone you don't really know to do something on your behalf. You can get thousands of people to sign up for a donor registry, because doing so is pretty easy. You have to send in a cheek swab and—in the highly unlikely event that your bone marrow is a good match for someone in need—spend a few hours at the hospital. Donating bone marrow isn't a trivial matter. But it doesn't involve financial or personal risk; it doesn't mean spending a summer being chased by armed men in pickup trucks. It doesn't require that you confront socially entrenched norms and practices. In fact, it's the kind of commitment that will bring only social acknowledgment and praise (Gladwell 2010).

Moreover, Gladwell sees the networking characteristic of new activism as a problem more than a solution. High-risk activism necessitates a hierarchal structure and discipline; this protects not only the cause but the participants themselves. Activism leaves "little room for conflict and error. The moment even one protester deviates from the script and responds to provocation, the moral legitimacy of the entire protest is compromised" (Gladwell 2010). This uniformity and discipline are what a network structure, which is made up of loose and weak ties without a hierarchical organisation, cannot provide.

Gladwell's article ends with an ironic comment on the activism described in the book *Here Comes Everybody* by Shirky, which recalls how a stolen telephone is recovered with the help of many anonymous people through social media. Gladwell's words accurately portray the narrow goals of this kind of activism:

> Shirky ends the story of the lost Sidekick by asking, portentously, "What happens next?"—no doubt imagining future waves of digital protesters. But he has already answered the question. What happens next is more of the same. A networked, weak-tie world is good at things like helping Wall Streeters get phones back from teen-age girls. *Viva la revolución.*

8   Digital Democracy

This chapter deals with the debate regarding the capabilities of digital media to foster democratic deliberation, focusing on the key concept of the "public sphere". Coined by Habermas, the term "public sphere" refers to the domain of social life in which public opinion is articulated through rational public discourse and debate. It points to a fundamental practice of democracy: the discussion of issues that constitutes the common. This chapter examines whether the concept of the public sphere fits the capabilities, affordances and functioning of the digital realm. To answer this question, it presents different positions ranging from the shift from a public sphere to a private one (Zizi Papacharissi) to the critical study of social media, particularly Twitter, as suitable platforms to deliberate on political issues (Christian Fuchs). The analysis highlights how specifics characteristics of social platforms such as stratification, the asymmetrical power of visibility, the lack of genuine interactivity, or the capital accumulation model can foster or prevent social media from complying with the model of the public sphere. Lastly, the chapter discusses the digital practices of "Anonymous" as an example of a wider set of political interventions orchestrated by geeks and hackers.

Keywords: public sphere, political deliberation, democracy, agonistic pluralism, Twitter, public/private dichotomy, Anonymous.

Digital Media and/as the Public Sphere

Digital activism—in the many forms of connective action described under the umbrella term *contentious politics*—has been at the centre of the debate regarding the potential of digital media to foster democratisation, but an equally important part of the debate has been devoted to the internet as a space of political deliberation. The space of (online) deliberation is the discursive space in which a fundamental practice of democracy can be carried out: deliberative democracy or the discussion of issues that constitutes the common. Dahlberg defines deliberative democracy as one of the four pillars of online democracy (Dahlberg 2011). Chadwick (2009) also highlights that deliberative democracy is one of the central concepts in contemporary discussions on democracy and digital technology (Strandberg and Grönlund 2018). Unlike in the study of connective actions, which continually assesses the relationship between online and off-line spaces, here the off-line dimension is less taken into account. The focus of examination is mainly the online arena. Through this approach, the particular structure and affordances of platforms, especially social media such as Twitter and Facebook, come to the fore. Platforms are computational and architectural concepts, but also, in a socio-cultural and political sense, political stages and performative infrastructures (Gillespie 2010). "A platform is a *mediator* rather than an intermediary: it shapes the performance of social acts instead of merely facilitating them," as Van Dijck asserts (2013, 29). The off-line world is actually not absent from the discussion but rather incorporated in a different way, assuming the form of an ideal or a norm against which the contemporary potential of the internet is assessed. The paradigmatic ideal has long been the *public sphere*.

Public sphere is the term that has dominated the debate regarding the capabilities of digital media to foster democratic deliberation. Coined by Jürgen Habermas in his seminal book, *The Structural Transformation of the Public Sphere* (1989), the term "public sphere" refers to the domain of social life in which public opinion is articulated through rational public discourse and debate. The final goal of the public sphere is consensus- and decision-making, though these objectives may not necessarily always be achieved. The public sphere is a space in between the society and the state—a sphere which mediates between society and the state, in which the public organises itself as the bearer of public opinion, it must not be confused with public space or with public opinion—though the three terms are closely related to each other. Public space is a pre-condition of the public sphere: it must exist in order for the public sphere to convene but it does not guarantee it. Public opinion, on the other hand, also depends on certain prerequisites to be achieved—first and foremost reasoning, since, according to Habermas, public opinion can come into existence only when a reasoning public is presupposed, this distinguishes public opinion from individual citizens expressing a multifarious set of points of view about public affairs even if they do so in a public setting. In sum, the main characteristics of the public sphere are: 1) it is a forum for discussion about matters of general interest in which the public opinion is formed; 2) it is a forum that operates autonomously from the state and/or the economy; 3) it is a forum to which all citizens have free and equal access; and 4) it is a forum in which discussion is ruled by informed and rational reasoning (Friess and Eilders 2015).

Since its initial formulation, the concept of the public sphere has been the object of diverse critiques that point to a series of alleged shortcomings in Habermas's formulation. Many claim that the public sphere as described by Habermas idealises citizen engagement in past societies and fails to take into account the exclusion of significant parts of the population from the public sphere. In this vein, Fuchs' *working-class* critique stresses that "Habermas focuses on the bourgeois movement and neglects other popular movements that existed in the seventeenth, eighteenth and nineteenth centuries, such as the working-class movement" (Fuchs 2014, 181–82) while the *feminist* critique, represented paradigmatically by Fraser (1992) points out that the public sphere has long been a sphere of educated, rich men from which women as well as gays, lesbians and minority ethnicities were excluded. The voices of these collective identities are expressed in a plurality of spheres, or what Fraser calls "subaltern counterpublics" (1992, 123).

A second critique has to do not with the exclusion of certain populations but rather with that of one of the main assumptions upon which the public sphere is based, that is, the centrality of rational deliberation and consensus. Drawing on Derrida and his emphasis on undecidability as the necessary constant in any form of public deliberation, Lyotard (1984) argued that it is anarchy and disagreement, rather than rational deliberation and consensus, which leads to a genuine democracy. Thus, the question is not only if consensus is possible but if it is desirable. In this regard, one of the most well-known theories is that advanced by Chantal Mouffe (2000; 2005). Her concept of *agonistic pluralism* opposes the traditional liberal conception of democracy as a negotiation among diverse interests, and also the Habermasian notion of consensus, in which the management of conflict is possible only if people are able to leave aside their particular interests and think as rational beings. On the contrary, Mouffe puts forward that democratic theory needs to acknowledge the ineradicability of antagonism and the impossibility of achieving a fully inclusive rational consensus. What the model of the public sphere conceals is the centrality of power in social relations or, rather, it posits an ideal model in which power relations have been eliminated. As Mouffe explains,

> By postulating the availability of a public sphere where power and antagonism would have been eliminated and where a rational consensus would have been realized, this model of democratic politics denies the central role in politics of the conflictual dimension and its crucial role in the formation of collective identities ... but if we accept that relations of power are constitutive of the social, then the main question for democratic politics is not how to eliminate power but how to constitute forms of power more compatible with democratic values (Mouffe 1999, 752–53).

The model of agonistic pluralism that Mouffe puts forward does not try to eliminate confrontation—that is impossible since it is constitutive of the political—but works to transform *antagonism* into *agonism,* that is, to change a relation between enemies into a relation between adversaries:

> An "agonistic" democratic approach acknowledges the real nature of its frontiers and recognizes the forms of exclusion that they embody, instead of trying to disguise them under the veil of rationality or morality. Awareness of the fact that difference allows us to constitute unity and totality while simultaneously providing essential limits is an agonistic approach that contributes in the subversion of the ever-present temptation that exists in democratic societies to naturalize their frontiers and essentialize their identities. Such an approach would, therefore, be much more receptive than the deliberative democracy model to the multiplicity of voices that a pluralist society encompasses, and to the complexity of the power structure that this network of differences implies (Mouffe 1999, 757).

These nodes of debate appear each time the deliberative potential of virtual space to become the new public sphere is discussed. In particular: 1) the question of the exclusion of certain voices or groups in the debate, and 2) the nature of the debate itself—is this a rational deliberation occurring in online conversations or is it more about noise, where voices manifest themselves in chaos and provide no real space for discussion?

A Private Sphere

The nature of the public sphere in the age of the digital is precisely the issue addressed by Zizi Papacharissi in her book *A Private Sphere: Democracy in a Digital Age* (2010). The title already anticipates her main argument: in the digital age, the public sphere has shifted into a private one.

Before presenting her thesis, Papacharissi reviews the vast literature on this topic to show that, as formulated by Habermas, the concept of the public sphere does not fit the capabilities, affordances and functioning of the digital realm. These arguments can be summarised as follows:

Firstly, although digital media provide a public space, they do not necessarily provide a public sphere. More access to information does not translate into more participation or political commitment. Furthermore, even if the digital divide—the social and economic inequality in the access to, use of or impact of the internet—had all lost relevance, there are still meaningful differences in usage beyond the issue of access. The internet is not that "outer world" described by John Barlow in his "Declaration of Independence," "a world that all may enter without privilege or prejudice accorded by race, economic power, military force, or station of birth" (Barlow 1996); in fact, it reproduces the inequalities of class, gender and race that exist in the offline public sphere. "Finally, the information access the internet provides also typically results in entertainment uses of the medium (Althaus and Tewksbury, 2000; Shah et al., 2001), the public sphere relevance of which is arguable (Moy et al., 2005; Dahlgren, 2005)" (Papacharissi 2009, 234).

Secondly, the occurrence of reciprocity in online discussions is also doubtful. Reciprocity implies that communication is a two-way bridge on a topic of interest to both parties, often governed by mutual compromise, with respect and rationality as guiding rules. However, it is not reciprocity that dominates online conversations. In actuality, online conversations tend to be unstructured, fragmented, dominated by a small number of voices, and too specific in focus to be close to the ideal of public sphere. Therefore, the result of the conversation is not a substantial discussion or of great political impact (Jones 1997; Schement and Curtis 1995; Papacharissi 2009, 235).

Finally, commercialisation presents a primary concern for researchers who examine the potential of the virtual sphere. The capitalist logic that governs the internet today is marked by commercial interests and hegemonic media conglomerates—what has been called FAANG: Facebook, Apple, Amazon, Netflix and Google, an acronym for grouping together currently high-performance technology companies that dominates the digital sphere. The objects and concerns of these companies are not necessarily in line with promoting the common good that is the basis of the Habermasian public sphere. Other arguments underline how mainstream legal tendencies can restrict the internet's democratising potential or how creative factions are colonised by commercial ones, with the result that content becomes standardised (Papacharissi 2009, 236).

This leads Papacharissi—in agreement with many other scholars—to conclude that, while online digital technologies create a public space, they do not inevitably enable a public sphere: "A new public space is not synonymous with a new public sphere, in that a virtual space simply enhances discussion; a virtual sphere should enhance democracy" (Papacharissi 2009, 236). This does not necessarily imply a failure of the internet, but rather an incorrect way of assessing the new possibilities offered by digital media: "[i]t is not online technologies that fail the public sphere test; rather it could be the other around. This does not necessarily suggest a failure of the online political apparatus; it could merely suggest that the language we use to describe online technologies routinely underestimates their potential" (Papacharissi 2009, 236). In order to capture what the genuine contribution of the internet to democracy is, Papacharissi proposes to understand the space previously defined as the public sphere as a new kind of space defined as the *private sphere*. Here, "private" does not simply stand in opposition to public—therefore representing the decline in or the loss of a common space—but rather it heralds a crucial shift in the articulation of the public/private dichotomy.

The distinction between public and private has long been one of the central concerns of political, social and moral analysis in Western thought, a binary opposition that subsumes a wide field of other distinctions and tries to dichotomise the social universe into clearly demarcated categories. To use Norberto Bobbio's useful phrase, the public/private distinction stands out as one of the "grand dichotomies" of Western thought (Bobbio 1996).

The public/private distinction is not unitary, but protean. Different conceptions of public and private emerge from different theoretical languages or universes of discourse, each with its own cargo of connotations and presuppositions (Weintraub 1997, 3–4). Yet, as Weintraub notes:

> At the deepest and most general level, lying behind the different forms of public/private distinction are (at least) *two* fundamental, and analytically quite distinct, kinds of imagery in terms of which "private" can be contrasted with "public": 1. What is hidden or withdrawn versus what is open, revealed, or accessible. 2. What is individual, or pertains only to an individual, versus what is collective, or affects the interests of a collectivity of individuals. This individual/collective distinction can, by extension, take the form of a distinction between part and whole (of some social collectivity). We might refer to these two underlying criteria as "visibility" (audibility being one component) and "collectivity" (Weintraub 1997, 4–5).

It is a commonplace to say that one of the most visible effects of the internet has been to call into question the boundaries between public and private. The changing parameters of this distinction are being played out today in the social, cultural and legal arenas—from the recent Facebook scandals with Cambridge Analytica to the new European laws on the protection of personal data. Papacharissi places this dichotomy at the centre of her proposal, effecting a displacement of the conventional question: her question is not to what extent the internet fits into the concept of the public as formulated in the Habermasian public sphere, but in what ways it compels us to rethink the public. In assessing this new space, Papacharissi seems to overlap two imaginaries of the public: the public as opposed to the individual, and the public as the contrary of what is hidden or withdrawn. This produces a displacement of the first imaginary into the second one. The political material that is posted online and starts conversations is not so much public in the sense that pertains to the common, but rather public because opinions that would otherwise remain hidden or withdrawn are now disclosed online.

One of the most persistent adjectives to describe internet culture has been "narcissistic." Digital media, as we described them in the previous chapter, promote the personalisation of (political) content: citizens define what is important to them, even if in principle it is not of concern to the broader community, and are encouraged to express their views, political opinions or concerns from the singularity of their own circumstances. Political opinions posted on blogs or social media are self-referential and motivated by personal fulfilment. While the narcissistic character of digital culture has been assessed negatively as an undermining of the public, Papacharissi, conversely, finds a positive connotation. Following *The Culture of Narcissism* (1979) by Christopher Lasch, she asserts that the self-preoccupation associated with our culture "arises not from complacency but from desperation" (Lasch, 1979, 26); the New Narcissus gazes at his/her own reflection "not so much in admiration as in unremitting search of flaws, signs of fatigue, decay" (Lasch quoted in Paparachissi 2009, 238). It is "*this particular breed of* narcissism [that] has a democratizing effect" (Papacharissi 2009, 238). That effect has to do with expanding the public agenda and making it more porous by incorporating a plurality of voices. Drawing on Mouffe's proposal of agonistic pluralism, Papacharissi asserts that the relevance of new media lies in these acts of dissent, the challenging of the distinction that separates public and private being at the core of them.

Strikingly, these potentially powerful acts of dissent emanate from a private sphere of interaction, meaning that the citizen engages and is enabled politically through a private media environment located within the individual's personal and private space. Whereas in the truest iterations of democracy the citizen was enabled through the public sphere, in contemporary democracy the citizen acts politically from a private sphere of reflection, expression and behaviour. Within this private sphere, the citizen is alone, but not lonely or isolated. Connected, the citizen operates in a mode and with political language determined by him or her. Primarily still monitorial in orientation, the citizen is able to become an agonist of democracy, if needed, but in an atomised mode (Papacharissi 2009, 244–245). What prevents us from becoming alienated in this exclusive private sphere or, in Arendt's words, what provides the specific and usually irreplaceable "in between" connecting the individual and his fellow men? Papacharissi's answer is somewhat tautological: "it is precisely this 'in-between', which, as individuals act civically from the locus of the private sphere, is filled in by online digital media" (2009, 244).

In Papacharissi's view, this private sphere contributes to achieving the agonistic model formulated by Mouffe. Therefore, even it does not contribute to the rational deliberation that defines the public sphere, Papacharissi nevertheless has a very positive assessment of the role of the internet because, in her view, Mouffe's model better captures a more authentic—and desirable—version of democracy than the

Habermasian model. From this perspective, Papacharissi can be placed on the side of the cyber-optimists.

Twitter and Democracy

Contrary to Papacharissi, Christian Fuchs's position represents a more sceptical view. He approaches the study of social media with a critical perspective, meaning, in his own words, a perspective "concerned with the question of power" (Fuchs 2014, 7). When examining social media or digital culture at large we can ask questions with or without a concern for power. For example, we can ask: Who uses social media? For what purposes are social media used? What do people communicate about on social media? What are the most popular social media platforms? How can politicians and parties best use social media to obtain more votes in the next elections? Or how can an NGO make use of social media to attract participants for a cause? These are typical questions that we normally encounter in the study of social media. According to Fuchs, the problem they share is that they do not interrogate power. Interrogating power means asking who benefits from using social media and how those benefits to a few are obtained to the detriment of others. Questions that neglect these kinds of power dynamics are based on a particularistic logic—to put it simply, they are concerned with only one side of the coin, while ignoring the other one.

One example is to be found in the uncritical question of how companies can take advantage of social media. What is overshadowed in this question is the working conditions within these companies that make these benefits possible - the wealth gap between the well-off managers and shareholders on the one hand, and the precarious situation of poorly-paid workers on the other. Asking critical questions means interrogating the economic, social and cultural conditions that produce and sustain inequalities, as well as how media is intertwined with these conditions.

That the history of digital technology "is deeply embedded into the history of capitalism, colonialism, warfare, exploitation and inequality" (Fuchs 2014, 10) is not a novelty. Yet we frequently forget the dark connections between technology and society. In *IBM and the Holocaust* (2001), Edwin Black—mentioned by Fuchs—exposed how the German and other European subsidiaries of the multi-national corporation International Business Machines (IBM) collaborated with the Nazis by selling them punched card systems which the Nazis used for numbering the victims and organising transport to the concentration and extermination camps. This works as a dark reminder that the origins of the internet are rooted in the military-industrial complex and first served the interests of war rather than of peace.

Coming back to what he views as the correct questions that a study on social media should pose, Fuchs gives the following examples, some of which take us back to the previous chapter on the role of digital media in alter-globalisation movements:

> Which power structures are underlying contemporary revolutions and protests? How do they influence the use of social media? Which problems and limits do alternative, non-profit and non-commercial platforms face in capitalist society, in which the control of resources (money, time, attention, influence, etc.) is asymmetrically distributed? How can activists best handle the contradiction between increased public visibility and increased police surveillance? How can Facebook use be labour even though it is so different from working in coal mine and feels more like singing with friends at a campfire? Can something be exploitation even though it does not feel like exploitation and is fun? Do users actually think about corporate social media use as labour? And how to trade unions, data protection agencies or privacy advocates react to the existence of this digital labour? (Fuchs 2014, 8–10).

Drawing on Critical Theory and informed by a Marxist approach, Fuchs interrogates the possibilities of the internet to constitute a public sphere. One of the differences with Papacharissi's approach is that Fuchs chooses to focus not on the internet at large, but on a particular platform, Twitter, which has often been considered to be the most political social media platform. There is an extensive body of literature on Twitter that ranges from case studies focusing on concrete social movements or particular topics—for example, Twitter Mini-Publics in the German National Election in 2013 (Einspänner-Pflock, Anastasiadis and Thimm 2016) or the role of Twitter ecology in the 2012 Local Elections in Belgium (D'heer and Verdegem 2014)—to more general studies that research the specificity of Twitter in relation to other platforms (Murthy 2013; Van Dijck 2013; Fuchs 2014). The dichotomy between cyber-optimists and cyber-pessimists is especially apparent in this research on Twitter, in which we find books where the platform is alternately heralded as a tool to fight against authoritarian regimes, as in Papacharissi's *Affective Publics. Sentiments, Technology and Politics* (2015), or a privileged instrument of other forms of authoritarianism, as in Fuchs's *Digital Demagogue: Authoritarian Capitalism in the Age of Trump and Twitter* (2018), to stick to the two authors we have already commented upon.

So why, for Fuchs, is Twitter not an update of the public sphere? To begin with, the typical Twitter user in 2013 was young (between 18 and 34 years old), had a university degree, and had no children. This typical user shows that unequal access to digital media—the digital divide—continues, despite all the announcements about its death. It should be noted, however, that inequality today is not so much to do with access itself but with a difference in the use of technology and in the skills required for that use. In this sense, Twitter does not guarantee equal access to deliberation; in other words, large segments of Twitter's user population do not participate in political debate.

Secondly, statistics show that Twitter topics are dominated by entertainment. Politics occupies a marginal place—in 2009, only 7% of the top Twitter trend topics were political topics; in 2010, only 3% were politics (Fuchs 2014, 190). The same goes for users with more followers: celebrities attract the most attention. In addition, the most popular political actors are influential mainstream political actors, such as Donald Trump, CNN or the *New York Times*, while alternative figures such as Michael Moore have comparatively much less visibility. In short, Twitter presents an asymmetric visibility: those who have power, fame, money or power outside Twitter tend to have many more followers and their tweets are re-tweeted much more frequently than those of ordinary people. The democratic potentials thus remain at a theoretical level. Thus far, the potential of ordinary people to amplify their voices and circulate their opinion in the form of re-tweets has not been realized—or at least not in a significant way—in the actual operation of the platform.

Thirdly, the degree of interaction is limited. This is crucial because the idea of deliberation does not consist in the mere expression of a political opinion but in the exchange of opinions. For example, Fuchs comments on his own analysis of the WikiLeaks and Egyptian revolution cases. To see the degree of interaction, the tweets were categorised as either purely informative, re-tweets of another post, or comments on another tweet (Fuchs 2014, 192–194). The results show that more than 50% of the postings are re-tweets in both cases and there is a low level of commenting (23.1% and 12.9% respectively) (Fuchs 2014, 193). As re-tweeting is also a form of information, the total level of information provision was 76.9% in the WikiLeaks case and 87.1% in the Egyptian case (Fuchs 2014, 193).

The same happens in the case of comments. This example shows that "mutual symbolic interaction is rare in political Twitter communication and that Twitter communication mostly consists of one-way comments" (Fuchs 2014, 193). Regardless of the potential of the platform, what is verified by looking at actual use once again highlights how Twitter falls short of the interactive ideal that underlies the public sphere.

Fourthly, the visibility of users also depends on the economic model that sustains Twitter. As Van Dijck points out in her analysis of social media, *The Culture of Connectivity: A Critical History of Social Media* (2013), platforms are both techno-cultural constructs and socio-economic structures. In approaching platforms as techno-cultural constructs, research must take into account technology, users and content, whereas, when highlighting platforms as socio-economic structures, the research focuses on their ownership status, governance and business models (Van Dijck 2013). As social media platforms evolve so do business models, which are constantly adapting, in a continuous negotiation between what the users accept and what the company needs.

In the case of Twitter, the platform started as a profit-oriented corporation without a business model, but after different experiences they implemented a business model in 2011 based on targeted advertising. There are three mechanisms through which someone can improve the visibility: *promoted tweets, promoted trends* and *promoted accounts*. Simply put, this means that when you search for trends or accounts, you will see not those trends or accounts that get more attention but those tweets, accounts and trends defined as significant by Twitter's advertising clients. If you are a user or a company with an advertising budget you can easily buy attention; on the contrary, if you are an ordinary citizen trying to make your opinion heard—even if your political opinion is a real contribution to the political debate—you will find it hard to gain attention.

In addition to all this, Fuchs raises the question whether meaningful political debates can be based on 140-character short messages (2014, 200).

In sum: stratification, the asymmetrical power of visibility, the lack of genuine interactivity, and the capital accumulation model prevent Twitter from complying with the model of the public sphere.

It is necessary to underline that Fuchs does not choose to replace the Habermasian formulation with another model of democracy—such as that of Chantal Mouffe, in the case of Papacharissi—suggesting that the achievements of the internet are proven if consensus and rational deliberation are not privileged above dissent and pluralism. Fuchs instead rehabilitates Habermas, underlining that the public sphere is a critical concept, coined by Habermas precisely to show the limits and contradictions that the public sphere acquired in bourgeoisie society.

In this sense, the public sphere is a useful concept "that helps to analyse whether modern society lives up to its own expectations" (Fuchs 2014, 207). As Fuchs notes,

> Twitter is not a public sphere. It should neither be the subject of hope for the renewal of democracy and publication, nor the cause of concerns about violence and riots. What should first and foremost concern us is inequality in society and how to alleviate inequality. Habermas's notion of the public sphere has not primarily been about the media, but about the creation of a concept that allows the criticism of structures that lack public concerns about common goods and limit the availability of the commons for all people ...
>
> Strengthening the commons requires common struggle, which also involves, among other things, common communication. The struggle for a commons-based society that overcomes neoliberalism should also be the struggle for communication commons. The stratified structures of Twitter are an expression of the limits of the public sphere. Another society is possible. Is another Twitter possible? (Fuchs 2014, 207).

Anonymous

On 21 January 2008, the video "Message to Scientology" was posted on YouTube. In the video, we see black clouds ploughing through a desolate urban landscape while we listen to a disembodied computer-generated voice that emits the following message:

> Hello, Scientology. We are Anonymous. Over the years, we have been watching you. Your campaigns of misinformation; your suppression of dissent; your litigious nature, these things have caught our eye. With the leakage of your latest propaganda video into mainstream circulation, the extent of your malign influence over those who have come to trust you as leaders has been made clear to us. Anonymous has therefore decided that your organization should be destroyed. For the good of your followers, for the good of mankind—and for our own enjoyment—we shall expel

> you from the Internet and systematically dismantle the Church of Scientology in its
> present form ... You have nowhere to hide because we are everywhere ...
> Knowledge is free. We are Anonymous. We are Legion. We do not forgive. We do
> not forget. Expect us (Church0fScientology 2008).

Part of a campaign against the Church of Scientology that included attacks on the organisation's website and street protests in which participants wore Guy Fawkes masks popularised by the V for Vendetta franchise, this was the first act that made Anonymous known in the public sphere. Two years later, in 2010, Anonymous gained notoriety with Operation Payback, in which they coordinated a series of DDoS attacks against PayPal, MasterCard, Amazon, Postfinance and Visa in support of WikiLeaks. The connection between WikiLeaks and Anonymous is significant. As Gabriella Coleman points out, both are examples of digital-based politics that are very different from each other while at the same time "belonging to the same family" (2011, 511). WikiLeaks is associated with one figure, Julian Assange, and his project. Anonymous, on the other hand, "is premised on a robust antileader, anticelebrity ethics, and its operations are open to all who care to contribute" (Coleman 2011, 511). Nonetheless, both are "examples of a much broader set of political interventions orchestrated by geeks and hackers" (Coleman 2011, 511).

The origins of Anonymous can be traced back to 4chan.org, a message board-based manga site founded by Christopher Pool in 2003. The board is dedicated to random posts, organised in different forums around particular interests that range from video to fashion, politics or even "random" posts. 4chan is not just a site in which people talk about their interests or discuss politics in a rational and educated manner, exchanging arguments and seeking to reach consensus that the description of the public sphere evokes—quite the contrary. To a certain extent, the kind of conversations that take place in the site could be considered the opposite of the idealised rational discourse of the public sphere. Here is an example of a conversation on 4chan.org:

> A rapper writes a new song and says that the first few minutes of the discussion
> in his thread will become part of the song. There is a story about a brother who
> tries to seduce his sister, but it turns out that his sister is a large arthropod. There
> is a thread with images of female buttocks, accompanied by an announcement that
> one of the portrayed girls receives prank phone calls. One sees a picture of a couple

having oral sex accompanied by the text "PORNO FUCK YEAH!" as well as a picture of a drunk sleeping man accompanied by the text "buddy passed out after 11 Coors lights and 2 bud lights" and the suggestion that a game will decide what the person who posted the picture will do to the drunk. There is a screenshot of a female teenager's profile on Facebook, suggesting "54, 72, 37 or 00 decides what I write," meaning that the fifty-fourth, seventy-second, thirty-seventh or hundredth posting determines what the person will write to the girl on Facebook. The subsequent interaction is posted online (e.g., "Hi, i liked you since high school i wanted to date you, but I was very young and very angry, perhaps that's no excuse. You're really hot and whenever i see you my wee wee goes woop, please go out with me or I'll skyrim myself"), the girl answers and each answer to her is determined in a new game. The girl temporarily closes her Facebook profile and the action ceases. Welcome to 4chan.org. (Fuchs 2015, 88–89).

Several features distinguish communication on the site, which has come to constitute a distinct digital culture. "The culture of the board was, and is, one of breaking limits, the grotesque, pornographic images, ironic humour, memes, trolling and lulz" (McDonald 2015, 972). For Fuchs, "4chan is at the same time anarchistic, mean, rude, absurd, pornographic, political, creative, playful, sarcastic, a display of black humour" (Fuchs 2015, 89). It was 4chan, for instance, that created the LOLcat meme, a macro image of a funny cat accompanied by a caption that is often grammatically incorrect. It was the first of many memes to find mainstream popularity outside 4chan, ultimately spawning other websites and even books (Olson 2012, 60). Olson comments that it was also in an online discussion on the site that the word 'lulz' was coined:

> In 2003, a forum moderator on another site was commenting on something funny when he suddenly typed "lulz!" Others in the chat room started repeating it, and it spread from there. "It was far superior to lol," Weev later remembered. Eventually, "I did it for the lulz" or just "for the lulz" would become a symbol of Internet culture and Anonymous itself, as well as an ever-popular catchphrase on 4chan (Olson 2012, 60).

'Lulz'—a corruption of Laugh Out Loud—is paradigmatic of the communicative practices that define 4chan and, as it spreads on the internet, a spirit that dominates much of internet discourse. The phrase "I did it for the lulz" conveys the idea that humour and fun are the main motivations—although not necessarily the only ones—behind an action, even if this action involves addressing themes as serious as the limiting of freedom of speech by authoritarian regimes. Humour becomes a political weapon that combines irony and critique, as well as a form of cruelty.

This is closely associated with the phenomenon of "trolling," which should not be equated to the common idea of online harassment. Trolling, as McDonald argues following Coleman, "is a form of action that seeks to trick the person being trolled into revealing a hidden identity. The aim of trolling is to provoke a reaction that is not one of simple frustration or anger, but a *reaction that reveals a truth* that the person reacting is either concealing, or may not even be aware of" (McDonald 2015, 973). Trolling could be another word to signal the sort of disruptions and practices that define Anonymous.

After attracting world-wide attention in 2010 with Operation Payback in support of WikiLeaks, Anonymous carried out many actions aimed at different targets. In 2010, Anonymous attacked Australian government websites in rejection of new laws that tried to censor the Internet. In the same year, they attacked the websites of organisations that defended intellectual property rights such as the Recording Industry Association of America (RIAA). In 2011, Anonymous organised a series of actions under the name of "Operation Tunisia" in support of the Arab Spring movements. For example, they created a script that the Tunisians could use to protect their web browsers from government surveillance and hacked-into government servers—including that of Prime Minister Mohamed Ghannouchi, which was replaced with an Anonymous message. They also attacked government websites in Bahrain, Egypt, Libya and Jordan. These actions were replicated with a variety of targets and practices that included not only the hacking of websites but also the publication of personal data—another method often used by Anonymous—as in the case of Nazi-Leaks, a platform which publishes data of alleged neo-Nazis and their supporters (Fuchs 2015, 90–91).

What values sustain Anonymous's digital activism? Although disputed and contradictory, these digital practices share a series of principles. First, and in a very general sense, Anonymous defends freedom—of expression, of information circulation, of access and ownership of the media. That freedom is played, exercised and disputed in the existential space of the web. Unlike the digital activism that we discussed earlier in relation to networked social movements or different types of connective actions, in which on-line and off-line dimensions are combined and fed back, Anonymous embodies an *essentially* digital activism. "Essentially digital" implies that, although protests or marches are also practices in which they participate, the main actors in the movement are so-called hackers and geeks.

Anonymous has made use of tactics such as DDoS attacks, anonymous phone calls, mobbing, publication of private data, death threats, sending black pages to fax addresses, ordering hundreds of pizzas to be delivered to one address simultaneously (Reissmann, Stöcker, and Lischka 2012), doxing (posting personal data about targets publicly on the internet), signing people up for junk mail, defacing websites, hacking into servers, downloading databases from servers with the help of SQL injection attacks, publishing e-mail and address lists (Fuchs 2015, 91).

These practices are characterised as digital activism not only because they imply a digital expertise, but also because they are practices that, by placing themselves in permanent tension with what is legal, question in that same gesture what is defined as legal and who defines what is legal in the digital world. For the members of the movement (or collective or anti-movement, as the very definition of what Anonymous is is in dispute) an association that defends copyright rights—such as the RIAA, the Motion Picture Association of America (MPAA) or Copyright Alliance, an anti-infringement group which was the target of Anonymous during 2010—become objects of attack inasmuch as they violate the free flow of information and therefore the right to access by users:

> Anonymous is tired of corporate interests controlling the internet and silencing the people's rights to spread information, but more importantly, the right to SHARE with one another. The RIAA and the MPAA feign to aid the artists and their cause; yet they do no such thing. In their eyes is not hope, only dollar signs. Anonymous will not stand this any longer (Tsotsis 2011).

The perspective of these organisations is, of course, a different one: copyright is a right protected by law and its defence is necessary, beyond the practices that enable the culture of the internet. Anonymous instead embodies a concept of freedom according to which the internet is—or should be—the space in which information circulates freely and to which everyone can have unrestricted access. Some of the principles of the movement that have been included in "5 Principles: An Anonymous Manifesto" underscore as essential that information must be "unrestricted and uncensored" and that the privacy of citizens "shall not be the target of any undue" surveillance" (Anonymous, quoted in Fuchs 2015, 95).

For some scholars, this position reflects a liberal sensibility that is at the base of Anonymous, since freedom, freedom of speech, privacy and individualism are also the values that liberalism promotes. However, rather than a full incarnation of the liberal ideology, what Anonymous expresses is its contradictions. As Fuchs states, "Anonymous to a certain degree aligns itself with the language of the free individual that characterizes contemporary liberalism, but at the same time expresses the contradictions of liberalism" (2015, 99). These contradictions are intrinsically linked not only with the fact that liberalism is already a contradictory ideology and that there are many "variants of liberalism," as stressed by Stuart Hall, but also with the evolution of the relationship between liberalism and technology, which during the 1980s transformed the 1970s countercultural ethos of public information into the ideology of "communicative capitalism" (Fuchs 2015, 99). Thus, although liberalism postulates individual freedoms as a universal value, its own reality permanently undermines this value, since material and political benefits are appropriated by an elite who profit from the supposed freedom of the public. Anonymous—among other movements, such as the politicised free software movement—argues that culture, code and technology are commons that should be available to all.

Another fundamental point, which is revealed both in the ethics and in the aesthetics of the movement, is the value given to anonymity. The name itself comes from 4chan.org where users are designated as anonymous by default. It condenses a complex core of debates around the issues of visibility, transparency and privacy on the web.

Anonymous designates at the same time an individual and a collective; by not being singularised, by not identifying a particular individual, Anonymous is anyone and at the same time (potentially) all—a legion. Unlike Facebook, where individuals are permanently forced to define themselves through the data they offer—the films they like, their political inclinations, their favourite pastimes, their life trajectories—thereby making themselves a commodity, Anonymous's refusal to identify itself challenges this logic of surveillance and commodification of the self. This logic is not simply concealment. It proposes a more complex dialectic between what is seen and what is hidden and the uniqueness that results from this game. McDonald (2015) points out the parallel between this strategy and the structure of the images that predominated in the "I am the 99%" campaign during the Occupy Wall Street protests. In these images, an individual holds a poster in which a message is read where he or she tells her or his personal experience and ends with the slogan "I am the 99%." The images put the poster in the foreground, while the face behind is only partially visible, eclipsed by the message itself. "I am the 99%" is a variant of "We are the 99%," although substantially different. It is not an individual representing a collective but individuals communicating their own specificity: "They're not just 'indebted students', 'the uninsured', 'the foreclosed'. They're THIS indebted student, they're THIS uninsured person, they're THIS person whose home was foreclosed. Specificity has great power" (Weinstein 2011, quoted in McDonald 2015, 977). It is in the singularity of the message itself—and not in the identity of the individual—that the communicative act is sustained. The notion of identity is questioned as "fragile and weak," "something that can be stolen or replaced" and thus susceptible of being refused: "Why not let it go and become Anonymous", invites one of Anon's posts (McDonald 2015, 978).

As the post makes clear, the way in which identity is defined is dependent on a digital self that is built by and through digital media, a self that is at the same time an object of surveillance and of commodification. If social media, as Van Dijck (2013) asserts, renders people's activities formal, manageable and manipulable, thereby enabling platforms to engineer sociality, then Anonymous's lack of identity points in the opposite direction, and marks the internet as the territory where this struggle takes place. In a more radical sense than any other form of digital politics, Anonymous makes the internet and digital media the space of dispute, contesting the laws, practices and impositions of governments and corporations.

To sum up: what is Anonymous? It has been called, among other things, a movement, an anti-movement, a collective, a group of geeks and hackers, a criminal organisation, human rights advocates who organise collective actions that advance political causes but also do them "for the lulz," a legion that fights for a fair and free (digital) society. The answer to this question depends on how we evaluate these political practices, and how we evaluate them is closely linked to the dichotomy between cyber-optimism and cyber-scepticism. If Anonymous demonstrates anything it is that the disputes raised by Barlow's 1996 "Declaration of the Independence of Cyberspace" around what is, can be and should be the role of the digital in the politics of our era are still alive. They continue to inform the way we think and shape technology, as well as the way technology shapes us.

9 Digital Self

This chapter seeks to delve into how digital technologies have impacted the construction of the self, giving rise to what can be termed a "digital self." The digital self refers to how we represent ourselves to others in a networked environment. This highlights the subject's agency, that is, their ability to choose which media to use, for what purpose, and to produce what knowledge about themselves. After examining the role of performativity and the characteristics of networked communities, we focus on three different modes of self-presentations in digital media: written, visual, and quantitative—texts, images, and numbers. These modes of self-presentation are placed in a long history, highlighting the continuities with previous forms, for example, the link between blogs and diaries, or the visual forms and self-portraits. Special attention is paid to the "selfie" as a paradigmatic visual representation in online culture. Although the selfie has been criticised for its narcissistic character, we claim here that this form goes beyond a mere example of banality: many of the forms of self-presentation contained in this allegedly modest formula clearly go beyond the stigma of narcissism.

Keywords: self-representation, relational self, identity, social interaction, performativity, social network sites, networked publics, (digital) diaries, selfie, narcissism.

This chapter seeks to delve into how digital technologies have impacted the construction of the self, giving rise to what can be termed a "digital self." This refers, broadly speaking, to the way in which we define ourselves—that is, what we individualise as a distinct and singular I—how others (including non-human others) define us, how the digital communities in which we participate provide us with or deprive us of intimacy, meaningful ties and a sense of belonging, and, finally, how the self becomes just another commodity in the digital landscape. The digital self thus refers, on the one hand, to how we represent ourselves to others in a networked environment. This highlights the subject's agency, that is, their ability to choose which media to use, for what purpose, and to produce what knowledge about themselves. On the other hand, it refers to the way in which digital technologies seemingly autonomously build a self through the collection of dispersed data, beyond our control and even beyond our agreement. These two selves are intertwined but, at the same time, they can collide. This is sharply illustrated, for instance, in the debates that surrounded the EU's Right to be Forgotten regulation. This chapter will first address the former component of the digital self, focusing on the mediated construction of the subject and the networked communities in which this construction is performed. In the last part of the chapter we will address the issue from the latter perspective, dealing with the self not as a subject but as an object of surveillance that results from the operations performed by digital media, in particular, interrogating the extent to which this object resembles or disturbingly mirrors what we consider to be ourselves.

The Relational Self and the "Networked Community"

The pronoun "I" designates a singular person, more concretely, the subject of the discourse who pronounces the word "I." This act, through which the subject distinguishes himself from the objects of the world as well as from other subjects, marks this entity as a singular one and promotes the illusion that the self is an autonomous entity that can be defined in isolation from the entities that surround it. The myth of autonomy makes us forget that identity is always a relational phenomenon and that, more than an entity that can be defined in isolation, the self is always defined by—and lives in terms of—its relations with others. The self is always a relational self (Eakin 1999).

Identity is not a fixed or essential entity that remains unchanged over time, nor is it a kind of essence or truth that constitutes the subject, which has to be discovered or unfolded over the course of a life. Identity is, on the contrary, a changing position that we constantly negotiate through social interaction. In face-to-face communication, a complex semiotic exchange takes place: we choose certain signs that seek to define ourselves, signs that become intelligible for others and say who we are—our clothing, gestures, vocabulary. These others read these signs and interpret them to decode our performance. In social interaction, we adapt our performance to the assumed expectations and cultural codes that are appropriate for that particular situation—let us think, for example, of the different performances involved in attending a formal party with our colleagues or an informal one with close friends. In his seminal work, *The Presentation of Self in Everyday Life* (1959), Erving Goffman stressed how face-to-face interaction is orchestrated as a theatrical representation in which the I *performs* its role in front of an audience while being at the same time an audience for its viewers' play. The self becomes an actor enacting a role on a setting composed of a stage and a backstage. They follow a script that carefully takes into account the setting in which the performance takes place, seeking to adapt themselves to this framework. As the self-presentation theory proposed by Goffman highlights, even face-to-face interaction, the most seemingly direct and unmediated interaction, is far from spontaneous or natural; on the contrary, it involves the conscious effort of the self to perform its role adequately. The idea that personal interaction is not mediated—or is less mediated—is thus a wrongful assumption. As Miller *et al.* put it when commenting on authenticity, "when we meet, face to face communication is thoroughly mediated by conventions and etiquette regarding appropriate behavior between those in conversation. Rules of kinship can limit what someone is allowed to say just as effectively as technological limits … For anthropologists, therefore, communicating online can be regarded as a shift in cultural mediation, but it does not make a relationship more mediated (Miller et al. 2016, 102). Similarly, Fortunati (2005) questions that face-to-face communication—or body-to-body communication, as she chooses to term it—should be the prototype for mediated communication. For her, body-to-body communication intermingles profoundly with forms of mediated communication, to the point that it becomes complicated to tell them apart. Moreover, mediated communication possesses a "great imitative capacity with regard to body-to-body communication" (Fortunati 2005, 53), a similarity that, according to Fortunati, is destined to grow in time. Nevertheless, even mediated, the advantage of face-to-face interaction relies on the fact that we are performing in front of a particular audience, or what Goffman refers to as a particular "frame" (1959, 33), which helps us to set boundaries by establishing rules and expectations to guide behaviour. We can therefore interpret the reaction of others and correct our behaviour if it is necessary.

In a digital environment, social interaction is technologically mediated. The theatrical performance described by Goffman as structuring social interaction remains valid in capturing the general picture; in fact, digital interaction strongly evokes this deliberate effort to perform a self in front of an audience which immediately "likes" or "dislikes" our presentation. At the same time, the scenery in which the digital self is enacted shows significant differences when compared not only to face-to-face exchange but also to other technologically mediated interactions. We should regard, as Miller *et al.* suggest, "offline and online as two 'frames' in our daily life that may trigger different attitudes and behaviors" (2016, 103–104). In this sense, we could state that in a digital environment the relational self becomes a networked self. The identity of this networked self is derived from the interactions that take place in the particular kind of audience or community that is made up primarily of social network sites. As social media—Facebook, Twitter, LinkedIn, Instagram, to name just the most well-known ones—are the main digital platforms on which we socially interact today, we will focus on social network sites to analyse the online self-presentation and the networked communities that these selves constitute. As the ideas of the networked individual and the networked public are interrelated, in what follows we will address first the main traits of a networked public as outlined by boyd (2011, styled lowercase) in order to then place the self as a node which is constituted by the links it establishes within this network.

According to boyd and Ellison (2008) social network sites are

> [W]eb-based services that allow individuals to (1) construct a public or semi-public profile within a bounded system, (2) articulate a list of other users with whom they share a connection, and (3) view and traverse their list of connections and those made by others within the system. The nature and nomenclature of these connections may vary from site to site (boyd and Ellison 2008, 211).

boyd and Ellison prefer the term "social network site" (SNS) to describe this phenomenon rather than "social *networking* site" because the adjective "networking" stresses relationship initiation, suggesting that people primarily use SNSs to establish new relationships with strangers. Establishing new relationships is not, nevertheless, the norm on SNSs. People use Facebook, Twitter or My Space to get in touch with friends, family members or acquaintances they know from the off-line world. Social media are embedded in our daily life and have an increasingly crucial role in sustaining personal relationships. In this sense, what makes social network sites distinctive is not that they allow individuals to meet new people, even if "latent ties" (Haythornthwaite 2005, 136) are sometimes cultivated, but rather that "they enable users to articulate and make visible their social networks" (boyd and Ellison 2008, 211).

For boyd, social network sites are to be understood as a genre of networked publics. Networked publics are, simultaneously "1) the space constructed through networked technologies and 2) the imagined collective that emerges as a result of the intersection of people, technology, and practice" (boyd 2011, 39). Therefore, networked publics designate at the same time a collection of people, an "imagined community" (Anderson 2006) and the particular space that is constructed through the practices of the members of that community. This space is not (only) *material geography*—we log on to Facebook to see the updates of our friends on the screens of our laptops or our smartphones—but also the *symbolic* and *imaginary geography* through which we attempt to make sense of our networked world. Drawing on Jackson, Crang and Dwyer's description of transnational spaces, we could assert that networked publics are also spaces that are "*complex, multidimensional and multiply inhabited*" (2004, 3).

What distinguishes SNSs is the combination of the following features: first, they allow the construction of a public or semi-public profile; second, they make it possible to articulate a list of users with whom the owner of the profile has a connection; and, finally, they make visible the connections that link users to each other—making what once could have been hidden into a visible entity.

The profile acts as the first presentation tool and, as such, it is fundamental as the first act of writing the self. On Facebook, for example, the profile includes not only a visual representation—the profile photo—but also a textual one—an abbreviated history of our life trajectory that includes which school or university we studied in, our previous jobs, our place of residence and our marital status. It also includes quantitative information, such as the number of friends displayed on the profile—the number of friends on Facebook or followers on Twitter quantifies our popularity on the network, although, as we will discuss later, this number is usually only nominal since it is only possible to interact with around 150 contacts actively. In addition to being a site of self-representation, the profile is a place of interaction, which our friends can use to post information—as on the Facebook wall—or to talk. As a result, control over self-representation is limited, since unless our settings prohibit comments, we cannot fully control the contribution of other users. It is here that the desire to control our self-representation and our desire to interact might be in tension.

The second feature is the friends list. As boyd argues, "the listing of Friends is both political and social" (boyd 2011, 44). Choosing whom we accept as friends and whom we reject implies a judgement about those we consider part of our social context and those we do not. While some individuals restrict their contacts to a small circle, others opt for a wider circle in which different social or cultural contexts coexist. However, beyond our intention to keep them separate, one of the defining features of social networks sites is what boyd calls "collapsed contexts" (2011, 49)—the breaking of the boundaries that separate our different circles. For example, in the off-line world, it is common to meet with our close friends at a place that our parents do not ordinarily frequent, such as a bar. The spheres of work and family are sharply separated—we do not take our children to work and, conversely, we do not share the school day with them. These different spaces can touch each other briefly in daily contact, but they remain differentiated, and any crossing is potentially experienced as an infraction or an intrusion into a space that does not belong to us. In an off-line environment, the transgression or fusion of spaces can be transformed into a political statement. For instance, when the Danish MEP Hanne Dahl took her three-month-old baby to the European Parliament session in March 2009 or the Italian MEP Licia Ronzulli took her seven-week-old baby to work at the European Parliament a year later; photographs of Ronzulli cradling her daughter in a sling as she voted on proposals to improve women's employment rights were broadcast around the world. On the other hand, social networking sites are the territory where the different characters of our lives—old friends, ex-lovers, actual ones, children, colleagues, family members, neighbours, and even pets—promiscuously share the same space.

In SNSs, the conversations we hold might resemble those taking place off-line, but there are critical differences that shape the experience of digital social interaction. First, while spoken conversations are ephemeral, digital conversations are—by default—recorded and stored. The digital culture has its memory, which frequently—and often dangerously—is a memory of banal utterances, of seemingly useless words, of small talk. However, what is banal in one context can be interpreted very differently in another one or when it is heard or viewed by a person for whom it was not intended. What boyd terms "persistence" accounts for this dynamic of automated storage, that "raises new concerns when it can be consumed outside of its original context" (2011, 47). Second, digital content can be replicated very easily. As Manovich contended in *The Language of New Media* (2001), this derives from the principles that define new media: because the elements of new media are modular, they can be assembled into larger units without losing their independence; this modularity also allows new media objects to be reproduced not as identical copies, as was the case with old media, but in different, potentially infinite, versions:

> Variability would also not be possible without modularity. Stored digitally, rather than in some fixed medium, media elements maintain their separate identity and can be assembled into numerous sequences under program control. In addition, because the elements themselves are broken into discrete samples (for instance, an image is represented as an array of pixels), they can be also created and customized on the fly (Manovich 2001, 56).

boyd highlights that the replicability that characterises SNSs raises concerns about the possibility of distinguishing between original and copy and therefore determining the source of the content. The third attribute of content in SNSs refers to scalability: the potential of content to scale, to be widely and immediately distributed across a broad audience. As boyd holds, the fact that the internet enables us to broadcast content and create audiences does not mean that it guarantees the visibility of that content. In other words, it does not guarantee that what becomes visible is what we expected or desired to be scaled—it may, on the contrary, be what the collective chooses to amplify (2011, 48). Fourth, the act of searching takes on a new role in a digital environment. The traces we leave, our digital footprints, might be easily available to anyone.

These affordances of networked publics give way to new dynamics that shape online interaction. Basically, what changes is the constitution of the audience—the homogeneity and visibility of the audience.

In face-to-face interaction, the subject acts according to the audience. In a job interview, at a family dinner, at a meeting of friends, at a protest, on a first date—

whatever the scene—we adapt our behaviour to the script and to the actors that make up the stage. Obviously, our ability to behave properly depends on knowing the codes, but even before this it depends on the fact that we are seeing those with whom we interact and therefore we can anticipate their response. In the digital ecology, on the other hand, the audience becomes mostly invisible. Given that content is persistent, replicable, scalable and searchable across broad swathes of space and time, in theory, it can be accessed by people who are there but are invisible to us. As boyd highlights, audience is critical to context:

> Without information about audience, it is often difficult to determine how to behave, let alone to make adjustments based on assessing reactions. To accommodate this, participants in networked publics often turn to an imagined audience to assess whether or not they believe their behaviour is socially appropriate, interesting, or relevant (boyd 2011, 50).

How do we assess whether the post we are going to make on Facebook is appropriate, interesting or relevant? For whom? For someone who imagines his Facebook audience as an informal group made up of his friends, it is fine—thus correct and appropriate—to post a comment about how boring his work is. Nevertheless, this assessment of one's audience could be completely wrong, as happened to an employee of Apple who was fired after posting how boring his work was.

Besides the impossibility of fully assessing who is part of the audience—now or in the future—networked publics are fundamentally heterogeneous, a mix of people from different spheres of life that cohabit, not necessary harmoniously. While previously contexts were segmented, now they have collapsed, which forces us to perform simultaneously for contrasting or even conflicting audiences. In networked publics, contexts often collide "such that the performer is unaware of audiences from different contexts, magnifying the awkwardness and making adjustments impossible" (boyd 2011, 51). Without the opportunity properly to assess the context, the self has to engage in a permanent evaluation of the multiple ways in which its performance could be interpreted. Without necessarily being conscious of it, in a networked public, the self is continuously renegotiating the boundaries that separate public and private. At the same time, the self is provided with different tools to present itself, modes of representation that allow it to see and be seen in distinct, complementary, but always distorted ways.

Modes of Self-presentation in Digital Media

These are the opening paragraphs of *Seeing Ourselves Through Technology*, a book devoted to examining how we represent ourselves in a digital environment:

> In 1524 Parmigianino painted his *Self-Portrait in a Convex Mirror*. Parmigianino used oil paints to paint on the hollow inside half a wooden ball, to mimic the shape of the mirror he copied his reflection from. The distortions of the convex mirror are exactly replicated in Parmigianino's self-portrait. His hand is in the foreground, grossly distorted by the fisheye perspective of the convex mirror he is looking into to see himself. We can just see the short pencil he is holding to sketch his own image. We see what he sees.
>
> Parmigianino used a convex mirror to see himself; today we use digital technologies (Rettberg 2014, 2).

In deciding to start a book on digital representations with the example of a self-portrait of the sixteenth century, Jill Walker Rettberg emphasizes three fundamental ideas: first, self-representations have a long history, whose origin probably goes back to the very origins of the species. The person who painted their body rudimentarily on the walls of a cavern did not do something very different from what a teenager does today when taking a selfie and uploading it to Facebook. Obviously, the technologies vary but the impulse of self-knowledge and representation that guides that act is similar. Second, all the images that we produce about ourselves are technologically mediated images—a mirror does not qualify as less of a technology than a camera—and this mediation always implies a degree of distortion, something that Parmigianino's self-portrait evidences in an exemplary way. Third, as the self-portrait genre demonstrates, and as is evident in the selfie, the images we produce about ourselves simultaneously serve two purposes: to see ourselves and to represent ourselves to others. In a complex game of mirrors, we see as spectators what once was seen by the self-reflective subject, although the judgment that we pass on that image is not necessarily the same. According to Rettberg, it is possible to distinguish three different modes of self-presentations in digital media: written, visual, and quantitative—texts, images, and numbers. Each one has its own history, one that the digital media summons at the same time as it rewrites.

The Self as Text

What does it mean to put our life into words? The extensive literature available in the autobiographical genre shows that the answer to this question implies navigating through the various forms that the words "life," "I" and "writing" assumed throughout history. Each historical epoch shapes the understanding of the self. Each epoch, then, writes its own self. But how can something as elusive as the self or as chaotic as life be transposed into words?

At the core of autobiographical writing lies the difficult task of transforming the raw data of our life into a meaningful narrative. The act of writing is precisely the technology that allows the self to come into existence since it is only the meaning constructed through this narrative that gives coherence—or, at least, a certain grade of coherence—to the apparently chaotic group of feelings, acts, likes, moods and relationships that make up an "I." The act of writing is primarily, then, an act of self-knowledge: we write to know who we are, even if this knowledge appears as elusive, insufficient, unsatisfactory and even if this knowledge is, by definition, impossible.

The digital self-representation inscribed in texts encompasses several forms such as blogs, micro-blogging forms like tweets, and Facebook updates, among many others. If we want to establish a link with previous forms of textual self-representations, online blogs can be regarded broadly as a contemporary form of autobiography, or, specifically, as an updated version of the old diaries. Rettberg refers to the growing practice of *automated diaries*, which are the many apps that automatically register our progresses around a concrete objective, such as, for example, daily exercises or the goal of eating healthily or a "to do list" app where we cross out the things already done.

Although Augustine's *Confessions* written in 397–8 AD is often recognised as the first autobiography, writing about oneself was a phenomenon reserved for only a few until the end of the 16th century. In Western society, the practice of regular journal writing is closely linked to spiritual and religious self-examination (Rettberg 2014, 4). It is in this practice of writing as a method to examine the achievements of the self, to measure how well or badly one is performing in relation to a series of self-improvement objectives, that a link to current digital forms of journalling can be observed. Beyond the formal features of a blog or the apps that write automated diaries, it is this underlying connection that I would like to focus upon.

The emergence of Protestantism and Puritanism introduced a new relationship of the subject with themselves in which self-examination occupied a central place. It is not that this relationship was absent in Catholicism; the Jesuits, for example, had a series of spiritual exercises designed for the believers to examine their sins in order to surpass themselves. Michelle Molina quotes a passage from the Spiritual Exercises initiated by Saint Ignatius, the founder of the Order:

> Consideration of oneself. Tuesday. Points: consideration of self and of time and place: Where are you? Who are you? Also, reflection on each phase of your life: the time, the place, the state of life, circumstances in which he then lived as a sinner in each period; the things he happened to witness, and how swiftly and unmindfully everything passed by. His state of mind then and now (Molina, quoted in Rettberg 2014, 6).

With the rise of Protestantism, the emphasis on self-examination was accentuated. The believers who could once confess their sins to a priest and be absolved now had to examine their own faults alone, through dialogue with themselves. Writing was then an indispensable instrument for this exercise of self-examination that allowed believers to identify faults, work on them, and overcome them. According to Viviane Serfaty (2004), blogs are a continuation of this puritanical tradition, although, obviously, it is now a secular practice in which sins are replaced by profane faults. The common narrative that links a puritanical diary, or a guide to Jesuit spiritual exercises, with a digital diary is one of self-improvement: the belief that the self can be continually improved, purified of its faults—whether we call them sins, lack of exercise, or the fulfilment of a long to-do list. The idea that the I can and must be perfected applies a technology of self-discipline based on rationalisation and efficiency. Spiritual journalling narratives did not record exceptional events; on the contrary, they recorded the banal, the everyday acts, the texture of everyday life, and the small changes that individuals experience. The record that the self carries of itself, trying to capture its own faults no matter how minimal, is not without an obsessive quality, a quality that digital media develop to its fullest extent. The different apps that we have today promise to free us from the heavy task of having to write our lives—we can finally relax while a simple device captures all the necessary data and writes the narrative for us. "The ultimate real-time diary is a diary that writes itself automatically, without needing your input," affirms Rettberg (2014, 46).

On the one hand, smartphones automatically store our data by default: "a phone can log our geographic location and thus where we go and how fast we are moving from place to place" (Rettberg, 2014, 46); it knows "when we make phone calls or send texts or emails, but also knows which apps we use and what we search online" (Rettberg 2014, 46), the music we play, the videos we watch and what we read. On the other hand, today we witness the emergence of "continuous, automated, real-time diaries, where our everyday use of technology is converted into a journal-like format" (Rettberg 2014, 46), such as HeyDay, Saga, Chronos or Step, that combine information to offer us organised diaries with little or no input from us. For instance, STEP journal's iTunes App Store claims: "Want to know yourself better? STEP Journal makes it easy to collect your life moments and manage them using quantified and visualized dashboard. It's a beautiful way to enrich your life" (Rettberg 2014, 47). Nevertheless, there is obviously an inherent tension between raw data—cumulative information about ourselves—and narrative in these apps' promises. They tell us that, by analysing our daily movements, habits and actions they can create meaning out of them, and, subsequently, enrich our lives, make us better, improve ourselves. Yet the narrative is not automatically derived out of these patterns. The anxiety behind the desire to record every moment of our lives, no matter how small or trivial, goes against the principle of narrative, which involves not only selection, and therefore remembering as well as forgetting, but also beginnings and ends—even if they are arbitrarily imposed over a continuum. In other words, the impulse to capture and record the "everything" promised by apps such as the Narrative Clip—a camera that clips onto your clothes and takes a photo every 30 seconds—goes against the old way in which we used to take photos, that is, recording ritualised, carefully selected moments. These carefully selected moments marked milestones in our lives, allowing us to see and give an order to significant steps in a narrative that revolves around a long-term script—our infancy, our marriage, the birth of our children, their first steps, and so on and so forth. On the contrary, the temporality underlying these apps and automated diaries is entirely pragmatic, aligned to the idea of continuous and indefinite self-improvement, which has to be achieved under the premises of rational choices and efficiency. It is a prospective narrative rather than a retrospective one. These kinds of apps give us the possibility of seeing our daily progress in achieving concrete goals, whatever they might be. This is what Rettberg, underscoring the similarity between the premises of apps and games, refers to as "gamified lives" (2014, 58),

> Many activity trackers use elements of gamification in the system mechanics. The basic premise of these trackers has a lot in common with games: you have a goal (lose three kilos or run a half-marathon) and you are given challenges through which you can earn points that move you towards that goal ... Paolo Pedercini argues that games are prime examples of the rationalisation Max Weber described in *The Protestant Ethic* and *The Spirit of Capitalism* at the end of the nineteenth century. 'If computer games,' Pedercini (2014) writes, 'in their immense variety, have anything in common, that may be their compulsion for efficiency and control. Computer games are the aesthetic form of rationalization' (Rettberg 2014, 58–59).

With these apps there is not, therefore, a lifelong temporality but rather a series of goals. Once one goal is achieved we must work towards the next. The temporality of digital diaries, be they in the form of automated diaries or social media status updates, is thus directed towards the future more than aimed at interpreting the past. Facebook continuously asking us "What's on your minds?" clearly reveals this hunger for the next post, the next update, the next bit of story. In this sense, although there is a powerful imagery of digital media as carriers of "total recall" (Roberts 2016), which would seem to convey an emphasis on the *past,* the temporality of the digital self seems to be more closely linked to the eternal present to which Ireneo Funes—the eponymous character from Jorge Luis Borges's short story "Funes, el memorioso" (Funes the Memorious) (1962)—is condemned.

"Funes the Memorious" is the tale of Ireneo Funes, a peasant from South America, who, after falling off his horse and receiving a bad head injury, acquires the incredible skill—or perhaps the curse—of remembering absolutely everything. The narrator meets Ireneo Funes and spends the whole night talking to him in the dark. The narrator describes how, after the accident, Funes's memory has become perfect, a total memory.

> We, at one glance, can perceive three glasses on a table; Funes, all the leaves and tendrils and fruit that make up a grape vine. He knew by heart the forms of the southern clouds at dawn on the 30th of April, 1882, and could compare them in his memory with the mottled streaks on a book in Spanish binding he had only seen once and with the outlines of the foam raised by an oar in the Río Negro the night before the Quebracho uprising. These memories were not simple ones; each visual image was linked to muscular sensations, thermal sensations, etc. He could reconstruct all his

dreams, all his half-dreams. Two or three times he had reconstructed a whole day; he never hesitated, but each reconstruction had required a whole day. He told me: "I alone have more memories than all mankind has probably had since the world has been the world". And again: "My dreams are like you people's waking hours". And again, toward dawn: "My memory, sir, is like a garbage heap" (Borges 1962, 69).

Borges's dystopic tale is about, among other things, the impossibility of forgetting. Funes seems to be burdened by an amount of information that he cannot manage—or perhaps, conversely, it becomes a problem because he can manage it so efficiently. Significantly, Funes appears as a solitary inhabitant of a present that seems to last forever, although without any desire or possibility of self-improvement—the very idea of self-improvement is parodied in the tale. His perfect register of every detail leads him to the eternal present in which he inhabits. What this perfect register seems to produce is not, as the STEP journal app promotes, "a beautiful way to enrich your life" but, conversely, a memory that is like a "garbage heap."

The Selfie

Among the many visual representations of the self that pervade the internet, the selfie stands out, undoubtedly, as a paradigm in online culture. The *Oxford Dictionaries* (2013) define it as "a photograph that one has taken of oneself, typically one taken with a smartphone or webcam and uploaded to a social media website." If we rely on this definition, many traits have to come together in order to form a selfie: "only photographs can count as selfies; drawings or paintings as well as moving pictures are ruled out" (Eckel *et al.* 2018, 4); thus the selfie must be a photograph in which the subject/author and object of the image coincide. The first part of the definition is ambiguous, however, regarding what counts as oneself: it does not affirm explicitly that the face has to be at the centre of the picture, leaving room for photographs that do not show the face of the photographer, but, for instance "their backside (a bum selfie, or belfie) or feet (a foot selfie, felfie or fooftie)" (Eckel *et al.* 2018, 5). In the same vein, a selfie is not necessarily restricted to oneself as it may—and often does—"stage more people than just the photographer (and consequently might be specified as usie, ussie, wefie, or groupfie)" (Eckel *et al.* 2018, 5). It is significant in this regard that this definition avoids linking the selfie with the long tradition of the self-portrait, in which the intention to capture the individual's personal identity is essential. If the first part of the definition refers to the character of the image, the second part testifies to the "fundamental communicative function of the selfie as a 'connected' and 'conversational' image: Social media sites link shared photos of one user to photos of many others and even invite them to react to an uploaded selfie by posting a selfie of their own (Gunther 2014)" (Eckel *et al.* 2018, 6). Hence, a selfie is not only a particular kind of visual object but a *practice*, a digital image *meant to be shared*. This is crucial since it is this practice of sharing, rather than any particular trait of the digital character of the image, that transforms the temporality of photography in a dramatic way. These two aspects—communicative practice and aesthetic features—which intersect in the practice of the selfie lead to two different approaches in selfie research: those interested in the technological and aesthetic dimension of the *image,* and those focusing on the communicative and social dimensions of the selfie *practice.* Although intertwined, they lead to different questions and concerns regarding the aesthetic nature, the social effects, or even the political and ethical implications of the apparently simple click of someone taking a photo of themselves.

One of the most persistent criticisms directed against the selfie has been—and still is—its narcissistic character: a practice that puts the self—a banal, inconsequential, ordinary self—at the centre of the scene. The millions of selfies that are uploaded to social networks every day seem to bear witness to a sickly fascination of the self with itself, obsessed with showing a singularity without noticing that this gesture, far from showing a singularity, indefinitely repeats the identical gestures of millions of other individuals. Obsessed with the contemplation of its own image occupying the centre of the scene, the I seems to be unable to see—in the most literal sense of the term—the scene or what surrounds it, that is, the world.

A clear example of this condemnation is found in the debates about selfies taken in seemingly inappropriate scenarios—for example, Auschwitz. "On June 20, 2014, an 18-year-old high school graduate from the US called Breanna Mitchell tweeted a selfie taken at Auschwitz," recalls Wulf Kansteiner (2017, 115). "The photo of the smiling teen with earbuds, loop earrings, and pink sweats in front of Auschwitz barracks went viral triggering an avalanche of critical and even hateful tweets indicting the teenager's alleged inappropriate narcissism and lackadaisical attitude at the site of so much suffering" (Kansteiner 2017, 115). Even though Breanna argued that taking the selfie at Auschwitz was an act of respect and mourning related to the death of her father, who had taught her about the Holocaust, the criticism it provoked was clear enough to show her how inappropriate the selfie was: "It's hard to think of anything less sensitive, less appropriate or less self-aware than a 'selfie in the Auschwitz Concentration Camp'—smiley—as if the suffering of millions of people was somehow subsumed by Breanna's own personal narrative," wrote a reporter from the *Washington Post* (quoted in Kansteiner 2017, 115). After these controversies, Holocaust selfies became less frequent on social media, and were replaced by more conventional portraits showing sombre faces looking at the remnants of the camps. Kansteiner argues that cases such as this one, rather than showing the narcissistic character of the selfie, demonstrate the orthodoxy of Holocaust memory:

> It is unlikely that the youths thus shamed into submission entertain more complex or self-reflexive feelings and thoughts about Nazi genocide than their selfie-loving predecessors but the examples demonstrate how the dynamic emergent environments of Facebook and Instagram generate and enforce their own standards of Holocaust orthodoxy through peer pressure and institutional policing. Breanna's selfie and its almost universal condemnation will exist in cyberspace as a stark exoskeletal warning and testament to the hate turn for many decades to come (Kansteiner 2017, 116).

Yet, it is fair to wonder whether or not the selfie is even a portrait of an individual. The question may seem rather obvious since what we evidently see in a selfie is the portrayal of a singular individual. Nevertheless, the repetition and seriality that characterise the selfie as a practice point to a different direction, one in which the selfie becomes "a communist form of expression" (Dean 2016). In her post on Fotomuseum, Jodi Dean warns us against the "critical reflex to dismiss selfies as yet another indication of a pervasive culture of narcissism" (2016), proposing instead that it should be understood as a common form, "a form that, insofar as it is inseparable from the practice of sharing selfies has a collective subject" (2016). Although, and here the example of Breanna Mitchell comes painfully to mind, "when we upload selfies, we are always vaguely aware that someone, when it is least opportune, may take an image out of its context and use it to our disadvantage" (Dean 2016), we nevertheless keep uploading our self-portraits because it is not really about ourselves as the subject of the photograph:

> It's my imitation of others and our imitation of each other. To consider the selfie as a singular image removed from the larger practice of sharing selfies is like approaching

a magazine through one word in one issue. A selfie is a photo of the selfie form, the repetition of a repeated practice (Dean 2016).

Drawing on Benjamin's distinction between the cult value and the exhibition value of an artwork, Dean adds a third category that she calls "circulation value" (2016). Based on the "shareability" of the image, access and transportability do not just increase, "they become ends in themselves" (Dean 2016). We upload selfies to participate in a conversation, following a communicative impulse instead of a desire to memorialise, something that the device itself testifies to, since, as Dean highlights, the fact "that the camera is a phone tells us that images are for communicating" (2016).

All this revolves around the unique and irreplaceable character of the face—our own face—that is depicted in the selfies, a face that ceases to be our own and becomes what we share with others; it becomes a common, an instance of "how one is like many, equal to any other" (Dean 2016). What is the status of this common? As Manovich argues, one of the defining features of new media is variability, that is, the generation of different versions of the same object: "new media objects assure users that their choices—and therefore, their underlying thoughts and desires—are unique, rather than preprogramed and shared with others" (Manovich 2001, 42). On the other hand, for Dean the selfie seems to defy this logic by transforming faces into common property. As we read in her conclusion:

> I would even say that the selfie demonstrates further the emancipation of the commonality of the object from the commodity form. To be common and reproducible is no longer a primary characteristic of the commodity—especially in a context where commodities are inscribed with individuality (personalized sneakers, designer this and that). To be common and reproducible is a characteristic of each of us, a realization we enact with every selfie and hashtag, even when we may not be fully aware that we are doing it (Dean 2016).

And, as her final sentence predicts, "Of course, the platforms through which our common property is produced and reproduced are still owned by a few—but not for long" (Dean 2016).

A different approach is proposed by Hagi Kenaan in "The Selfie and the Face" (2018). Unlike Dean, Kenaan considers the face depicted in the selfie to be representing an individual and not any kind of collective, but rather than the question of singularity and uniqueness, it is representation that is at stake here.

Before turning to the selfie, let us consider the face as an object of vision. What makes faces visually different from most other objects that surround us is that they remain unseen by their own bearers. "While we constantly see the faces of others, our own face does not directly appear in our field of vision," says Kenaan (2018, 116). Faces are particular objects intrinsically embedded in the interaction in which they appear. A face is never a "self-sufficient entity" but is "an intrinsically environmental being" (Kenaan 2018, 118). Always already in the mode of self-presenting, "always geared toward and affected by its surroundings" (Kenaan 2018, 118), and always changing to respond to the gestures that we read in other faces, the face is, like the self, "primarily an inter-face" (Kenaan 2018, 118). Thus, while we constantly see, read and interpret others' faces, that which serves as our *carte de visite* "is something to which we ourselves do not have direct access ... the self's primarily blind spot" (Kenaan 2018, 118). This blind spot accounts for the realisation that the self has a relationship with its own face that is always mediated. It is either mediated by the way others see us, and consequently the way in which we decode their reactions, or mediated by instruments, like the mirror, which allow us to see that which does not offer itself to sight directly. Naturally, the selfie can be read as a form of self-presentation in the public sphere, a means of self-promotion in a setting that expands the possibilities of appearing in public. Kenaan does not dispute this; however, he argues that this focus on self-presentation comes at the expense of understanding the selfie as something equally, or possibly even more, fundamental: a means of accessing the appearance of our own faces. Being unable to register our faces is not just a neutral fact about us, but constitutive, perhaps even part of what defines our humanity: "we are the kind of creatures who are aware of and affected by the lacuna that the face creates in their field of vision" (Kenaan 2018, 121) and therefore creatures who are constantly negotiating means to solve this lacuna. In this vein, selfies are objects aimed at fulfilling this primary need of seeing ourselves. Therefore, they should not be placed under the rubric of "representation," in the same way that a mirror does not "re-present to us something that is already present in our visual field but rather transforms the invisibility of our face in a manner that allows it to become part of the realm that lends itself to our vision" (Kenaan 2018, 121).

What is involved in the act of seeing ourselves reflected in a mirror? This question leads us to a much-visited topic in selfie research: that of the relationships between the selfie and the self-portrait. Kenaan is keen to re-visit this well-worn path in order to capture the specificity of the selfie.

In making a self-portrait—a task with specific challenges, as Kenaan highlights—the painter is trying to answer a question that, by definition, lacks a positive answer: Who am I? The I appears as an enigma whose impossible resolution implies the complex play between the appearance and the truth of the self, to which the self-portrait adds a second layer—that of a reflection on the identity of the painter as an artist: "[t]he self-portrait's confrontation with the question of identity is thus traditionally inseparable from a domain of questions about one's identity as an artist, about the meaning of being an artist, and, ultimately, it is inseparable from the artist's view on what art is" (Kenaan 2018, 123–24). If a painter is successful in capturing his own self through the looking glass, it is not because he is able to provide a transparent picture through which we have access to the secret of his personality; rather, it is because of his ability to locate himself within—and give us an inside glimpse into—the "unresolvable dialectics" (Kenaan 2018, 124) between appearance and truth. In other words, the value of the self-portrait lies not in the answer it provides but in the way in which it poses the question.

At first sight, the selfie does not seem to be involved in this process of exploration. On the contrary, and in line with the most common criticisms levelled against it, the selfie appears to rely on a simplistic notion of identity in which the face unequivocally represents the "I" to which it refers. There are no intrinsic difficulties, questions or dilemmas, nor any complex play between appearance and truth—only transparency and immediacy. The inherent uncertainty involved in the act of self-representation seems to be absent in the image we come across on Facebook or Instagram: "this is me." This is me on the beach, this is me on my vacation, this is me climbing, this is me in my graduation, this is me at a party with friends, and so on. This identity is confirmed by the insistence with which the image repeats itself. This raises the question whether this photographic picture can be more than a mere simplistic gesture of auto-promotion:

> Can the visuality of the selfie come close to containing, for example, modalities of exploration, of self-questioning and scepticism toward one's identity, as the self-portrait often does? Can the selfie subvert and offer an alternative to the common, ready-at-hand and well-packaged, replicas of the affirmation of selfhood, or is it ultimately condemned only to repeat and duplicate these simplistic figures of identity? (Kenaan 2018, 125).

As Kenaan warns us, there is no "conclusive or univocal way to answer the above questions" (2018, 126). Yet he appears to be optimistic about the possibilities of this photographic form to go beyond plain exhibitionism. It is not only that the selfie—like any other cultural form—is open and therefore susceptible to changing over time and acquiring new meanings; for Kenaan, it is the centrality of the face that keeps the selfie from closure or sheer banality:

> [H]aving the face at its center, the selfie finds itself—whether it wants it or not—intertwined with an enigma: the enigma of a subjectivity that not only manifests itself visually but that is always already embedded in the appearances that it cannot control or contain. Consequently, even if the selfie is effective in leveling the face's complex presence, the enigma is still there waiting to be rediscovered. ... What possibilities can the selfie open for the appearance of the face? What would it mean for the selfie to look after the face and keep its humanity alive? These questions need to be asked as part of philosophy's role—a role that it shares with art—in opening for us new ways of resisting an unprecedented kind of reification that gradually prevails over the sphere of the visual (Kenaan 2018, 126–127).

There is yet another form of self-presentation that the selfie delivers beyond the easy identification of the "I" and the picture. Alise Tifentale and Lev Manovich find it in what they call "competitive photography" (2018, 171), a subgenre in a liminal space between avant-garde photography and amateur photography. Competitive photography emerged after World War II and was aimed at an audience "consisting of a of peer group of more or less like-minded photographers" (Tifentale & Manovich 2018, 171), a group in which the pictures circulated and were evaluated "on the basis of the mastery of photographic technique, aesthetics, and creativity" (Tifentale & Manovich 2018, 171)—unlike family photos, which have value and circulate only among family and friends, whose aesthetic qualities are less important than those of the people and the events depicted. Although, naturally, many things have changed since then, competitive photography is a term that can be used to describe a segment of contemporary Instagram photographs and selfies. This practice can be art but it does not pertain to the elite circles of advanced art; it is amateur, in the sense that its authors are not professional photographers who profit from their work. These photos are aesthetically sophisticated and "the images are explicitly made for public display and critical evaluation of their technical and aesthetic qualities" (Tifentale & Manovich 2018, 173).

These aesthetic photos, however, do not dominate Instagram. Based on their project *Selfiecity,* in which they analysed large samples of Instagram that encompassed over 20 million images shared in 17 global cities, Tifentale and Manovich assert that most of the photographs and selfies posted on this platform follow the "home mode" (2018, 178) of 20th-century photography, namely, photos that are of interest for the authors themselves, their friends and families, or, at best, a circle of acquaintances. Yet even if the majority of the photos shared on Instagram belong to the non-competitive category, a significant proportion can be assigned to the competitive one—approximately 20%, compared to the 80% of home mode photographs, according to an "informal count" using a random sample of geotagged photos during one week in London in September 2015 (Tifentale & Manovich 2018, 179).

The most basic question that arises when looking at this variety of photographic practices on Instagram is: are all selfies really self-portraits? The answer these authors give is clearly no. The selfies we encounter do not comply with the traditional self-portrait because, instead of depicting a person deprived of the environment that surrounds her, they show, at the same time, the person—or persons—and the place, the person *at* the place,

> They do not show *a person isolated from their environment*, as both self-portraits and portraits often did historically (think, e.g., of self-portraits by Rembrandt and van Gogh). Instead, they are *records of places, events, activities, experiences and situations that include the photo's author.*
> The backgrounds of many selfie photos identify the place and show the activity and the ambience of this place. In this way, the person(s) in the selfie becomes part of a situation rather than being shown in isolation (Tifentale & Manovich 2018, 180).

A selfie, thus, is not just a photo showing a person looking towards the camera but rather depicts a "person/people in a situation/experience" (Tifentale & Manovich 2018, 181), in which the self appears metonymically, showing parts of its body instead of the face. Tifentale and Manovich call this genre "anti-selfie" (2018, 181). There are different versions:

> One variation of this genre shows the author of the Instagram account in a landscape or another space looking into this landscape or space. The person is looking away from the camera, so we do not see the face. Another variation shows the author's

free hand pointing (or making some other, often comical, gesture) to a landscape or city space. Yet another variation shows hands or other parts of the body as part of an arrangement of objects. (Such arrangements in Instagram are often called flatlays.) In all these situations, the person may be the author of the account or somebody else photographed by the author. By not displaying the author's face, these photos clearly signal their goal—to show person's participation in a situation or an experience. By including a part of the body of a person who is in this situation/experience cut by a frame, a photo includes you in the experience. You are not the disembodied eye observing the world from the distance, as in Renaissance perspective, but the body that is part of the pictured world (Tifentale & Manovich 2018, 181).

So, while a typical selfie—or, simply, a selfie—displays a face as the sign of identity, an anti-selfie shows "the world experienced through the first-person point of view" (Tifentale & Manovich 2018, 182). The photographer uses a singular visual style that conveys "a single consciousness experiencing the world" (Tifentale & Manovich 2018, 182). It is this particular consciousness experiencing the world, a world that is out there but looked at through the senses of this self—and expressed in her particular visual style—that stands as the representation of the I. "In other words: Anti-selfies on Instagram are not photographs of something out there; they and their author's life are supposed to be the same in terms of values, interests, and aesthetics" (Tifentale & Manovich 2018, 182).

To conclude, Tifentale and Manovich call for acknowledging that we cannot speak of the selfie as if it were a homogeneous and fixed genre; the genre of the anti-selfie demonstrates that there are many forms of self-presentation contained in this supposedly simple form and that many of them clearly go beyond the stigma of narcissism.

10   The Digital Person, the Panopticon and Kafka

The digital self refers, on the one hand, to how define ourselves – that is, what we individualise as a distinct and singular I – in a networked environment. On the other hand, it points to the way in which digital technologies seemingly autonomously build a self through the collection of dispersed data, beyond our control and even beyond our agreement. While the former highlights the subject's agency, the latter points out the other side of self-representation, the way in which each of us is represented by other entities that gather, store and aggregate this information in ways that we cannot fully access. In this chapter we address the issue from the latter perspective, dealing with the self not as a subject but as an object of surveillance that results from the operations performed by digital media, in particular, interrogating the extent to which this object resembles or disturbingly mirrors what we consider to be ourselves. Drawing on the work of Orwell and Kafka, the chapter further discusses the nature of digital surveillance: is it a central power that watches and controls everything or is rather a much subtler and ungraspable power, that of bureaucracy?

Keywords: digital self, digital dossier, surveillance, sousveillance, Panopticon, reputation, Kafka, Orwell, privacy interfaces.

In the previous chapters, we have explored the self-representations we create of ourselves, in the forms of texts, photographs and numbers. Their mediated character makes us think that we have full control—or at least more control than before—since we are able to choose what, how and when we create and share these representations. Before uploading a selfie to Instagram, we can take as many as we want, we can choose a filter, improve it, add a text explaining the situation, or just a funny comment, and, finally, choose the platform on which we want to share "ourselves" with our circle of friends, relatives, or simply the world out there. Through these acts of self-representation, we are permanently leaving digital footprints, fragments of our persons dispersed across the web. If, separately, they cannot provide a coherent representation of who we are, put together they can create a powerful and useful—although the question here is useful for what and for whom—representation of ourselves. This is the other side of self-representation, the way in which each of us is represented by other entities that gather, store and aggregate this information in ways that we cannot fully access.

In *The Digital Person* (2004), Daniel Solove invites us to:

> Imagine that the government had the power to compel individuals to reveal a vast amount of personal information about themselves—where they live; their phone numbers; their physical description; their photograph; their age; their medical problems; all of their legal transgressions throughout their lifetimes; the names of their parents, children, and spouses; their political party affiliations; where they work and what they do; the property that they own and its value; and sometimes even their psychotherapists' notes, doctors' records, and financial information.
>
> Then imagine that the government routinely poured this information into the public domain—by posting it on the Internet where it could be accessed from all over the world ... Imagine as well that this information would be traded among hundreds of private-sector companies that would combine it with a host of other information such as one's hobbits, purchases, magazines, organizations, credit history, and so on. This expanded profile would then be sold back to the government in order to investigate and monitor individuals more efficiently.
>
> Stop imagining. What I described is a growing reality in the United States, ante the thread posed to privacy is rapidly becoming worse (Solove 2004, 4–5).

In the years since Solove wrote this book we have discussed the revelation in 2005 that the NSA was monitoring American phone calls through an illegal programme, the Snowden leaks in 2013, and the Facebook-Cambridge Analytica data scandal in 2018—to name just a few of the most heated cases. This suggests that Solove was right in 2004 when he predicted that this growing reality "is rapidly becoming worse" (Solove 2004, 5). We are constantly under surveillance: our information is collected, stored and aggregated without our consent or even our knowledge following complex trajectories and flows.

In *Critical Theory and the Digital* (2014), David Berry stresses the necessity of thinking of the computational society in terms of flows instead of objects. "The world is transitioning from analogue, structured in most part by the physicality of destination, to the digital. A new *industrial internet* is emerging, a computational, real-time streaming ecology that is reconfigured in terms of digital flows, fluidities and movement" (Berry 2014, 1). We need to stop thinking about the digital "as something static and object-like and instead consider its 'trajectories'" (Berry 2014, 1). Under the stable representations that we commonly think of as digital objects, or, to put it simply, under the surface of our screen, "there is a constant stream of processing, a movement and trajectory, a series of lines that are being followed and computed" (Berry 2014, 1). These flows of information, more than each separated piece of it, are what matter in the digital environment. This is because the question of privacy is not so much about the nature of the information being shared but the way in which different spheres of our lives are transgressed by these flows.

Based on the work of Helen Nissenbaum, Vaidhyanathan (2011) proposes the notion of "privacy interfaces" to describe the domains in which we live our privacy and through which we negotiate what is known about us, each of them offering different levels of control and surveillance.

The first privacy interface is what he calls "person to peer" (Vaidhyanathan 2011, 94). It refers to the most personal sphere of friends and family, and how we learn early on how to manage what we want or do not want these people to know. For example, "a boy growing up gay in a homophobic family learns to exert control over others' knowledge of his sexual orientation. A teenager smoking marijuana in her bedroom learns to hide the evidence" (Vaidhyanathan 2011, 94). The second one, "person to power", refers to those persons such as teachers, parents and employers who represent authority and who could use the information to punish us. For example, "an employee may find it prudent to conceal a serious medical condition from her employer to prevent being dismissed to protect the company's insurance costs" (Vaidhyanathan 2011, 94). The third privacy interface is "person to firm", and it involves the information we wish to be known—or not known—by companies. It is interesting to observe that in many cases we are unaware of the data we provide to companies and that this does not only occur in the digital environment. When we accept, for example, a discount card at a supermarket or another store, these are used for recording our purchases in order to have a detailed record of our consumer habits. The fourth interface, "person to state", is the most important "because the consequences of error and abuse are so high" (Vaidhyanathan 2011, 94). Through several bureaucratic functions, the state tracks data that can be used against us; it is quite obvious what we are referring to here. Finally, the fifth privacy interface is what he calls "person to public", which can be considered the most characteristic of our online environment. Through this interface, we can find our lives exposed, our names ridiculed. Fuelled by digital media, a very small incident or mistake can be propagated—viralised—to an extent that was unthinkable decades before, damaging our reputation with unpredictable harm. This is related to the juxtapositions of spheres we addressed in the previous chapters, that is, how networked communities are promiscuous spaces where our social lives are blended. We are only beginning to understand what is at stake here and how to deal with it. Of course, this not only has to do with the structure of networked communities or the obscure desires of companies to profit from us, but also with our social behaviour.

Vaidhyanathan devotes a section of his book to commenting on the case of the "Star Wars kid", which was previously addressed by Solove in *The Future of Reputation* (2007):

> In November 2002, a Canadian teenager used a school camera to record himself acting like a character from *Star Wars*, wielding a golf-ball retriever as a light saber. Some months later, other students at his school discovered the recording and posted it on a file-sharing network. Within days, the image of a geeky teen playing at *Star Wars* became the hit of the Internet. Thousands—perhaps millions—downloaded the video. Soon, many downloaders used their computers to enhance the video, adding costumes, special effects, and even opponents for the young man to slay. Hundreds of versions still haunt the Web. ... By the time YouTube debuted in 2005, the "Star Wars Kid" was a miserable and unwilling star of user-generated culture. He had to quit school. The real-world harassment drove his family to move to a new town (Vaidhyanathan 2011, 95–96).

Thus, an ostensibly harmless video recorded by an adolescent in the supposed privacy of his high school studio became, thanks to the internet, not so private and not so harmless. Since 2006, when the video was uploaded to YouTube, it has acquired over 34,000,000 views. Hundreds of parodies, like the "drunken Jedi" (fantom81z28 2006) which added a real light sabre, or "fighting Yoda" (AlexstrifePE 2006) or "Agent Smith Fight" (Israel Alejandro 2006) got millions of views. Ghyslain Raza, the protagonist of the original clip, has described the negative comments he received online. In an interview in 2013, he stated that one commenter called him "a pox on humanity" (Taylor 2013). Others suggested he commit suicide: "'On the Internet, there are no limits,' Raza said. 'It was poison. … I couldn't help but feel worthless … it was a very dark period for me'" (Taylor 2013).

As Vaidhyanathan contends, the very nature of digital images and the flows of circulation made it impossible for the adolescent to erase what had been an innocent video of himself imitating Darth Maul's light sabre moves. Vaidhyanathan adds that, nevertheless, "it was not the technology that was at fault, Solove reminds us. It was our willingness to ridicule others publicly and our ease at appealing to free-speech principles to justify the spreading of everything everywhere, exposing and hurting the innocent along the way. … Our appetite for public humiliation of others (undeserved or otherwise) should trouble us deeply" (Vaidhyanathan 2011, 96). Importantly, Raza's video was not intended to be public. He just recorded a videotape and left it in a basement by accident. It was later found by a schoolmate who created an electronic file and distributed it amongst the students. On 14 April 2003, it was uploaded to the Internet and the rest is history—not exactly a happy ending for Raza.

The sad story of the "Star Wars Kid" is revealing in showing the distinction between the nature and the use of information. The video was not disclosing any type of information that would be conventionally regarded as private in terms of secret. What was harmful was the way in which this information was used by peers instead of the nature of the information itself. This distinction is crucial and leads to distinct metaphors aimed at conceptualising the digital representations that we cannot control, and yet define us more and more, shaping fundamental aspects of our lives. Yet, I do not want to focus on this type of disclosure, though anyone interested can read Daniel Solove's book *The Future of Reputation: Gossip, Rumor, and Privacy on the Internet* (2007), which provides an excellent discussion about what is at stake in this matter. Instead I will concentrate on the first types of privacy interfaces.

Orwell and Kafka

One of the essential functions of the state has always been to collect and accumulate information about its citizens for different purposes. This information is needed both to design more effective public policies and to discipline those individuals whose behaviour does not conform to the law. Companies, on the other hand, have always been interested in knowing more about us, basically in order to understand our consumption habits and thus to be able to optimise the products they offer us—consequently increasing their sales. What has changed in the digital age is not, therefore, the fact that we are under the scrutiny of these actors but rather the extent of the information that is collected—or can be potentially collected—as well as the capacity to store such information, the way it circulates, and its accessibility to anyone who wants to consult it. Today, the quantity, trajectory and cycles of information are what differentiate the impact of the digital age and directly affect our ability to oppose or at least control which representations define us.

The fact—or the potential—of being permanently observed has made the Panopticon—the Bentham design that Foucault popularised in *Discipline and Punishment*—one of the most used metaphors to describe the kind of surveillance we are exposed to in the digital age. The Panopticon is a type of prison that replaces darkness with visibility. It consists of a series of individual cells making up a circular perimeter in the centre of which there is a guard. The guard is capable of simultaneously seeing all the prisoners, who, for their part, are unable to see if the guard is actually watching them or not. It is this knowing and not knowing that keeps them disciplined. As Foucault describes it:

> All that is needed, then, is to place a supervisor in a central tower and to shut up in each cell a madman, a patient, a condemned man, a worker or a schoolboy. By the effect of backlighting, one can observe from the tower, standing out precisely against the light, the small captive shadows in the cells of the periphery. They are like so many cages, so many small theatres, in which each actor is alone, perfectly individualized and constantly visible. The panoptic mechanism arranges spatial unities that make it possible to see constantly and to recognize immediately. In short, it reverses the principle of the dungeon; or rather of its three functions—to enclose, to deprive of light and to hide—it preserves only the first and eliminates the other two. Full

lighting and the eye of a supervisor capture better than darkness, which ultimately protected. Visibility is a trap (Foucault 1995, 200).

Since Foucault wrote about the Panopticon, the nature of surveillance has changed. Above all, it is not clear that the Panopticon's essential purpose of disciplining the observed person is the same purpose that prevails today. Based on these changes, new terms that replace or complement the concept of surveillance have been proposed, such as "dataveillance," a term coined by Roger Clark (1988) to refer to "the systematic monitoring of people's actions or communications through the application of information technology" (Clark, quoted in Rettberg 2014, 85), "sousveillance," which refers to citizens' control over authorities, and "coveillance" which describes the monitoring of peers by each other (Mann, Nolan, and Wellman, cited in Rettberg 2014, 85).

The figure of the Panopticon as a metaphor is still ubiquitous, as are references to the Big Brother figure from *1984*, the famous novel by George Orwell, to which it is closely related. As with the Panopticon, the dystopian society that Orwell imagines in *1984* is dominated by a central power that scrupulously subjects its citizens to maximum control, leaving no room for intimate life or any dimension that could be considered private. In this society all citizens are permanently observed, in the public space, through vigilantes who walk the streets, and—and this is crucial—in the private sphere of their own homes. Not coincidentally, the representation of this enormous power is a face "with eyes [that] follow you about when you move" and the caption "BIG BROTHER IS WATCHING YOU" (Orwell 1949, 3). Inside each house, this surveillance operates through a screen called the "tele-screen," which consists of a two-way television—individuals can see it but it also allows Big Brother to see them:

> There was of course no way of knowing whether you were being watched at any given moment. How often, or on what system, the Thought Police plugged in on any individual wire was guesswork. It was even conceivable that they watched everybody all the time. You had to live—did live, from habit that became instinct—in the assumption that every sound you made was overheard, and, except in darkness, every movement scrutinized (Orwell, quoted in Solove 2004, 29).

As Solove emphasises, the collection of information on the web can be easily analogised with the telescreen. While browsing the web, we are being watched but we are never sure exactly by whom or to what extent. Big Brother tries to control private life because it is key to manipulating the entire existence of individuals: their ideas, their actions. This mechanism of observation is certainly useful in thinking our digital landscape; however, Solove questions whether this is the most appropriate metaphor to conceptualise the phenomenon and suggests that it is at least not the only one.

The main problem with the Big Brother metaphor is the kind of power it describes: an absolute power, whose main purpose is to discipline the population. However, many of the practices associated with databases have a different character. For example, when collecting information, sellers seek to know which products would best fit our consumption habits. While they try to get us to act in a certain way—that is, they seek to condition us to buy certain products instead of others—their purpose is not to control us in the manner of the oppressive power that Orwell describes. Another fundamental aspect that renders the metaphor inadequate is the absence of human judgement on that which is observed. If, in Orwell's case, observation is directly linked to judging behaviour as right or wrong and punishing it, in the case of the internet that judgement is largely absent. As Solove points out, "being observed by an insect on the wall is not invasive of privacy; rather, privacy is threatened by being subject to human observation, which involves judgments that can affect one's life and reputation" (2004, 34). On the web, much of the action of observation is performed and processed by computers, which are totally indifferent to our good or bad behaviour. This impersonality makes surveillance less invasive. The danger is then elsewhere rather than in the kind of innocuous personal information that is collected—such as marital status, hobbies, profession, personal tastes—which in principle could not be subject to any punishment for inappropriate behaviour. For Solove:

> the surveillance model does not explain why the recording of this non-taboo information poses a problem. ... Digital dossiers do cause a serious problem that is overlooked by the Big Brother metaphor, one that poses a threat not just to our freedom to explore the taboo, but to freedom in general. It is a problem that implicates the type of society we are becoming, the way we think, our place in the larger social order, and our ability to exercise meaningful control over our lives (Solove 2004, 35).

Solove then proposes the work of Kafka, specifically *The Trial,* to conceptualise this phenomenon. The central figure of *The Trial* is not an absolute central power that watches and controls everything but rather a much subtler and ungraspable power: bureaucracy. The story is well known: Joseph K wakes up one day with two officers at his door informing him that he is under arrest, although they do not tell him why. In fact, the guards do not seem to know either. When K asks who is accusing him and what he is accused of, they limit themselves to answering "You are under arrest, certainly, more than that I do not know" (Kafka, quoted in Solove 2004, 36). They do not take him prisoner either, instead they simply leave. For the rest of the novel, Joseph K unsuccessfully tries to find out the reasons for his arrest and resolve the situation. At each step he faces a vast bureaucratic machinery that has produced a dossier about him, which K naturally does not have access to but which theoretically contains the secret of his arrest.

According to Solove, "Kafka's *The Trial* best captures the scope, nature, and effects of the type of power relationship created by databases" (2004, 37), because it depicts an "indifferent bureaucracy, where individuals are pawns, not knowing what is happening, having no say or ability to exercise meaningful control over the process" (2004, 38). *The Trial* "captures the sense of helplessness, frustration, and vulnerability one experiences when a large bureaucratic organization has control over a vast dossier of details about one's life" (Solove 2004, 9), and in that sense it becomes a metaphor that digital dossiers posit, "the way the bureaucratic process treats individuals and their information" (Solove 2004, 38).

What does bureaucracy mean in this context? It indicates not a type of institution but a series of practices or processes of decision-making, standardised to make the system efficient according to previously established categories. The bureaucracy does not exercise the kind of manipulative power typical of Orwell—or Huxley's *Brave New World*, in which manipulation is exercised through pleasure and entertainment instead of force—but an indifferent power, a power that does not bother to inform K what he is accused of. It is indeed likely that the reason for his arrest does not exist or, if it exists, it is absurd. What is discernible, and for Solove this is the main point, are the social effects of the power relationship between Joseph K and the bureaucracy:

> The power depicted in *The Trial* is not so much a force as it is an element of relationships between individuals and society and government. These relationships have balances of power. What *The Trial* illustrates is that power is not merely exercised in totalitarian forms, and that relationships to bureaucracies which are unbalanced in

power can have debilitating effects upon individuals—regardless of the bureaucracies' purposes (which may, in fact, turn out to be quite benign). On this view, the problem with databases and the practices currently associated with them is that they disempower people. They make people vulnerable by stripping them of control over their personal information. There is no diabolical motive or secret plan for domination; rather, there is a web of thoughtless decisions made by low-level bureaucrats, standardised policies, rigid routines, and a way of relating to individuals and their information that often becomes indifferent to their welfare (Solove 2004, 40–41).

The problem then lies in our defencelessness before the digital self that results from the indiscriminate aggregation of our data. These representations are not only reductive, but also potentially erroneous. The information on the internet, so carefully collected and gathered, is not capable of distinguishing nuances, or providing contexts, but only supposed facts. For example, as Solove emphasises, a record of an arrest without any explanation of context or reason is "misleading" (2004, 49). That arrest could have been in the 1960s—or today—for civil disobedience while participating in a demonstration to defend a cause, but if this information does not appear, the datum 'arrest' will be interpreted simply as a sign of a criminal act.

In short, we are reconstituted in databases as digital persons composed of data. The privacy problem stems paradoxically from the pervasiveness of these data—the fact that they encompass much of our lives—as well as from their limitations—how they fail to capture us and distort who we are (Solove 2004, 49).

> In sum, the privacy problem created by the use of databases stems from an often careless and unconcerned bureaucratic process—one that has little judgment or accountability—and is driven by ends other than the protection of people's dignity. We are not just heading towards a world of Big Brother or one composed of Little Brothers, but also towards a more mindless process—of bureaucratic indifference, arbitrary errors, and dehumanisation—a world that is beginning to resemble Kafka's vision in *The Trial* (Solove 2004, 55).

To conclude and connect the two chapters, the question of the digital self and its modes of representation seems to be the other side of the question about digital politics and its modes of action but, in fact, it is not. The question of the self is always, at the same time, a question about "we"; as Vaidhyanathan claims,

Almost every major marketing campaign these days is likewise framed as being about "you". "You" have freedom of choice. "You" can let yourself be profiled so that "you" receive solicitations only from companies that interest "you." "You" could customize "your" mobile phone with a ringtone. "You" go to the Nike Store to design your own shoes. This emphasis on "you," however, is only a smokescreen for what is actually happening online. As I have stressed throughout this book, the Googlization of everything entails the harvesting, copying, aggregating, and ranking of information about and contributions made by each of us. This process exploits our profound need to connect and share, and our remarkable ability to create together—each person contributing a little bit to a poem, a song, a quilt, or a conversation. It is not about "you" at all. It should be about "us"—the Googlization of us (Vaidhyanathan 2011, 83).

It is about us, indeed, and above all about our possibilities to choose: the relevance and irrelevance of choice, the architecture of choice. The same world that constantly praises our unlimited choices seems to remain silent about the fact that we can only choose among the things that are not relevant. We cannot choose our privacy options on the internet, even if it seems so. We cannot control the information that is collected or circulated about us, and it is far from clear what influence we can have on the way it is being or will be used. Beyond any apocalyptic vision, the digital turn invites us to consider, perhaps more urgently or with a new urgency, an old problem: what our possibilities to choose really are, how we exercise that freedom, and, especially, how together we design the technologies that help us eliminate oppressions, or, on the contrary, increase them.

The research leading to Part 3 has received funding from the European Research Council (ERC) under the European Union's Horizon 2020 research and innovation programme ("Digital Memories", Grant agreement n° 677955)

Notes

NOTES INTRODUCTION

1. Paleo-anthropologists are still debating whether *Homo sapiens* speciated 200,000 or 500,000 years ago, or anywhere in between. Fascinating in its own right, this debate should not detain us here.

NOTES PART ONE: MASS MEANING

1. There is irony in the fact (if it is a fact) that this objection to linguistic error itself mistakenly calls the King *Caesar* rather than *Rex* (Ludwig got his promotion to Emperor only in 1433). But then Julius Caesar was never an emperor either. So it goes.
2. For a recent comprehensive account of (anti-)social media see Vaidhyanathan 2018. The first half of the book is not particularly enlightening in its kicking at open doors, but the second half contains perceptive and troubling diagnoses of the mess we are in.
3. For further comments on Smith's account of sympathy see de Graef 2003.
4. It obviously is not. For a fine succinct account of the afterlife in economic theory of this separation between economic self-interest and human decency, and its challenge (with qualified success) by behaviourial science see Haldar 2018.
5. See also Ypi 2014, 270–71.
6. See also Lehman 2009, 66–68.
7. Much the same can be said of the role of Facebook messages in the so-called "Arab Spring" or other protests in the first decades of the 21st century (Vaidhyanathan 2018, 128–45).
8. For an excellent account of the stakes of the Huxley-Arnold debate with specific emphasis on the lasting relevance of 19th-century thinking about education see Small 2013.
9. On the rise of sociology and its role in the Huxley-Arnold debate see Lepenies 1988, 155–74.
10. To be fair, Huxley himself admitted as much in his preface to the 1946 re-edition of the novel. (Aldous Huxley 2005, 6).
11. As Lee & Lee 1979 demonstrate, despite its short-lived existence the IPA has had a lasting influence on propaganda studies. Today, its legacy is still online: https://propagandacritic.com/.

12. "*So act that you use humanity, whether in your own person or in the person of any other, always at the same time as an end, never merely as a means*" Kant 1785, 80. The "Greatest Happiness principle" Huxley mentions is a reference to the Utilitarian philosophy of Jeremy Bentham (1748-1832), who argued that the greatest happiness of the greatest number is the measure of right and wrong.

13. "The Uniqueness of Man" is the title essay of a 1941 volume by Julian Huxley. The title of its US edition adds extra emphasis to its phallocentric incorrectness: *Man Stands Alone*.

14. For an account of Wells as heir to Thomas Henry Huxley see Vanvelk 2015.

15. It still is not. As I write this, in January 2019, Israel and the United States have just left UNESCO.

16. Huxley was commendably critical of the concept of "race" and co-authored a book published in the first year of World War II rubbishing "claims to 'racial unity' [...] in recent nationalist controversy" (Huxley, Haddon & Carr-Saunders 1939, 15–19).

17. Wikipedia contributors. "Mentifact." Wikipedia, The Free Encyclopedia. Wikipedia, The Free Encyclopedia, 7 Sep. 2019. Web. 22 Oct. 2019, from: https://en.wikipedia.org/wiki/Mentifact

18. "meme, n." OED Online, Oxford University Press, December 2018, www.oed.com/view/Entry/239909. Accessed 1 February 2019.

19. For a fascinating history of images in science, unfortunately not dealing with the double helix diagram, see Daston & Galison 2007.

20. The scans and comments can be consulted on Newberg's website: http://www.andrewnewberg.com/research/.

21. For a more extensive discussion see de Graef 2014.

22. https://www.publicbooks.org/about/.

23. For a fine critical account of big data also recommended by Underwood see boyd & Crawford 2012; for a salutary note of caution about over-eager adoption of computational techniques in cultural scholarship see Da 2019 and the online forum in response to this article https://critinq.wordpress.com/2019/03/31/computational-literary-studies-a-critical-inquiry-online-forum/.

NOTES PART TWO: MEDIUM

1. https://en.wikipedia.org/wiki/The_Book_of_Sand. The eponymous collection that contains the story was initially published in Spanish in 1975 (Buenos Aires: Emecé). English version: Borges 2001.

2. It is crucial in this regard to observe that this story about infinite meanings is a... *short* story. Borges, who did not like James Joyce, has made strong claims against authors writing 500 pages on subjects one would prefer to read in their abridged, five-page version (he will exemplify this claim by reviewing invented books, a high-brow version of the lower middle *Reader's Digest* ideology). Size matters, and the anxiety of information overload in the digital era proves a key issue in contemporary thinking on words and images. *The Book of Sand* illustrates Borges's conviction that literature is infinite, not because of the infinite number of books, but because each book is infinite.

3. In the most literal sense of the word: Marshall McLuhan actually did participate in a TV show inspired by *The Medium is the Massage*, a typographically truly revolutionary "reader's digest" version of the author's ideas. This is how his biographer, Philip Marchand, explains his role in it:

"[a]lmost simultaneous with the publication of the book was the release of the CBS Records version of *The Medium is the Massage* and a one-hour NBC television documentary on McLuhan, which aired on March 19, 1967. The NBC film featured clips of McLuhan delivering one-liners, thrown into a stew of pop art, animated visuals, newspaper headlines, and other images and edited with the fast-cut technique coming into vogue in both movies and television. (Beatles' movies had led the way). McLuhan detested the film, produced by Ernest Pintoff, calling it 'grotesque trash'" (Marchand 1998: 203).

Available on youtube: https://archive.org/details/thisismarshallmcluhanthemediumisthemessage (part 1) and https://archive.org/details/thisismarshallmcluhanthemediumisthemessage/thisismarshallmcluhanthemediumisthemessagereel1/thisismarshallmcluhanthemediumisthemessagereel2.mov (part 2).

4.   Bound non-periodical publication having 49 or more pages.

5.   The following lines rework some passages from Baetens & Sánchez-Mesa (2015).

6.   There exist of course many other proposals to organise the field. A very famous, and an equally simple, one is the article by Irina Rajewsky from 2005. Its scope is however that of intermediality alone, not that of transmediality.

7.   In the aesthetic theory of Nelson Goodman, the distinction of the terms autographic vs allographic is defined this way: "a work of art is autographic if and only if the distinction between original and forgery of it is significant; or better, if and only if even the most exact duplication of it does not thereby count as genuine" (1976, 113).

8.   In spite of their apparent synonymy, the notions of "culture industry" and "cultural industry" are dramatically different. The first one refers to the commercial and ideological standardisation of culture in modern capitalist societies, as introduced by Adorno and Horkheimer in their book, *Dialectic of Englightenment* (1947). The second refers to the way in which cultural goods and services are created, produced and distributed. Within the broad field of the cultural industries, a further distinction is made between cultural industries in the narrow sense of the word and creative industries, which entail the management of intellectual property rights.

9.   Actually, all important scholars in the field do so. The difference between Kirschenbaum and others such as Manovich and Hayles is just a matter of focus: all of them directly address issues of code, but the former is doing it more extensively than the latter. Other examples can be found in Moulthrop and Grigar (2017).

10.   "The Garden of Forking Paths" (original Spanish title: *"El jardín de los senderos que se bifurcan"*) is a 1941 short story by Argentine writer and poet, Jorge Luis Borges. It is the title story in the collection *El jardín de los senderos que se bifurcan* (1941), which was republished in its entirety in *Ficciones* (*Fictions*) in 1944. It was the first of Borges's works to be translated into English by Anthony Boucher when it appeared in *Ellery Queen's Mystery Magazine* in August 1948 (Wikiedia, accessed on 8 April 2019).

11.   See the synoptic tableau on page 106.

12.   To open the black box is not just a metaphor, as shown by Robert Sikoryak's "unauthorized adaptation" of Apple's user contract, *Terms and Conditions* (Montreal: Drawn and Quarterly, 2017).

13.   For a parodical view of the newly hegemonic role of the curator in visual arts see the 2005 performance "Licking Curator's Ass" by Ondrej Brody and Kristofer Paetau: https://iffr.com/en/2007/films/licking-curators-ass.

14.   This project has been "creatively copied" by Kenneth Goldsmith in his book on New York (2015a).

15. The French system definitely gives more rights to the individual author or copyright owner than the Anglo-Saxon system, which in its turn is rapidly evolving towards a trade-mark system that unquestionably favours intermediary institutions (read: companies). And in our globalising world, the French legal approach is certainly not gaining points...

16. Second Life is an online virtual world, developed and owned by Linden Lab and launched in 2003. By 2013, *Second Life* had approximately one million regular users. In many ways, *Second Life* is similar to massively multiplayer online role-playing games; however, Linden Lab is emphatic that its creation is not a game. See: https://secondlife.com/.

17. In a dramatically influential and still frequently quoted essay, Krauss (1979) claims that post-modern sculpture can no longer be analysed as an object or a practice in itself (as the traditional Modernist paradigm would like to have it). Post-modern sculpture is a practice that blurs the boundaries between work and material context as well as between media, hence the necessity to study it in an "expanded field" that also includes notions such as landscape and architecture. The appeal to situate artistic media in some kind of "expanded field" has rapidly become a basic feature of contemporary criticism.

18. It should be stressed however that digital self-publishing remains quite rare, at least for successful or important writers. The example of Stephen King, whose experiments with self-publishing on the net were short-lived and, one may assume, not very positive, seems to suggest that the traditional structures are more resilient than one thought at the launch of the e-book hype. As far as literature in print is concerned, and given the complexity of physical storage and distribution structures, self-publishing has never been a real option in the modern publishing business.

19. An inspiring example is the *EXTRA!* Festival organised by the Centre Pompidou in Paris. See https://www.centrepompidou.fr/cpv/resource/cdAaBnj/r5nd5g4.

20. http://nt2.uqam.ca/fr/search/site/?f%5B0%5D=type%3Arepertoire&retain-filters=1   (the acronym NT2 stands for: Nouvelles Technologies + Nouvelles Textualités).

21. http://collection.eliterature.org/, where one finds the three volumes (2006, 2011, 2016) of the *"Electronic Literature Organization" Collection*.

22. https://elmcip.net/ (the acronym ELMCIP stands for: Electronic Literature as a Model of Creativity and Innovation in Practice).

23. http://www.ubu.com/resources/index.html
Of course the nod to Alfred Jarry's bitingly absurdist farce *Ubu Roi* (1896) is key to the name of the site, which also refers, on a more sober note, to the institution (the State University of New York at Buffalo) that first hosted it.

24. Quoted from Rilke's *8th Duino Elegy*:
"And we: always and everywhere spectators,
turned toward the stuff of our lives, and never outward.
It all spills over us. We put it to order.
It falls apart. We order it again
and fall apart ourselves."
(Translated by Joanna Macy & Anita Barrows)

25. The project was a collaboration between the University of Leiden, the University of Utrecht and the Stedelijk Museum Amsterdam. More information is available at https://www.stedelijk.nl/en/dig-deeper/research/photographs-and-preservation.

26. The video recordings of the proceedings can be found here: day 1: https://vimeo.com/270085856, and day 2: https://vimeo.com/278105994.
27. The point had not escaped Borges either, see his short story "The Wall and the Books" (1975).

NOTES PART 3: COMMUNITY

1. In a different domain, that of digital memory, Andrew Hoskins (2017) also replaces the "collective" in "collective memory" with "connective memory," which he uses to describe the shift in how collective memory is shaped under the impact of digital ecology.
2. For a discussion on the differences between "cyberactivism," "online advocacy," "e-activism" and "social media for social change" see the introduction "How to Think about Digital Activism", by Mary Joyce (2010) in *Digital Activism Decoded: The New Mechanics of Change*.

Works Cited

Aarseth, Espen J. (1997). *Cybertext—Perspectives on Ergodic Literature.* Baltimore, Maryland: Johns Hopkins University Press.

AlexstrifePE. (2006). "Star Wars Kid VS Yoda." YouTube. 6 December. https://www.youtube.com/watch?v=2URImmLYAsQ.

Althaus, Scott L., and David Tewksbury (2000). "Patterns of Internet and Traditional News Media Use in a Networked Community". *Political Communication* 17 (1): 21–45.

Amerika, Mark (2011). *remixthebook.* Minneapolis, Minnesota: Minnesota University Press.

Anderson, Benedict (2006[1991]). *Imagined Communities: Reflections on the Origin and Spread of Nationalism.* Revised edition. London: Verso.

Appadurai, Arjun (1996). *Modernity at Large: Cultural Dimensions of Globalization.* Minneapolis, Minnesota: University of Minnesota Press.

Arnold, Matthew (1861). "Democracy", in Arnold 1993, 1–25.

—— (1864). "The Function of Criticism at the Present Time", in Arnold 1993, 26–51.

—— (1869). "Culture and Anarchy: An Essay in Political and Social Criticism", in Arnold 1993, 53–187.

—— (1882). "Literature and Science", in Matthew Arnold (1974). *Philistinism in England and America*, ed. R.H. Super. Ann Arbor, Michigan: University of Michigan Press, 53–73.

—— (1993). *Culture and Anarchy and Other Writings*, ed. Stefan Collini. Cambridge: Cambridge University Press.

Austin, J.L. (1976). *How to Do Things with Words.* Oxford: Oxford University Press.

Baetens, Jan (2014). "Le médium n'est pas soluble dans les médias de masse". *Hermès* 70, 40–45.

—— (2016). *À voix haute. Poésie et lecture publique.* Brussels: Les Impressions Nouvelles.

—— (2017). "Les livres de poche: une littérature 'exposée'?". *Image (&) Narrative*, 18:4, 55–62. http://www.imageandnarrative.be/index.php/imagenarrative/article/view/1651.

—— (2018 [2008]). *Novelization. From Film to Novel*, trans. Mary Feeney. Columbus, Ohio: Ohio State University Press.

Baetens, Jan, and Ben de Bruyn (2018). "In Defense of Canonization", in *Writing Literary History*, ed Matthias Somers and Bram Lambrecht. Leuven: Peeters, 39–53.

Baetens, Jan, and Hugo Frey (2015). *The Graphic Novel.* New York: Cambridge University Press.

Baetens, Jan, and Domingo Sánchez-Mesa (2015). "Literature in the Expanded Field: Intermediality at the Crossroads of Literary Theory and Comparative Literature". *Interfaces* 36, 289–304.

Barlow, John Perry (1996). "A Declaration of the Independence of Cyberspace". https://www.eff.org/nl/cyberspace-independence.

Baron-Cohen, Simon (2012). *Zero Degrees of Empathy: A New Theory of Human Cruelty and Kindness.* London: Penguin.

Barras, Colin (2018). "World's oldest drawing is Stone Age crayon doodle". *Nature* online, 12 September 2018, doi: 10.1038/d41586-018-06664-y.

Baym, Nancy K. (2010). *Personal Connections in the Digital Age.* Cambridge: Polity Press.

Benjamin, Walter (1969 [1935]). "The Work of Art in the Age of Technical Reproduction", in *Illuminations*, ed. Hannah Arendt, trans. Harry Zohn, from the 1935 essay. New York: Schocken Books.

—— (2002). *The Arcades Project,* trans. Howard Eiland and Kevin McLaughlin. Cambridge, Massachusetts: Belknap Press.

Bennett, Lance W., and Alexandra Segerberg (2012). "The Logic of Connective Action". *Information, Communication & Society* 15:5, 739–768.

—— (2013) *The Logic of Connective Action. Digital Media and the Personalization of Contentious Politics.* Cambridge, Massachusetts: Cambridge University Press.

Bennington, Geoffrey, and Jacques Derrida (1991). *Jacques Derrida.* Paris: Seuil.

Berland, Jody (2009). *North of Empire: Essays on the Cultural Technologies of Space.* Durham, North Carolina: Duke University Press.

Beronä, David (2008). *Wordless Books. The Original Graphic Novels.* New York: Abrams.

Berry, David M. (2014). *Critical Theory and the Digital.* London: Bloomsbury. Kindle edition.

Bianchini, Samuel (2012). "La Performation–Quand faire, c'est dire", in *L'Ère post-média. Humanités digitales et cultures numériques,* ed. Jean-Paul Fourmentraux. Paris: Hermann, 137–162.

Bijker, Wiebe E., Thomas P. Hughes and Trevor J. Pinch (eds) (1987). *The Social Construction of Technological Systems: New Directions in the Sociology and History of Technology.* Cambridge, Massachusetts, MIT Press.

Black, Edwin (2001). *IBM and the Holocaust: The Strategic Alliance between Nazi Germany and America's Most Powerful Corporation.* New York: Crown.

Bloomfield, Camille (2017). *Raconter l'Oulipo. 1960–2000.* Paris: Honoré Champion.

Bobbio, Norberto. (1996 [1994]). *Left and Right: The Significance of a Political Distinction.* Cambridge: Polity Press.

Bolter, Jay D., and Richard Grusin (1999). *Remediation. Understanding New Media,* Cambridge, Massachusetts: MIT Press.

Bonnet, Gilles (2017). *Pour une poétique numérique. Littérature et Internet.* Paris: Hermann.

Borges, Jorge Luis (1975 [1952]). *Other Inquisitions, 1937–1952,* trans. Ruth L.C. Simms. Austin, Texas: Texas University Press.

—— (2001). *The Book of Sand* (2001 [1975], trans. Andrew Hurley. London: Penguin.

—— (1962). "Funes the Memorious", in *Labyrinths.* New York, New Directions Publishing Company, 65–71.

boyd, danah (2011). "Social Network Sites as Networked Publics: Affordances, Dynamics, and Implications", in *A Networked Self: Identity, Community, and Culture on Social Network Sites*, ed. Zizi Papacharissi. New York: Routledge, 39–58.

boyd, danah, and Nicole B. Ellison (2008). "Social Network Sites: Definition, History, and Scholarship". *Journal of Computer-Mediated Communication* 13, 210–230.

boyd, danah, and Kate Crawford (2012). "Critical Questions for Big Data". *Information, Communication & Society* 15:5, 662–679. doi: 10.1080/1369118X.2012.678878.

Burman, Jeremy Trevelyan (2012). "The misunderstanding of memes: Biography of an unscientific object, 1976–1999". *Perspectives on Science* 20:1, 75–104.

Carroll, Noel (1996). "Medium Specificity Arguments and the Self-Consciously Invented Arts. Film, Video, and Photography", in Noel Caroll, *Theorizing the Moving Image*, Cambridge: University of Cambridge Press.

Cavell, Stanley (1979). *The World Viewed*, Cambridge, Massachusetts, Harvard University Press.

Cayley, John (2018). "The Code Is Not the Text (Unless It Is the Text)", in John Cayley, *Grammalepsy. Essays on Digital Language Art*. New York: Bloomsbury, 53–66.

Chadwick, Andrew (2009). "Web 2.0: New Challenges for the Study of e-Democracy in the Era of Informational Exuberance". *I/S: A Journal of Law and Policy for the Information Society* 5.1, 9–41.

—— (2013). *The Hybrid Media System*. Oxford: Oxford University Press.

Chandler, David (2004). *Constructing Global Civil Society. Morality and Power in International Relations.* Basingstoke: Palgrave Macmillan.

Christin, Anne-Marie (1995). *L'image écrite ou la déraison graphique*. Paris: Flammarion.

—— (2009). *Poétique du blanc*. Paris: Vrin.

Church0fScientology (2008). "Message to Scientology," YouTube video, 2:03, 21 January 2008, https://youtu.be/JCbKv9yiLiQ.

Cohen, B.R. (2018). "Public Thinker: Siva Vaidhyanathan on Facebook and Other 'Antisocial' Media". *Public Books* 12 September 2018. https://www.publicbooks.org/books-of-the-year-2018-public-thinker-siva-vaidhyanathan-on-facebook-and-other-antisocial-media/.

Coleman, Gabriella (2011). "Hacker Politics and Publics". *Public Culture* 23:3, 511–516.

—— (2014). *The Many Faces of Anonymous*. London: Verso.

Collins, Jim (2010). *Bring on the Books for Everybody. How Literary Culture Became Popular Culture*. Durham, North Carolina: Duke University Press.

Cortázar, Julio (1966 [1963]). *Hopscotch*, trans. Gregory Rabassa. New York: Pantheon.

Costello, Diarmuid (2008). "On the Very Idea of a 'Specific' Medium: Michael Fried and Stanley Cavell on Painting and Photography as Arts". *Critical Inquiry* 34:2, 274–312.

D'heer, Evelien, and Pier Verdegem (2014). "An Intermedia Understanding of the Networked Twitter Ecology. The 2012 Local elections in Belgium", in *Social Media in Politics. Case Studies on the Political Power of Social Media*, ed. Bogdan Patrut and Monica Patrut. New York: Springer.

Da, Nan Z. (2019). "The Computational Case against Computational Literary Studies," *Critical Inquiry* 45:3, 601–639.

Dahlberg, Lincoln (2011). "Re-Constructing Digital Democracy: An Outline of Four 'Positions'". *New Media and Society* 13, 855–872.

Dahlgren, Peter (2005). "The Internet, Public Spheres, and Political Communication: Dispersion and Deliberation". *Political Communication* 22, 147–162.

Dalton, Russell J. (2014). *Citizen Politics*: *Public Opinion and Political Parties in Advanced Industrial Democracies*. London: Sage.

Daston, Lorraine, and Peter Galison (2007). *Objectivity*. New York: Zone Books.

Dawkins, Richard (2006). *The Selfish Gene*. 30th anniversary edition. Oxford: Oxford University Press.

De Graef, Ortwin (2003). "Suffering, Sympathy, Circulation: Smith, Wordsworth, Coetzee (But there's a dog)". *European Journal of English Studies* 7:3, 311–31.

—— (2014). "Spectre Disorder: Neuro-Marxism and the State of the Soul", in *Marxism and the Future: Proceedings of the Sino-British Bilateral Forum on Marxist Aesthetics,* ed. Wang Jie *et al*. Shanghai: Central Compilation and Translation, 107–123.

De Kosnik, Abigail (2016). *Rogue Archives: Digital Cultural Memory and Media Fandom.* Cambridge, Massachusetts: MIT Press.

Dean, Jodi (2016). "Images without Viewers: Selfie Communism" https://www.fotomuseum.ch/en/explore/still-searching/articles/26420_images_without_viewers_selfie_communism.

Debray, Régis (1995). "The Three Ages of Looking". *Critical Inquiry* 21:3, 529–555.

Delius, Juan D. (1989). "Of mind memes and brain bugs; a natural history of culture", in *The nature of culture: proceedings of the international and interdisciplinary symposium, October 7–11, 1986 in Bochum*, ed. Walter A. Koch. Bochum: Studienverlag Brockmeyer. 26–79.

—— (1991). "The nature of culture", in *The Tinbergen Legacy*, ed. Marian Stamp Dawkins, T.R. Halliday and Richard Dawkins. London: Chapman & Hall, 75–99.

DeSilvey, Caitlin (2017). *Curated Decay. Heritage Beyond Saving.* Minneapolis, Minnesota: Minnesota University Press.

Di Fraia, Guido, and Maria Carlotta Missaglia (2016). "Two Step Flow Twitter Communication in 2013 Italian Political Election: A Missed Opportunity for Citizen Participation", in *Citizen Participation and Political Communication in a Digital World*, ed. Alex Frame and Gilles Brachotte. New York and London: Routledge. Kindle edition. 25–41.

Dworkin, Craig (2013). *No Medium.* Cambridge, Massachusetts: MIT Press.

—— (2018). "Poetry in the Age of Consumer-Generated Content". *Critical Inquiry* 44:4, 674–705.

Eakin, Paul John (1999). *How Our Lives Becomes Stories: Making Selves.* Ithaca: Cornell University Press.

Earl, Jennifer, and Katrina Kimport (2011). *Digitally Enabled Social Change: Activism in the Internet Age.* Cambridge, Massachusetts: MIT Press.

Earl, Jennifer, Jayson Hunt, R. Kelly Garrett, and Aysenur Dal (2015). "New Technologies and Social Movements", in *The Oxford Handbook of Social Movements*, ed. Donatella Della Porta and Mario Diani. Oxford: Oxford University Press.

Eckel, Julia, Jens Ruchatz and Sabine Wirth (eds) (2018). *Exploring the Selfie: Historical, Theoretical, and Analytical Approaches to Digital Self-Photography.* London: Palgrave Macmillan.

—— (2018). "The Selfie as Image (and) Practice: Approaching Digital Self-Photography", in *Exploring the Selfie: Historical, Theoretical, and Analytical Approaches to Digital Self-Photography*, ed. Eckel, Ruchatz and Wirth. London: Palgrave Macmillan, 1–23.

Eco, Umberto (1989 [1962]). *The Open Work*, trans. Anna Cancogni. Cambridge, Massachusetts: Harvard University Press.

Eco, Umberto, and Jean-Claude Carrière. 2012 [2009]. *This Is Not the End of the Book*, trans. Polly McLean. Evanston, Illinois: Northwestern University Press.

Edwards, Michael (ed.) (2011). *The Oxford Handbook of Civil Society.* New York: Oxford University Press.

Einspänner-Pflock, Jessica, Mario Anastasiadis and Caja Thimm (2016). "Ad Hoc Mini-Publics on Twitter Citizen Participation or Political Communication? Examples from the German National Election 2013", in *Citizen Participation and Political Communication in a Digital World*, ed. Alex Frame and Gilles Brachotte. New York and London: Routledge. Kindle edition, 42–59.

Elsaesser, Thomas (2006). "Early Film Theory and Multi-Media: An Archaeology of Possible Futures?", in *New media, Old Media. A History and Theory Reader*, ed. Wendy Hui Kyong Chun and Thomans Kennan. New York: Routledge, 13–25.

Emerson, Lori (2014). *Reading Writing Interfaces: From the Digital to the Bookbound.* Minneapolis, Minnesota: Minnesota University Press.

Engels, Friedrich, and Karl Marx (1848). *Manifesto of the Communist Party*. https://www.marxists.org/archive/marx/works/1848/communist-manifesto/.

fantom81z28 (2006). "Star Wars Kid Drunken Jedi." *YouTube*. 16 February. https://www.youtube.com/watch?v=3GJOVPjhXMY.

Foucault, Michel (1995 [1975]). *Discipline and Punish: The Birth of the Prison*, trans. Alan Sheridan. New York: Random House.

Flusser, Vilém (2000 [1983]). *Towards a Philosophy of Photography*. trans. Anthony Mathews, London: Reaktion Books.

Fortunati, Leopoldina (2005). "Is body to body communication still the prototype?" *The Information Society* 21, 53–61.

Foucault, Michel (1982). *The Archeology of Knowledge*, trans. A.M. Sheridan Smith. New York: Pantheon Books.

Frame, Alex, and Gilles Brachotte, eds (2016). *Citizen Participation and Political Communication in a Digital World*. New York and London: Routledge. Kindle edition.

Fraser, Nancy (1992). "Rethinking the Public Sphere: A Contribution to the Critique of Actually Existing Democracy", in *Habermas and the Public Sphere*, ed. Craig Calhoun Cambridge, Massachusetts: MIT Press, 109–142.

Friess, Dennis, and Christiane Eilders (2015). "A Systematic Review of Online Deliberation Research". *Policy and Internet* 7.3, 319–39.

Fuchs, Christian (2015). "Anonymous. Hacktivism and Contemporary Politics", in *Social Media, Politics and the State. Protests, Revolutions, Riots, Crime and Policing in the Age of Facebook, Twitter and YouTube.*, ed. Daniel Trottier and Christian Fuchs. New York: Routledge, 88–106.

—— (2014). *Social Media: A Critical Introduction*. London: Sage.

—— (2018). *Digital Demagogue. Authoritarian Capitalism in the Age of Trump and Twitter*. London: Pluto Press.

Gagnon, Monika Kin, and Janine Marchessault (eds) (2014). *Reimagining Cinema: Film at Expo 67*. Montreal and Kingston: McGill and Queen's University Press.

Gardner, Jared (2012a). *The Rise and Fall of Early American Magazine Culture*. Chicago, Illinois: University of Illinois Press.

—— (2012b). *Projections Comics and the History of Twenty-First-Century Storytelling*. Stanford, California: Stanford University Press.

Gaudreault, André, and Philippe Marion (2015 [2013]). *The End of Cinema?: A Medium in Crisis in the Digital Age*, trans. Timothy Bernard. New York: Columbia University Press.

Gillespie, Tarleton (2010). "The Politics of 'Platforms'". *New Media & Society* 12:3, 347–64.

Gitelman, Lisa (2008 [2006]). *Always Already New; Media, History, and the Data of Culture*. Cambridge, Massachusetts: MIT Press.

—— (2014). *Paper Knowledge: Toward a Media History of Documents*. Durham, North Carolina: Duke University Press.

Gladwell, Malcolm (2010). "Small Change: Why the revolution will not be tweeted". *The New Yorker*, 4 October.

Goffman, Erving (1959). *The Presentation of Self in Everyday Life*. New York: Anchor Books.

Goldsmith, Kenneth (2011). "Why Conceptual Writing? Why Now?", in *Against Expression. An Anthology of Conceptual Writing*, ed. Craig Dworkin and Kenneth Goldsmith. Evanston, Illinois: Northwestern University Press, xvii–xxii.

—— (2012). *Uncreative Writing*. New York: Columbia University Press.

—— (2015a). *Capital: New York, Capital of the 20th Century*. London: Verso.

—— (2015b). *Seven American Deaths and Disasters*. New York: powerhouse books.

—— (n.d). "Being Boring", http://writing.upenn.edu/library/Goldsmith-Kenny_Being-Boring. html (retrieved 20 July 2018).

Goodman, Nelson (1976). *Languages of Art*. 2nd edition. Indianapolis, Indiana: Hackett.

Gray, John (2008). "The Atheist Delusion". *The Guardian*,15 March 2008. https://www.theguardian. com/books/2008/mar/15/society.

Grusin, Richard (2015). "Radical Mediation". *Critical Inquiry* 42:1, 124–148.

Habermas, Jürgen (1989) [1962], *The Structural Transformation of the Public Sphere: An Inquiry into a Category of Bourgeois Society*, trans. Thomas Burger and Frederick Lawrence. Cambridge, Massachusetts: The MIT Press.

—— (2006). "The Public Sphere: An Encyclopedia Article". In *Media and Cultural Studies: Keyworks*, ed. Meenakshi Gigi Durham and Douglas M. Kellner. Malden: Blackwell.

Haig, David (2006). "The Gene Meme", in *Richard Dawkins: How a Scientist Changed the Way We Think,* ed. Alan Grafen and Mark Ridley. Oxford: Oxford University Press, 50–65.

Haldar, Antara (2018). "Intrinsic goodness: Why we might behave better than we think". *Times Literary Supplement*, 2 November 2018, 10–11.

Harari, Yuval Noah (2014). *Sapiens: A Brief History of Mankind*. London: Vintage.

Hayles, N. Katherine (1999). *How We Became Posthuman: Virtual Bodies in Cybernetics, Literature and Informatics*. Chicago, Illinois: Chicago University Press.

—— (2002). *Writing Machines*. Cambridge, Massachusetts: MIT Press.

—— (2007). "Narrative and Database: Natural Symbionts". *PMLA* 122:5, 1603–1608

—— (2008). *Electronic Literature*. Notre-Dame, Indiana: Notre-Dame University Press.

Hayles, N. Katherine and Jessica Pressman (eds) (2013). *Comparative Textual Media. Transforming the Humanities in the Postprint Era*. Minneapolis, Minnesota: Minnesota University Press.

Haythornthwaite, Caroline (2005). "Social networks and Internet connectivity effects". *Information, Communication & Society* 8:2, 125–147.

Henkin, David (2018). "The Book is a Time Machine." *Public Books* 19 July 2018. http://www.publicbooks.org/the-book-is-a-time-machine/.

Henshilwood, Christopher S., Francesco d'Errico, Karen L. van Niekerk, Laure Dayet, Alain Queffelec and Luca Pollarolo (2018). "An abstract drawing from the 73,000-year-old levels at Blombos Cave, South Africa". *Nature* 562, 115–118.

Heylighen, Francis (2011). "Conceptions of a Global Brain: An Historical Review". *Evolution: Cosmic, Biological, and Social*, ed. Leonid E. Grinin, Robert L. Carneiro, Andrey V. Korotayev and Fred Spier. Volgograd: 'Uchitel' Publishing House, 274–89.

Hobbes, Thomas ([1651], 1996). *Leviathan*. Revised student edition, ed. Richard Tuck. Cambridge: Cambridge University Press.

Hoskins, Andrew (ed.) (2017). *Digital Memory Studies. Media Pasts in Transition*. New York: Routledge.

Hrdy, Sarah Blaffer (2009). *Mothers and Others: The Evolutionary Origins of Mutual Understanding*. Cambridge, Massachusetts: Harvard University Press.

Huthamo, Erkki, and Jussi Parikka (eds) (2011). *Media Archaeology: Approaches, Applications, and Implications*. Berkeley, California: University of California Press.

Humboldt, Wilhelm von (1993 [1852]). *The Limits of State Action*, ed. J. W. Burrow. Indianapolis, Indiana: Liberty Fund.

Huxley, Aldous (2005 [1932]). *Brave New World and Brave New World Revisited*. Foreword Christopher Hitchens. New York: Harper Perennial.

Huxley, Julian (1941). *The Uniqueness of Man*. London: Chatto & Windus.

—— (2010 [1946]). "UNESCO: Its Purpose and Its Philosophy", in *UNESCO: Its Purpose and Philosophy: facsimiles of English and French editions of this visionary policy document.* London: Euston Grove Press, 1–62.

—— (1957). *New Bottles for New Wine*. London: Chatto & Windus.

Huxley, Julian, Alfred Cort Haddon and A.M. Carr-Saunders (1939). *We Europeans: A Survey of "Racial" Problems*. Harmondsworth: Penguin.

Huxley, Thomas Henry (1881 [1880]). *Science and Culture, and Other Essays*. New York: Appleton and Company. http://aleph0.clarku.edu/huxley/CE3/S-C.html.

Israel, Alejandro (2006). "Star Wars Kid- Agent Smith Fight." YouTube. 26 June. https://www.youtube.com/watch?v=YvEibGgp-GA.

Jackson, Peter, Philip Crang and Claire Dwyer (2004). "Introduction: the spaces of transnationality", in *Transnational Spaces,* ed. Peter Jackson, Philip Crang and Claire Dwyer. London and New York: Routledge, 1–24.

Janssen, Peter, and Elsie Premereur (2018). "Kijken in je hoofd: hoe kan hersenonderzoek onze samenleving veranderen?" *Karakter* 61. http://www.tijdschriftkarakter.be/kijken-in-je-hoofd-hoe-kan-hersenonderzoek-onze-samenleving-veranderen/.

Jenkins, Henry (2003). "Transmedia storytelling. Moving characters from books to films to video games can make them stronger and more compelling". *MIT Technology Review*. http://www.technologyreview.com/biotech/13052/

—— (2006). *Convergence Culture. Where Old Media and New Media Collide*, New York, New York University Press.

—— (2009). "The Revenge of the Origami Unicorn". *Confessions of an Aca-Fan*: http://henryjenkins.org/blog/2009/12/the_revenge_of_the_origami_uni.html

Jolles, André (2017 [1930]). *Simple Forms*, trans. Peter J. Schwartz. London-New York: Verso.

Jones, Steven (1997). "The Internet and its social landscape", in *Virtual Culture: Identity and Communication in Cybersociety*, ed. Steven Jones. Thousand Oaks, California: Sage. 7–35.

Jordan, Lisa (2011). "Global Civil Society", in *The Oxford Handbook of Civil Society*, ed. Michael Edwards. New York: Oxford University Press, 93–105.

Joyce, Mary (ed.) (2010a). *Digital Activism Decoded: The New Mechanics of Change*. New York: International Debate Education Association.

—— (2010b). "Introduction: How to Think About Digital Activism", in *Digital Activism Decoded: The New Mechanics of Change*, ed. Mary Joyce. New York: International Debate Education Association, 1–15.

Kaldor, Mary (2011). "Social Movements, NGOs, and Networks", in *Global Activism Reader*, ed. Luc Reydams. New York and London: Continuum, 3–23.

—— (2003). *Global Civil Society: an Answer to War*. Cambridge: Polity Press.

Kalifa, Dominique, Philippe Régnier, Marie-Ève Thérenty and Alain Vaillant (eds) (2011). *La Civilisation du journal: Histoire culturelle et littéraire de la presse française au XIXe siècle*. Paris: Nouveau Monde.

Kansteiner, Wulf (2017). "The Holocaust in the 21st Century: Digital anxiety, transnational cosmopolitanism, and never again genocide without memory", in *Digital Memory Studies. Media Pasts in Transition,* ed. Andrew Hoskins. New York: Routledge, 116–149.

Kant, Immanuel (1784a). "Idea for a Universal History with a Cosmopolitan Purpose", in Kant 1991, 41–53.

—— (1784b). "An Answer to the Question: 'What Is Enlightenment?'", in Kant 1991, 54–60.

—— (1785)." Groundwork of the Metaphysics of Morals", in Kant 1996, 37–108.

—— (1788). "Critique of Practical Reason", in Kant 1996, 133-271.

—— (2001 [1790]). *Critique of the Power of Judgment,* ed. Paul Guyer, trans. Paul Guyer and Eric Matthews. Cambridge: Cambridge University Press.

—— (1798). "A Renewed Attempt to Answer the Question: 'Is the Human Race Continually Improving?'", in Kant 1991, 177–90.

—— (1991). *Political Writings*, ed. Hans S. Reiss, trans. H.B. Nisbett. Second, enlarged ed. Cambridge: Cambridge University Press.

—— (1996). *Practical Philosophy*, trans. and ed. Mary J. Gregor, gen. ed. Allen Wood. Cambridge: Cambridge University Press.

Kavada, Anastasia (2010). "Activism Transforms Digital: The Social Movement Perspective", in *Digital Activism Decoded: The New Mechanics of Change*, ed. May Joyce. New York: International Debate Education Association, 101–118.

Kawase, Hiroshi, Okata Yoji and Kimiaki Ito (2013). "Role of Huge Geometric Circular Structures in the Reproduction of a Marine Pufferfish". *Scientific Reports* 3, 2106. doi:10.1038/srep02106 (2013).

Kellaway, Kate (2010). "How the Observer brought the WWF into being". *The Observer,* 7 November 2010. https://www.theguardian.com/environment/2010/nov/07/wwf-world-wildlife-fund-huxley.

Kelsey, Robin (2007). *Archive Style. Photographs and Illustrations for U.S. Surveys, 1850–1890*. Berkeley, California: University of California Press.

Kenaan, Hagi (2018). "The Selfie and the Face", in *Exploring the Selfie: Historical, Theoretical, and Analytical Approaches to Digital Self-Photography,* ed. Julia Eckel, Jens Ruchatz and Sabine Wirth. London: Palgrave Macmillan. 113–130.

Kittler, Friedrich (1992 [1985]). *Discourse Networks, 1800/1900*, trans. Michael Metteer. Stanford, California: Stanford University Press.

—— (1999 [1986]). *Gramophone, Film, Typewriter (Writing Science),* trans. Geoffrey Winthrop-Young and Michael Wutz. Stanford, California: Stanford University Press.

Krauss, Rosalind (1979). "Sculpture in the Expanded Field". *October* 8, 30–44.

—— (1999). *"A Voyage on the North Sea". Art in the Age of the Post-Medium Condition*. London: Thames and Hudson.

Landow, George (2006 [1992]). *Hypertext.3.0. Critical Theory and New Media in an Era of Globalization*. Baltimore, Maryland: Johns Hopkins University Press.

Lapham, Lewis (1997). "Introduction to the MIT Press Edition. The Eternal Ow", in Marshall McLuhan, *Understanding Media* [1964]. Cambridge, Massachusetts: MIT Press, i-xxiii.

Lasch, Christopher (1979). *The Culture of Narcissism: American Life in an Age of Diminishing Expectations*. New York: Norton & Co.

Lee, Elizabeth Briant, and Alfred McClung Lee (1979). "The Fine Arts of Propaganda Analysis—Then and Now". *ETC: A Review of General Semantics* 36:2, 117–127.

Lehman, Robert S. (2009). "Finite States: Toward a Kantian Theory of the Event". *Diacritics* 39:1, 61–74.

Lepenies, Wolf (1988). *Between Literature and Science: The Rise of Sociology,* trans. Reginald John Hollingdale. Cambridge: Cambridge University Press.

Letourneux, Matthieu (2017). *Fictions à la chaîne. Littératures sérielles et culture* médiatique. Paris: Seuil.

Leys, Simon (2018). *La Chine, la mer, la littérature*. Brussels: Espace Nord & Les Impressions Nouvelles.

Lilleker, Darren G. (2016). "Re-Imagining the Meaning of Participation for a Digital Age", in *Citizen Participation and Political Communication in a Digital World*, ed. Alex Frame and Gilles Brachotte. New York and London: Routledge, 109–124.

Lotman, Yuri, and Boris Uspensky (1978 [1971]). "On the Semiotic Mechanism of Culture". *New Literary History* 9:2, 211–232.

Lunenfeld, Peter (2001). *Snap to Grid. A User's Guide to Digital Arts, Media and Cultures*. Cambridge, Massachusetts: MIT Press.

—— (2006). "Godscan", in *Sensorium: Embodied Experience, Technology, and Contemporary Art*, ed. Caroline A. Jones. Cambridge, Massachusetts: MIT Press.

Lyotard, Jean François (1984). *The Postmodern Condition*, trans. Geoff Bennington and Brian Massumi. Minneapolis, Minnesota: University of Minnesota Press.

Malraux, André (1954 [1953]). *Museum Without Walls*. London: Martin Secker and Warburg.

Manovich, Lev (2001). *The Language of New Media*. Cambridge, Massachusetts: MIT Press.

Marchand, Philip (1998). *Marshall McLuhan: The Medium and the Messenger*. Cambridge, Massachusetts: MIT Press.

McDonald, Kevin (2015). "From Indymedia to Anonymous: rethinking action and identity in digital cultures". *Information, Communication & Society* 18:8, 968–982.

McLuhan, Marshall (1951). *The Mechanical Bride*. New York: The Vanguard Press.

—— (1962). *The Gutenberg Galaxy. The Making of Typographic Man*. Toronto: Toronto University Press.

—— (1994 [1964]). *Understanding Media: The Extensions of Man*. Cambridge, Massachusetts: MIT Press.

McLuhan, Marshall and Quentin Fiore (1967). *The Medium is the Massage. An Inventory of Effects*. London: Penguin.

Meyer, David S., and Sidney Tarrow (eds) (1998). *The Social Movement Society. Contentious Politics for a New Century*. Lanham, Maryland: Rowman and Littlefield.

Meyrowitz, Joshua (1994). "Medium Theory", in *Communication Theory Today*, ed. David Crowley and David Mitchell. Stanford, California: Stanford University Press, 50–77.

Micheletti, Michele. (2003). *Political virtue and shopping: Individuals, consumerism and collective action*. Basingstoke: Palgrave.

Miller, Daniel, Elisabetta Costa, Nell Haynes, Tom McDonald, Razvan Nicolescu, Jolynna Sinanan, Juliano Spyer, Shriram Venkatraman and Xinyuan Wang (2016). *How the World Changed Social Media*. London: UCL Press.

Mitchell, W.J.T. (2005). "There Are No Visual Media." *Journal of Visual Culture* 4:2, 257–266.

Montherlant, Henry de (1975). *Tous feux éteints. Carnets 1965, 1966, 1967. Carnets sans dates et 1972*. Paris: Gallimard.

Moretti, Franco (2013). *Distant Reading*. London and New York: Verso.

Motte, Warren, ed. (1988). *Oulipo: A primer in potential literature*. Lincoln, Nebraska: University of Nebraska Press.

Mouffe, Chantal (1999). "Deliberative Democracy or Agonistic Pluralism?". *Social Research* 66:3, 745–758.

—— (2000). *The Democratic Paradox*. London: Verso.

—— (2005). *On the Political*. London: Routledge.

Mougin, Pascal (ed.) (2016). *La Tentation littéraire de l'art contemporain*. Dijon: Les presses du réel.

Moulthrop, Stuart, and Dene Grigar (2017). *Traversals: The Use of Preservation for Early Electronic Writing*. Cambridge, Massachusetts.: MIT Press.

Murphet, Julian (2016). "Medium", in *Literature Now. Key Terms and Methods for Literary History*, ed. Sascha Bru, Ben de Bruyn and Michel Delville. Edinburgh: Edinburgh University Press.

Murray, Janet H. (1997). *Hamlet on the Holodeck. The Future of Narrative in Cyberspace*. New York: The Free Press.

Murray, Simone (2011). *The Adaptation Industry*, London: Routledge.

Murthy, Dhiraj (2013). *Twitter: Social Communication in the Twitter Age*. Cambridge: Polity Press.

Nachtergael, Magali (2015). "Écritures plastiques et performances du texte: une néolittérature?", in *Le Bal des arts*, ed. Elisa Brico. Macerata: Quodlibet. https://books.openedition.org/quodlibet/506.

National Academies of Sciences, Engineering, and Medicine (2018). *The Integration of the Humanities and Arts with Sciences, Engineering, and Medicine in Higher Education: Branches from the Same Tree*. Washington, DC: The National Academies Press. https://doi.org/10.17226/24988.

Norris, Pippa. (2002). *Democratic Phoenix*: *Reiventing Political Activism.* Cambridge: Cambridge University Press.

Nunberg, Geoffrey (ed.) (1996). *The Future of the Book*. Berkeley, California: The University of California Press.

Nys, Michiel (2011). *Julian Huxley: Evolution's Representative Man*. Leuven, unpublished doctoral dissertation.

Olson, Parmy (2012). *We Are Anonymous: Inside the Hacker World of LulzSec, Anonymous, and the Global Cyber Insurgency*. New York: Little, Brown and Company.

Orwell, George (1949). *1984*. London: Secker & Warburg.

Oxford Dictionaries (2013). "The Oxford Dictionaries Word of the Year 2013." OxfordWords Blog. 2013. https://blog.oxforddictionaries.com/press-releases/oxford-dictionaries-word-of-the-year-2013/.

Papacharissi, Zizi (2010). *A Private Sphere: Democracy in a Digital Age*. Cambridge: Polity Press.

—— (2009). "The Virtual Sphere 2.0: The Internet, the Public Sphere, and Beyond", in *Routledge Handbook of Internet Politics*, ed. Andrew Chadwick and Philip Howard. London: Taylor & Francis, 230–245.

—— (2015). *Affective Publics: Sentiment, Technology, and Politics*. Oxford: Oxford University Press.

Parikka, Jussi (2012). *What Is Media Archaeology?* London: Polity.

Pavić, Milorad (1988 [1984]). *Dictionary of the Khazars*, trans. Christina Pribicevic-Zoric. New York: Knopf.

Perloff, Marjorie (1994). *Radical Artifice. Writing Poetry in the Age of Media*. Chicago, Illinois: University of Chicago Press.

—— (2006). "Screening the Page/Paging the Screen: Digital Poetics and the Differential Text", in *New Media Poetics. Contexts, Technotexts, and Theories*, ed. Adelaide Morris and Thomas Swiss. Cambridge, Massachusetts, MIT Press, 143–164.

—— (2010). *Unoriginal Genius. Poetry by Other Means in the New Century*. Chicago, Illinois: University of Chicago Press.

Portela, Manuel (2013). *Scripting Reading Motions: The Codex and the Computer as Self-Reflexive Machines*. Cambridge, Massachusetts: MIT Press.

Postill, John (2012). "Digital Politics and Political Engagement", in *Digital Anthropology*, ed. Heather Horst and Daniel Miller. London: Berg.

Pratten, Robert (2011). *Getting Started in Transmedia Storytelling. A Practical Guide to Beginners*. Scotts Valley, California: CreateSpace Amazon.

Queneau, Raymond (1961). *Cent mille milliards de poèmes*. Paris: Gallimard.

Rajewsky, Irina O. (2005). "Intermediality, Intertextuality, and Remediation: A Literary Perspective on Intermediality". *Intermédialités/Intermedialities* 6, 43–64.

Ramos, Howard, and Kathleen Rodgers (eds) (2015). *Protest and Politics: The Promise of Social Movement Societies*. Vancouver: UBC Press.

Rayward, W. Boyd (2008). "The March of the Modern and the Reconstitution of the World's Knowledge Apparatus: H.G. Wells, Encyclopedism and the World Brain", in *European Modernism and the Information Society: Informing the Present, Understanding the Past*, ed. W. Boyd Rayward. Farnham: Ashgate, 223–39.

Rettberg, Jill Walker (2014). *Seeing Ourselves Through Technology: How We Use Selfies, Blogs and Wearable Devices to See and Shape Ourselves*. Basingstoke: Palgrave Macmillan.

Rettberg, Scott (2019). *Electronic Literature*. London: Polity.

Reverseau, Anne (ed.) (n.d.). "L'Exporateur littéraire". *Littératures modes d'emploi* (portal site).: http://www.litteraturesmodesdemploi.org/presentation/.

Reydams, Luc (ed.) (2011). *Global Activism Reader*. New York and London: Continuum.

Roberts, Adam (2016). "'We Can Remember It, Funes, Wholesale': Borges, Total Recall and the Logic of Memory", in *Memory in the Twenty-First Century: New Critical Perspectives from the Arts, Humanities and Sciences*, ed. Sebastian Groes. London: Palgrave Macmillan, 218–228.

Rudd, Damien, and Cécile Coulon (2018). *Triste Tropique.* Paris: Jean Boîte editions.

Sainte-Beuve, Charles Augustin (2013 [1839]). *De la littérature industrielle*. Paris: Allia.

Saint-Gelais, Richard (2005). "Transfictionality", in *The Routledge Encyclopedia of Narrative Theory*, ed. David Herman *et al*. London: Routledge, 612–13.

Scheible, Jeff (2015). *Digital Shift: The Cultural Logic of Punctuation*. Minneapolis, Minnesota: University of Minnesota Press.

Schement, Jorge Reina, and Terry Curtis (1995). *Tendencies and Tensions of the Information Age: The Production and Distribution of the Information in the United States*. New Brunswick: Transaction Publishers.

Scott, James C. (1998). *Seeing Like a State: How Certain Schemes to Improve the Human Condition Have Failed*. New Haven, Connecticut: Yale University Press.

Scull, Andrew (2012). "Blood Flow". *Times Literary Supplement,* 17 February. https://www.the-tls.co.uk/articles/private/blood-flow/.

—— (2018). "What is empathy?". *Times Literary Supplement*, 10 April. https://www.the-tls.co.uk/articles/public/what-is-empathy/.

Serfaty, Viviane (2004). *The Mirror and the Veil: An Overview of American Online Diaries and Blogs*. Amsterdam: Amsterdam Monographs in American Studies.

Shermer, Michael (2006). "The Skeptic's Chaplain: Richard Dawkins as a Fountainhead of Skepticism", in *Richard Dawkins: How a Scientist Changed the Way We Think,* ed. Alan Grafen and Mark Ridley. Oxford: Oxford University Press. 227–35.

Sikoryak, Robert (2017). *Terms and Conditions*. Montreal: Drawn and Quarterly.

Small, Helen (2013). *The Value of the Humanities*. Oxford: Oxford University Press.

Smith, Adam (1976a [1759]). *The Theory of Moral Sentiments*, ed. D. Daiches Raphael and Alexander Lyon Macfie. Oxford: Clarendon Press.

—— (1976b [1776]). *An Inquiry into the Nature and Causes of the Wealth of Nations*, ed. R.H. Campbell, Andrew S. Skinner and W.B. Todd. Oxford: Clarendon Press.

Solove, Daniel J. (2004). *The Digital Person: Technology and Privacy in the Information Age*. New York: New York University Press.

Stephens, Paul (2015). *The Poetics of Information Overload: From Gertrude Stein to Conceptual Writing*. Minneapolis, Minnesota: University of Minnesota Press.

Stewart, Garrett (2010). "Bookwork as Demediation". *Critical Inquiry* 36:3, 410–457.

Strandberg, Kim, and Kimmo Grönlund (2018). "Online Deliberation", in *The Oxford Handbook of Deliberative Democracy*, ed. Andre Bächtiger, John S. Dryzek, Jane Mansbridge and Mark Warren. Oxford: Oxford University Press. doi: 10.1093/oxfordhb/9780198747369.013.28.

Sweet, Paul R. (1980). *Wilhelm von Humboldt: A Biography, vol. 2, 1808–1835*. Columbus, Ohio: Ohio State University Press.

Tabbi, Joseph (2017). "Relocating the Literary: Ion Networks, Knowledge Bases, Global Systems, Material, and Mental Environments", in *The Bloomsbury Handbook of Electronic Literatur,* ed. Joseph Tabbi. London: Bloomsbury, 399–419.

Tarrow, Sidney (2015). "Contentious Politics", in *The Oxford Handbook of Social Movements*, ed. Donatella Della Porta and Mario Diani. Oxford: Oxford University Press. doi: 10.1093/oxfordhb/9780199678402.013.8.

Taylor, Chris (2013). "'Star Wars Kid' Blasts Bullies, Jedi Knights Defend Him. *Mashable*". https://mashable.com/2013/05/10/star-wars-kid-interview-cyberbullying/?europe=true#KJrcwSRwLGqS.

Thompson, John B. (2010). *Merchants of Culture*. London: Polity Press.

Tifentale, Alise, and Lev Manovich (2018). "Competitive Photography and the Presentation of the Self", in *Exploring the Selfie: Historical, Theoretical, and Analytical Approaches to Digital Self-Photography,* ed. Julia Eckel, Jens Ruchatz and Sabine Wirth. London: Palgrave Macmillan, 167–187.

Timby, Kim (2015). *3D and Animated Lenticular Photography: Between Utopia and Entertainment*. Berlin: De Gruyter.

Tomasello, Michael (2016). *A Natural History of Human Morality*. Cambridge, Massachusetts: Harvard University Press.

Trottier, Daniel, and Christian Fuchs (eds) (2015). *Social Media, Politics and the State. Protests, Revolutions, Riots, Crime and Policing in the Age of Facebook, Twitter and YouTube*. New York: Routledge.

Tsotsis, Alexia (2011). "RIAA Goes Offline, Joins MPAA As Latest Victim Of Successful DDoS Attacks. TechCrunch". https://techcrunch.com/2010/09/19/riaa-attack/.

Underwood, Ted (2017). "A Genealogy of Distant Reading." *Digital Humanities Quarterly* 11:2. http://www.digitalhumanities.org/dhq/vol/11/2/000317/000317.html.

—— (2018). "Why an Age of Machine Learning Needs the Humanities". *Public Books* 5 December. https://www.publicbooks.org/why-an-age-of-machine-learning-needs-the-humanities/.

Vaidhyanathan, Siva (2018). *Anti-Social Media: How Facebook Disconnects Us and Undermines Democracy*. Oxford: Oxford University Press.

—— (2011). *The Googlization of Everything (and why we should worry)*. Berkeley: University of California Press.

Van Dijck, José (2013). *The Culture of Connectivity: A Critical History of Social Media*. Oxford: Oxford University Press.

Vanvelk, Jan (2015). "Listening to the Silence: Huxley, Arnold, and Wells' Scientific Humanity". *Victoriographies* 5:1, 72–93.

Virilio, Paul (1989 [1984]). *War and Cinema: The Logistics of Perception*, trans. Patrick Camiller. London: Verso.

Vlavo, Fidèle A. (2018). *Performing Digital Activism. New Aesthetics and Discourses of Resistance.* New York and London: Routledge.

Vromen, Ariadne (2017). *Digital Citizenship and Political Engagement. The Challenge from Online Campaigning and Advocacy Organisations*. London: Palgrave Macmillan.

Walgrave, Stefaan, and Joris Verhulst (2009). "Government Stance and Internal Diversity of Protest: A Comparative Study of Protest against the War in Iraq in Eight Countries". *Social Forces* 87:3, 1355–87.

Waters, Lindsay (2004). *Enemies of Promise. Publishing, Perishing, and the Eclipse of Scholarship.* Chicago, Illinois: University of Chicago Press.

Watson, James D., and Francis H.C. Crick (1953). "A Structure for Deoxyribose Nucleic Acid". *Nature* 4356, April 25, 737–738.

Weintraub, Jeff (1997). "The Theory and Politics of the Public/Private Distinction", in *Public and Private in Thought and Practice. Perspectives on a Grand Dichotomy*, ed. Jeff Weintraub and Krishan Kumar. Chicago, Illinois, and London: University of Chicago Press, 1–42.

Wells, Herbert George (1920). *The Outline of History, Being a Plain History of Life and Mankind*. Volume 2. New York: Macmillan.

White, Paul (2005). "Ministers of Culture: Arnold, Huxley and Liberal Anglican Reform of Learning". *History of Science* 43, 115–138.

Williams, Raymond (1975). *Television: Technology and Cultural Form*. London: Schocken.

Wulf, Andrea (2015). *The Invention of Nature: The Adventures of Alexander von Humboldt, the Lost Hero of Science*. London: John Murray.

Yates, Simeon (2016). "Foreword: 'Ideologies' and 'Utopias' in the Discourses and Practices of Digital Politics". In *Citizen Participation and Political Communication in a Digital World*, ed. Alex Frame and Gilles Brachotte. New York and London: Routledge, ix-xvii.

Ypi, Lea (2014). "On Revolution in Kant and Marx". *Political Theory* 42:3, 262–87.

Zielinski, Siegfried (2006). *Deep Time of the Media: Toward an Archaeology of Hearing and Seeing by Technical Means*. Cambridge, Massachusetts: MIT Press.

Index

Subject Index

Index of Names